THE SUFI MESSAGE
OF
HAZRAT INAYAT KHAN

Pir-o-Murshid
Hazrat Inayat Khan

THE SUFI MESSAGE

OF

HAZRAT INAYAT KHAN

THE PATH OF INITIATION

Published for
International Headquarters of the Sufi Movement, Geneva

First published by Barry and Rockliff 1964
Second Impression 1973
Third Impression (revised) 1979
Published by Servire BV, Secr. Varkevisserstraat 52,
2225 LE Katwijk aan Zee, Netherlands

© 1979 in its re-edited form by
International Headquarters Sufi Movement, Geneva
ISBN 90 6325 098 3
Series ISBN 90 6325 101 7
Library of Congress Catalog Card Number 79-67752

Set in 12 on 13 point Bembo
Printed in USA by Delta Lithograph Company, Van Nuys, California

CONTENTS

PREFACE

THE EIGHT chapters of *Sufi Mysticism* consist of lectures, delivered on various occasions, in which Hazrat Inayat Khan tried to explain something of the essence of mysticism, and also to give a glimpse of the life and work on earth of the mystics, those beings who through their advanced state of evolution and their constant contact with the unseen and the unknown 'hold aloft the light of truth through the darkness of human ignorance', in the words of the Sufi invocation.

Because so many people are apprehensive of the word 'initiation', believing it to mean a kind of mysterious ordeal one has to go through, Inayat Khan repeatedly explained its real significance, for example, in *The Way of Illumination* (Vol. I of this series, pp. 46-53). When asked what initiation involved, he often replied that it was 'a blessing and a welcome'. *The Path of Initiation and Discipleship* is a collection of lectures and papers in which the different stages and aspects of initiation and discipleship are set forth in a comprehensive form. It may serve as a guide to those who wish to learn more about the esoteric activity of the Sufi Movement.

Coming himself from a long line of Sufis, both on his father's and his mother's side, it is natural that Inayat Khan should have greatly revered the Sufi mystics and poets of the past, who have not only left an indelible mark on the poetry, religion, and philosophy of the East, but have also in their own age and later deeply influenced Western thought. In *Sufi Poetry* some of the greatest of these poets are described, their lives and work, their experiences and characteristics.

The divinity of art, its mystical aspects, and its social significance were subjects which were never far from Inayat Khan's mind. Before he left India in 1910 he was a famous musician, singer, and poet; and when he arrived in the West to bring his message of Sufi wisdom, he used his art, especially during the first years, not only as a means of livelihood but also to convey the basic Sufi philosophical and mystical concepts to those who came to see and hear him. Thus one of the first series of lectures to appear in book form was *The Mysticism of Sound*; another early series called *Music* is published together with it in Volume II of the present edition. In order to make people in the West better acquainted with Sufi ideas, the Sufi Movement also published in those early years several small volumes containing poetry by Persian and Indian Sufis, including translations of Inayat Khan's own poems. These will be re-published in a later volume.

Then, during the last two years of his life, the Pir-o-Murshid delivered a series of lectures on many different aspects of art, including painting, sculpture, and architecture, which were published after his death under the title *Yesterday, Today, and Tomorrow*. It is this book which appears in the present volume in a slightly modified form.

Hazrat Inayat Khan's aesthetic standards differ on some points from the values which are generally accepted in the Western world, as does the terminology he uses. It is necessary to bear this in mind when following the Sufi mystic's trend of thought. In fact, Inayat Khan always approached his subject as a mystic, whose principal aim in this case was to place art in its proper perspective, not so much as an achievement of man but as a manifestation of God through man. Therefore he does not describe ancient forms of art as a historian would, nor does he speak as an art critic about modern art; he merely takes some instances and examples to illustrate the points he wants to emphasize. To make this clearer several chapters of a more general character have been included, and a few passages have been deleted which referred to situations and art movements of the beginning of the century which have lost most of their actuality.

The Problem of the Day forms the last part of this volume. It consists of lectures on the present need of mankind; in these Inayat Khan stresses the fact that if in our times man has gone so far astray morally, it is principally because of his declining interest in religion and his lack of a higher ideal.

SUFI MYSTICISM

CONTENTS

MYSTICISM

MYSTICISM is the essence and the basis of all knowledge, science, art, philosophy, religion, and literature. These all come under the heading of mysticism.

When one traces the origin of medicine, which has developed into the pure science it is today, one will find that its source was in intuition. It is the mystics who have given it to the world. For instance Avicenna, the great Persian mystic, has contributed more to medicine than any other man in the world history of medicine. We know the meaning of science to be a clear knowledge based on reason and logic; but at the same time, where did it start? Was it by reason and logic? First there was intuition, then came reason, and finally logic was applied to it. Furthermore, in the lower creation there are no doctors, yet the creatures are their own physicians. The animals know whether they will best be cured by standing in the sun, by bathing in a pool of water, by running in the free air, or by sitting quietly under the shade of a tree. I once knew a sensible dog who used to fast every Thursday. No doubt many people of the East would say he was an incarnation of a Brahmin, but to me it was a puzzle how the dog knew it was Thursday!

People think a mystic means a dreamer, an unpractical person who has no knowledge of worldly affairs. But such a mystic I would call only half a mystic. A mystic in the full sense of the word must have balance; he must be as wise in worldly matters as in spiritual things. People have had many misconceptions of what a mystic is. They have called a fortune-teller a mystic, or a medium, a clairvoyant, a visionary. I do not mean that a mystic does not possess all these qualities, but these qualities do not make a mystic. A real mystic should prove to be an inspired artist, a wonderful scientist, an influential statesman. He should have just as good qualifications for business, for industry, for social and political life, as the materially minded man. When people say to me, 'You are a mystic, I thought you would take no notice of this or that', I do not like it. Why should I not take notice of it? I take notice of every little detail, although every little detail does not occupy my mind so much that I take notice of nothing else. It is not necessary to be unconscious of the world while being conscious of God. With our two eyes we see one vision; so we should see both aspects, God and the world, as a clear vision at the same time. It is difficult, but not impossible.

Mysticism is an outlook on life. Things which seem real to an average person are unreal in the eyes of the mystic; and the things that seem unreal in the eyes of the average person are real in the eyes of the mystic.

For the mystic God is the source and goal of all. God is all, and all is God; but a real mystic does not say, as an intellectual student of philosophy does, 'I do not believe in God, although I believe in the abstract'. Such a man is unpoetic and without an ideal. He may have got hold of some truth, but it is a flower without fragrance. One cannot worship the abstract; no one can communicate with the abstract, give anything to it, nor take anything from it. To worship in that way is meaningless. We must have something before us to love, to worship, to adhere to, to look up to, to raise high. But while it is true if we say, 'God is everything and all', yet at the same time, from another point of view, 'everything' means 'nothing'.

The mystic says, 'If you have no God, make one.' It is the man without an ideal and without imagination who ignores God. A cup of water is as interesting as the ocean, or perhaps even more so when one is thirsty. A personal God is as important as, or even more important than, the idea of the abstract from which we gain nothing. We human beings have our limited mind. We can grasp the idea of God inasmuch as we can conceive of God. For instance we may have a friend whom we love and whom we wish to praise; and yet he is above our praise. All we can do is to say, 'How kind, how good, how patient, or how wonderful is my friend.' That is all. Our words cannot make him greater. Our words cannot even express fully what we ourselves think of him. All we can do is to make a conception of our friend for our own understanding.

It is the same with God. Man cannot comprehend God fully. All he can do is to form a conception of God for himself in order to make comprehensible something which is unlimited. That is why the mystic does not say, 'My realization of God is higher than yours, therefore I keep away from you.' I have seen a mystic walking in a religious procession with the peasants, singing hymns with them before an idol of stone. He himself was greater than the god in the procession and yet he was singing with the same reverence as everybody else. He never had any desire to show that his belief, his realization, was higher or greater than the realization of the others.

God is not abstract for the mystic; to him He is a reality. The mystic does not think of God as abstract, although he knows God to be so. It is not a question of knowing, but of being. God for the mystic is the stepping-stone to self-realization. He is the gate, He is the door, the entrance to the heavens. God, for the mystic, is a key with which to open the secret of life, the abode from whence he comes and to which he returns and where he finds himself at home.

Once a Western seeker of truth went to a sage in China and said to him, 'I have come to learn from you what truth is.' The sage said, 'Many of your missionaries come to us here and teach your faith. Why do you come to me?' 'Well,' he said, 'what they teach about is God. We know about God; but now I come to you to ask you about the mystery of life.' The sage said, 'If you know God, that is all there is to be known, there is nothing more. That is all the mystery there is.'

There is the question of the mystic's conception of Christ. Do we not know that one person is better than another, and is it not true that God is in man? If that is true, the mystic says, what objection is there if one person calls Christ God, and if the other believes Christ to be man? If God is in man, then if Christ is called God, what does it matter? And if Christ is called man, it only raises man, whom God has created, to that stature. Both have their reasons, and both are right, and yet they oppose one another. Some object to Christ being called divine; but if divinity is not sought in man, then in what shall we seek God? Can divinity be found in the tree, in the plant, in the stone? Yes indeed, God is in all; but at the same time it is in man that divinity is awakened, that God is awakened, that God can be seen.

The tolerance of the mystic is different. The people of a certain nation, race, or religion may say, 'In Jesus Christ we see the Lord.' Under that name they recognize their ideal. People of other countries have seen their divine ideal in Buddha. For their consolation and in support of their ideal they can all find in history the name of someone who has once existed. The Muslim says that Mohammad is the object of his worship, the Hindu says Krishna. As long as they have not realized the spirit of their ideal they will dispute, quarrel, and fight; and they will say, 'My Teacher is great,' 'Mine is greater still.' But they do not see that it is one and the same spirit, manifesting in greater excellence. We exalt the teacher to the extent that we have understood him, but we do not exalt him enough if we call him by a certain name and thus limit him to a certain part of the world. But when we see the unlimited, we can call him by all names and say, 'You are Krishna, you are Christ, and you are Buddha', just as the loving mother can call her child 'My prince'. She can give the most beautiful names to her child.

Once four little girls were disputing. One said, 'My mother is better than yours.' The second girl said, 'My mother is better than your mother.' So they were arguing and being quite disagreeable to one another. But someone who was passing by said to them, 'It is not your mother or their mother, it is *the* mother who is always the best. It is the mother quality, her love and affection for her children.' This is the point of view of the mystic in regard to the divine ideal.

The moral principle of the mystic is the love principle. He says, 'The greater your love, the greater your moral. If we are forced to be virtuous according to a certain principle, a certain regulation, certain laws or rules, that is not real virtue. It must come from the depths of our heart; our own heart must teach us the true moral.' Thus the mystic leaves morality to the deepening of the heart quality. The mystic says that the more loving someone's heart is, the greater is his morality.

There is no greater teacher of morals than love itself, for the first lesson that one learns from love is: I am not, you are. This is self-denial, self-abnegation, without which we cannot take the first step in love's path. One may claim to be a great lover, to be a great admirer, to be very affectionate, but it all means nothing; as long as the thought of self is there, there is no love. But when the thought of self is removed then every action, every deed that one performs in life, becomes a virtue. It cannot be otherwise. A loving person cannot be unjust, a loving person cannot be cruel. Even if what he does seems wrong in the eyes of a thousand people it cannot be wrong in reality. In reality it will be right, for it is inspired by love.

What is religion to the mystic? The religion of the mystic is a steady progress towards unity. How does he make this progress? In two ways. In the first way he sees himself in others, in the good, in the bad, in all; and thus he expands the horizon of his vision. This study goes on throughout his lifetime, and as he progresses he comes closer to the oneness of all things. And the other way of developing is to become conscious of one's own self in God, and of God in one's self, which means deepening the consciousness of our innermost being. This process takes place in two directions: outwardly by being one with all we see, and inwardly by being in touch with that one Life which is everlasting, by dissolving into it, and by being conscious of that one Spirit being *the* existence, the only existence.

The law of the mystic is the understanding of the law. The average man says, 'This person has got the better of me. I will show him!' The mystic's outlook is different; he believes that no one can get away with anything in this world without paying for it. For every gain, the food one eats, every drop one drinks, every breath of air one takes, there is a tax to be paid. One is continually paying, and yet one does not know it. This shows that behind it all there is a perfect justice working. One cannot get the slightest comfort and pleasure without having to pay for it, and every pain has its own reward, though few seem to realize this. Therefore behind all this falsehood and injustice we see that there is a perfect wisdom working continually day and night. The mystic sees it in everything with open eyes; and that is the great miracle. For in the first place the mystical life is a puzzle, in the second place a bewilderment, and in the third place a miracle.

It is a puzzle when the law is not understood, a very interesting puzzle. There is no better game than to be occupied with that puzzle, to try and understand it, to solve it. It is so interesting that there is no sport or game that can be compared with it. Then it is a bewilderment, because of the difference between the way everybody looks at life and how it is in reality. There comes a stage when a person says, 'Either they are all mad, or I am mad; but someone must be mad!'

The mystic can see from the point of view of everyone else as well as from his own, which may be quite the contrary. For instance, in his teachings Christ says, 'If anyone asks you for your coat, give him your overcoat also.' A worldly man will say, 'It is not practical; if someone asked this of me every day I would be continually buying new coats!' Yet at the same time it is more than practical from the point of view of the Master, for according to his view we cannot give anything, in whatever form, without getting it back in some way or other. Pure thought, good will, our service, our time, whatever we give, is never lost. It comes back to us according to our willingness to give; it comes back to us a thousandfold. That is why one is never the loser by being generous; one only gains.

The mystic sees the law in all things and this gives him an insight into life. He begins to see why this misery has come upon him, why that pleasure has come; why one person is prospering and another not, why one is progressing and not the other. All these things become clear to him because he sees the law working in all things. The law of the mystic is not the law of the people. It is the law of nature; it is the real law.

A mystic never restricts himself to a certain rule, for instance to the rule of celibacy, although for certain experiences celibacy is of great importance. But if it is necessary for him to fast, practise celibacy, live on a vegetarian diet, or stay in a remote place in seclusion, or any other such thing, he can prescribe it for himself and be benefited by it. But one cannot say a mystic *must* do this or that, or that he must live a certain life; Solomon with his kingdom and all his grandeur was as great a mystic and as wise a man as many hermits in the forest. One cannot judge a mystic by his appearance. If he is a real mystic, he will be a king whether he is in the midst of the treasures of a court or sitting clad in a ragged mantle. He is a king just the same wherever he is. Neither money, a court, nor life in the world can take away his kingship from him. If he chooses to live in solitude, it is his own affair. If he wishes to be in the crowd, he may just as well be there. Whether a person sits in a remote place in the forest or in a baker's shop, if he is thinking of a high ideal his surroundings cannot touch him; he does not see them. There is no aspect of life that can deprive a mystic of his mystical spirit. He may be rich or poor, in the midst of the world or away from everything, he is a mystic just the same.

The way to perfection for the mystic is by the annihilation of the false ego. He understands that in man there is a real ego, that this ego is divine, but that the divine ego is covered by a false ego; and every man has a false ego because it begins to grow from his birth.

Man develops in himself a false idea, and that false idea is identification with something which he calls himself. He says, 'I am a professor, a lawyer, a barrister, a doctor,' or, 'I am a king, a lord, or something.' But whatever he claims, he is not that. His claim may be humble or proud, but in reality he is not that.

The mystic on the spiritual path perseveres in wiping out this false ego as much as he can, by meditation, by concentration, by prayer, by study, by everything he does. His one aim is to wipe out so much, that one day reality, which is always there buried under the false ego, may manifest. And by calling on the Name of God, in the form of prayer, or in Zikr, or in any other form, what the mystic does is to awaken the spirit of the real ego in order that it may manifest. It is just like a spring which rises out of the rock and which, as soon as the water has gained power and strength, breaks even through stone and becomes a stream. So it is with the divine spark in man. Through concentration, through meditation, it breaks out and manifests; and where it manifests it washes away the stains of the false ego and turns into a greater and greater stream, which in turn becomes the source of comfort, consolation, healing, and happiness for all who come into contact with that spirit.

CHAPTER II

THE MYSTIC

MYSTICISM is neither a faith nor a belief, nor is it a principle or a dogma. A mystic is born; being a mystic means having a certain temperament, a certain outlook on life. It is for this reason that many are confused by the word mystic, because mysticism cannot be explained in plain words.

To a mystic, impulse has divine significance. In every impulse a mystic sees the divine direction. What people call free will is something that does not exist for a mystic. He sees one plan, working and making its way towards a desired result, and every person, whether willingly or unwillingly, contributes towards the accomplishment of that plan; and this contribution to the plan is considered by one to be free will and by another accident. The one who feels, 'This is my impulse; this is my idea; this I must bring into action', only knows of the idea from the moment it has become manifest to his view. He therefore calls it free will. But from whence did that idea come to him? Where does impulse come from? It comes, directly or indirectly, from within. Sometimes it may seem to come from outside, but it always starts from within, and thus every impulse for a mystic is a divine impulse. One may ask, why is not every impulse divine for everybody, since every impulse has its origin within? It is because not everybody knows it to be so. The divine part of the impulse is in realizing it is divine. The moment we are conscious of the divine origin of the impulse, from that moment it is divine. Although all through life it has come from within, it is the fact of knowing this which makes it divine.

A mystic removes the barrier that stands between himself and another person by trying to look at life, not only from his own point of view, but also from the point of view of another. All disputes and disagreements arise from people's misunderstanding of each other, and mostly people misunderstand each other because they have their fixed point of view and are not willing to move from it. This is a rigid condition of mind. The more dense a person, the more he is fixed in his own point of view. Therefore it is easy to change the mind of an intelligent person, but it is most difficult to change the mind of a foolish person once it is fixed. It is the dense quality of mind which becomes fixed in a certain idea, and that clouds the eyes so that they cannot see from the point of view of another person.

Many fear that by looking at things from the point of view of someone else they lose their own point of view, but I would rather lose my point of view if it was a wrong one. Why must one stick to one's point of view simply because it is one's own? And why should it be one's own point of view and not all points of view, the point of view of one and the same Spirit? For just as two eyes are needed to make the sight complete and two ears are necessary to make the hearing complete, so it is the understanding of two points of view, the opposite points of view, which gives a fuller insight into life.

A mystic calls this unlearning. What we call learning is fixing ideas in our mind. This learning is not freeing the soul; it is limiting the soul. By this I do not mean to say that learning has no place in life, but only that learning is not all that is needed in the spiritual path; there is something besides, there is something beyond learning, and to this we can only attain by unlearning. Learning is just like making knots of ideas, and the thread is not smooth as long as the knots are there. They must be unravelled, and when the thread is smooth one can treat it in any way one likes. A mind with knots cannot have a smooth circulation of truth; the ideas which are fixed in one's mind block it. A mystic, therefore, is willing to see from all points of view in order to clarify his knowledge. It is that willingness which is called unlearning.

The sense of understanding is one and the same in all of us, and if we are willing to understand, then understanding is within our reach. Very often we are not willing to understand, and that is why we do not understand. Mankind suffers from a sort of stubbornness. A man goes against what he thinks comes from another person. And yet everything he has learned has come from others; he has not learned one word from himself. All the same he calls it his argument, his idea, and his view, although it is no such thing; he has always taken it from somewhere. It is by accepting this fact that a mystic understands all, and it is this which makes him a friend of all.

A mystic does not look at reasons as everybody else does, because he sees that the first reason that comes to his mind is only a cover over another reason which is hidden behind it. He has patience, therefore, to wait until he has lifted the veil from the first reason, until he sees the reason behind it. Then again he sees that this reason which was hidden behind the first reason is more powerful, but that there is a still greater reason behind it. And so he goes from one reason to another, and sees in reason nothing but a veil to cover reality. And as he goes further, penetrating the several veils of reason, he reaches the essence of reason. By touching the essence he sees the reason in everything, good and bad.

Compare a mystic with an average person who argues and disputes and fights and quarrels over the first reason, which is nothing but a cover. Compare the two. The one is ready to form an opinion, to praise and to condemn; while the other patiently waits until reality gradually unfolds itself. A mystic believes in the unknown and unseen, not only in the form of God, but the unknown that is to come, the unseen that is not yet seen; whereas the other has no patience to wait until he knows the unknown, until he sees the unseen. A mystic does not urge the knowledge of the unknown or unseen upon another, but he sees the hand of the unknown working through all things. For instance, if a mystic has the impulse to go out and walk towards the North, he thinks there must be some purpose in it. He does not think it is only a whim, a foolish fancy, although the reason for it he does not know. But he will go to the North, and he will try to find the purpose of his going there in the result that comes from it.

The whole life of the mystic is mapped on this principle, and it is by this principle that he can arrive at the stage where his impulse becomes a voice from within that tells him 'go here', 'go there', or 'leave', 'move', or 'stay'. Therefore while others are prepared to explain why they are doing something or going somewhere or what they wish to do, the mystic cannot explain, because he himself does not know. And yet he knows more than the person who is ready to answer why he is going and what he is going to accomplish, for what does man know about what will happen to him? He makes his programme and plans, but he does not know.

Man proposes and God disposes. Many say this every day, yet at the same time they make their programmes and lay out their plans. A mystic is not particular about it. He is working on the plan which is laid out already and he knows that there is a plan. He may not know the plan in detail; but if anyone can and will know the plan, it is the mystic. This again tells us something: that the one who knows little, knows most; and those who seem to know more, know the least.

The outlook of the mystic is like that of a man standing on a mountain-top and looking at the world from a great height. And if a mystic looks upon everyone as being not much different one from another, because they are all like children to him, it is like what we see from the top of a mountain. All people whether tall or short seem to be of the same size; they appear like little beings moving about; and an average man is frightened of truth in the same way that a person who has never been on a great height gets frightened at the sight of the immensity of space. The truth is immense, and when a person reaches the top of understanding he becomes frightened and he does not want to look at it.

Many have told me, 'Eastern philosophy interests us very much, but the conception of Nirvana is very frightening.' And I have answered, 'Yes, it is frightening. Truth is just the same: truth is also frightening, but truth is reality.' Besides man is so fond of illusion that he so to speak revels in it. If someone awakens a man who is having an interesting dream, that man will say, 'O let me sleep on!' He likes looking at his dream; he does not want to wake up to reality because reality is not as interesting as the dream. Thus among the seekers after truth we find only one in a thousand who is courageous enough to look at the immensity of truth. But there are many who take an interest in illusion, and they are inclined, out of curiosity, to look at mental illusions, because these are different from the illusion of the physical life. And they are apt to call this mysticism, but it is not mysticism.

No one can be a mystic and call himself a Christian mystic, a Jewish mystic or a Mohammadan mystic. For what is mysticism? Mysticism is something which erases from one's mind all idea of separateness, and if a person claims to be this mystic or that mystic he is not a mystic; he is only playing with a name.

People say that a mystic is someone who dreams and who lives in the clouds; my answer to this is that the real mystic stands on earth, but his head is in heaven. It is not true that the wise man is not intellectual, or that the wise man is not clever. A clever man is not necessarily wise, but the one who has the higher knowledge has no difficulty in gaining knowledge of worldly things. It is the man who has knowledge of worldly things only who has great difficulty in absorbing the higher knowledge. Mr. Ford was very wise when he said to me, 'If you had been a business man, I am sure you would have been successful.' Furthermore, he said, 'I have tried all my life to solve the problem which you appear to have solved.' This again gives us an insight into the idea that higher wisdom does not debar a person from having worldly wisdom, though worldly wisdom does not qualify a person to attain to the higher wisdom.

And now let us come to the mystic's vision. People think that to see colours or spirits or visions is mystical. But mysticism cannot be restricted to this, and those who see these things are not necessarily mystics. Besides those who can see and whose vision is clear, say so little about it. The mystic will be the last to claim that he sees or does wonderful things; his vision and his power would be diminished as soon as he began to feed his vanity by claiming to know or do things which others cannot know or do. The main thing that the mystic has to accomplish is to get rid of the false ego, so that if he feeds it on claiming such things he will lose all his power and virtue and greatness.

To a mystic every person is like an open letter, just as to an experienced physician a person's face tells his condition. And yet a mystic would never say to someone else, 'In this person I see this or that', for the more he knows the greater trust is put in him by God. He covers all that should be covered; he only says what has to be said. A mystic will know most and yet will act innocently. It is the ones who know little who make a fuss about their knowledge. The more a person knows, the less he shows to others. Besides a mystic is never ready to correct people for their follies, to condemn them for their errors, or to accuse them of foolishness. He sees so much of errors and follies and foolishness that he never feels inclined to point them out; he just sees life in its different aspects, and understands the process an individual goes through in life. It is by mistakes and errors that one learns in the end, and a mystic never feels that he should condemn anyone for them; he only feels that they are natural. Some are advancing rapidly, others are going slowly. Foolishness is just like light and darkness: it is through darkness that the sun rises, and through ignorance wisdom will rise one day. A mystic, therefore, need not learn patience; he is taught patience by life from the beginning till the end. A mystic need not learn tolerance; his outlook gives him tolerance, it is natural for him. He need not learn forgiveness; he cannot do anything but forgive.

Man loves complexity and calls it knowledge. A great many societies and institutions in the world which call themselves occult and esoteric and psychic and by various other names, knowing that everyone is interested in complexity, cover the truth; and instead of covering it with one cover they cover it with a thousand covers to make it more interesting. It is just like customs which were followed in ancient times when people came to worship and asked the priest how they should do it, and he would say, 'How far do you live from the shrine?' And when they said, 'Two miles,' he answered, 'You must come on foot to the shrine and walk around it a hundred times before you may enter it.' He gave them a good exercise before they were allowed to come in. And even today they do the same thing. When a person says, 'I want to see truth', but wishes to look for truth in complexity, they cover truth under a thousand covers and then they give him the problem to solve. Are there not many people interested in the Mahatmas of the Himalayas, are there not many interested in the holy souls in remote places of Persia, many who look for a master in the centre of Australia? Perhaps next year an article will appear declaring that a great soul has been born in Siberia. What is it all about? It is all the love of complexity, queer notions, strange ideas which do not lead souls any further.

Therefore a mystic very often appears to be simple, because sincerity makes him feel inclined to express the truth in simple language and in simple ideas. But because people value complexity, they think that what he says is too simple and that it is something which they have always known, that it is nothing new. But, as Solomon said, there is nothing new under the sun.

Besides truth belongs to the soul and the soul knows it, and as soon as the truth is spoken the soul recognizes it; it is not new, not foreign to it. If a person says, 'This is something I already know', even if his soul has known it, it can never be repeated too often for him. The great saints of the East have repeated one phrase, for instance, 'God is One', perhaps a million times in their lives. Should we believe that they were so foolish as not to be able to understand the meaning of it by saying it once? Why then do they repeat it a million times? The reason is that it is never enough. We live in the midst of illusion from morning till evening when we go to sleep. What we do not know is the illusion in which we are from morning till evening. It is not the truth we do not know; truth is all we know—if we know anything fully. The mystic, therefore, instead of learning truth, instead of looking for truth, wishes to maintain truth; he wishes to cling to the idea of truth, to keep the vision of reality before him lest it may be covered by the thousand veils of illusion.

Does the mystic make any effort to reach the highest realization? Yes. It is an art which is passed on from teacher to pupil, and so this art is handed down through the ages from one person to another. One might ask why, if truth is within oneself, is there any necessity for such an art. But, after all, art is not nature. The animals and birds do not need an art; they are happy, they are peaceful, they are innocent, they are spiritual, really spiritual. They live in nature, their life is natural. We live far away from nature, we have made our artificial world to live in; and that is why we require an art to free ourselves from it. I do not mean to say that we must abandon life, or that we must not have anything to do with life in order to be mystics, but we have to practise that art which enables us to get in touch with reality.

That art is in the first place concentration. Concentration does not mean closing the eyes and sitting in church on Sunday. Many know how to close their eyes and sit there, yet their mind wanders about, specially when they have closed their eyes. Concentration means that every atom of the body and of the mind is centred in one spot.

The next step is contemplation; that is to be able to retain an idea which raises one's consciousness from the dense world. The third stage is meditation, and that is to purify oneself, to free oneself, and to open oneself to the light of truth, in order that it may abide in one's spirit. And the fourth step is realization. Then the mystic is no longer the knower of truth, but is truth itself.

CHAPTER III

REALIZATION

THERE IS one God and one truth, one religion and one mysticism; call it Sufism or Christianity or Hinduism or Buddhism, whatever you wish. As God cannot be divided, so mysticism cannot be divided.

It is an error when a person says, 'My religion is different from yours.' He does not know what religion means. Neither can there be many mysticisms, just as there cannot be many wisdoms; there is one wisdom. It is an error of mankind to say: this is Eastern and that is Western; this only shows lack of wisdom.

It is the same divine truth that man inherits, no matter to what part of the world he belongs. To distinguish between occultism and mysticism is also an error, just as it would be an error to say of one's eyes: this is my eye and that is yours. The two eyes belong to one soul. When a person pictures mysticism as a branch of a tree which is truth, he is wrong in thinking it to be a branch; for mysticism is the stem which unites all branches. Mysticism is the way by which to realize the truth. Jesus Christ said, 'I am the Way and the Truth.' He did not say, 'I am the Ways and the Truths'; for there is only one way, and any other way would be the wrong way. Many religions there are, but not many wisdoms.

Many houses of the Lord for worship, but only one God. Many scriptures, but only one truth. So there are many methods, but only one way.

The methods of gaining that realization are many, but there are four principal ones: by the heart, by the head, by action, by repose. A person must choose from among these four different methods of developing himself and preparing himself to journey on the way, the only way, which is called mysticism. No religion can call it its own, but it is the way of all religions. No church can say that it owns it, for it belongs to all churches. No one can say that his is the only way. It is the same way as all others have to go.

People have often imagined that a mystic means an ascetic, that a mystic is someone who dreams, a person who lives in the air, someone who does not dwell here on the earth, a person who is not practical; or that a person who is an ascetic must be a hermit. This is not the case. And very often people think of the mystic as a peculiar sort of man, and if they meet someone who is peculiar, they say that he must be a mystic! This is a wrong conception, an exaggeration, for a real mystic must show equilibrium, balance. He will have his head in the heavens but his feet will be on the earth. The real mystic is as wide awake in this world as in the other. A mystic is not someone who dreams. He is wide awake; yet he is capable of dreaming when others are not, and of keeping awake when the rest cannot do so. A mystic strikes the balance between two things: power and beauty. He does not sacrifice power for beauty, nor beauty for power. He possesses power and enjoys beauty.

There are no restrictions in the life of the mystic; everything there shows balance, reason, love, and harmony. The religion of the mystic is every religion, and yet he is above what people call their religion. In point of fact he *is* religion, and his moral is that of all religions: reciprocity; to reciprocate all the kindness we receive from others, to do an act of kindness to others without wanting any appreciation or return for it, and to make every sacrifice, however great, for love, harmony, and beauty.

The God of the mystic is to be found in his own heart; the truth of the mystic is beyond words. People argue and debate about things of little importance, but mysticism is not to be discussed. People want to talk in order to know, and then they forget it all. Very often it is not the one who knows who talks so much, but the one who wants to know. The one who knows but does not discuss is the mystic. He knows that happiness is in his own heart; but to put this into words is like putting the ocean into a drop of water.

Yet there is a wine which the mystic drinks, and that wine is ecstasy. A wine so powerful that the presence of the mystic becomes as wine for everyone who comes into his presence. This wine is the wine of the real sacrament, whose symbol is found in the church. What is it, where does it come from, what is it made of? It may be called a power, life, a strength which comes through the mystic, through the spheres which every man is attached to. By his attachment to these spheres the mystic drinks the wine which is the sustenance of the human soul, and that wine is ecstasy, the mystic's intoxication. That intoxication is the love which manifests in the human heart. What does it matter, once a mystic has drunk that wine, whether he is sitting among the rocks in the wilderness or in a palace? It is all the same. The palace does not deprive him of the mystic's pleasures, neither does the rock take them away. He has found the kingdom of God on earth, about which Jesus Christ has said, 'Seek ye first the kingdom of God and all these things shall be added unto you.'

People strive for many different things in this world but last of all they seek the spiritual path. And there are some indifferent ones who say, 'There is a long life before us and when the time comes that I must awake I shall wake up.' But the mystic knows that this is the one thing he must attend to, that all other things come after that. It is of the greatest importance in his life.

Should he, by working for realization of God, neglect his duties in the world? It is not necessary. There is nothing that a mystic need renounce in order to have the realization of life. He only needs to attach the greatest importance to what is most important in life.

The life of a mystic is meditative, but to him meditation is like the winding of a clock. It is wound for only a moment, yet all day long it goes by itself. He does not have to think about it all day long. He does not trouble about it.

A Shah of Persia used to sit up at night for his vigils and prayers. And a friend who was visiting him wondered at his long meditations after the whole day's work. 'It is too much,' he said, 'you do not need so much meditation.' 'Do not say so,' was the answer, 'you do not know. For at night I pursue God, and during the day God follows me.' The moments of meditation set the whole mechanism in running order, like a stream running into the ocean. They do not in the least keep the mystic from his duty; they only bless every word he speaks with the thought of God.

In all he thinks or does there is the perfume of God, which becomes a healing and a blessing. And if one asks how a mystic, who has become so kind and helpful, gets on among the crowd in everyday life, since the rough edges of everyday life rubbing against him must necessarily make him heartsore, the answer is that they certainly do, and the heart of the mystic is even more sore than that of anybody else. Where there is only kindness and patience all the thorns will come. But just as the diamond by being cut becomes brilliant so does the heart; and when the heart has been sufficiently cut it becomes a flame which illuminates not only the life of the mystic, but also that of others.

CHAPTER IV

THE NATURE AND WORK OF A MYSTIC

THERE IS a difference between a philosopher, a wise man, a mystic, and a sage. From a mystical point of view the philosopher is a person who knows the nature and character of things and beings, who has studied this, who has reasoned it out, and who understands it. A wise man is he who has been the pupil of life. Life has been his teacher; its sorrows and troubles and experiences have brought him to a certain understanding of life. A mystic, however, need not have had experience of life to teach him, nor the study of life to make him intellectual enough to understand it better. The mystic is born with the mystical temperament. His language is a different language, his experience a different experience; he so to speak communicates with life, with conditions, things, and beings. But the sage has all three of these qualities. The sage is a philosopher, a wise man, a mystic, all three combined.

It is possible that a mystic may be no philosopher; though the mystic always has a clear vision and understanding, he may not have the philosopher's means of expression. The difference is like that between short sight and long sight. The mystic may not see the outline of things distinctly, a philosopher may observe only the detail, while the wise man may not be a philosopher but has learnt wisdom from life, and he may be different from the mystic as well.

And yet, when they arrive at the stage of the culmination of knowledge, they all come closer together. For instance, I was once talking to a business man, a man who had spent nearly fifty years of his life in commerce, and had made a success of it. He had never believed in any religion, he had never studied any philosophy, except that sometimes he read the works of great poets. But after we had talked for about an hour on subjects concerning the inner life, he discovered that he was not very far from my own beliefs; that after all, the patience which is required to make money, the sacrifices one has to make in order to be successful, and the experiences one has to go through with those whom one works with daily in business, had been for him both a practice and a study. And I found that he was not very far from the conclusions to which a wise man, a philosopher, a mystic would come. It is he whom I would call a wise man, for by his wisdom he had reached that truth which is studied by the philosopher and which is attained by the mystic through meditation.

The meaning of philosophy has changed in modern times. People generally understand by philosophy that which one finds in the books written by European philosophers and which are read and studied at universities. But spiritual philosophy is different; it is a different kind of knowledge, an understanding of the origin, the nature, and character of things and beings. It necessitates the study of human nature, the study of conditions of life. It is the deeper insight into life which makes one a philosopher.

Mysticism is neither taught nor learned. A mystic is born; it is a temperament, it is a certain outlook on life, it is a certain attitude towards life that makes a man a mystic. His chief characteristic is that he knows the meaning of every action, whether it is by intuition or by accident, although to a mystic nothing is an accident. Every action, every condition, everything that happens has a meaning and a purpose. Very often people find that a mystic has a queer temperament. He may suddenly think during the night, 'I must go to the North', and in the morning he sets out on his journey; he does not know why, he does not know what he is to accomplish there, he only knows that he must go. By going there he finds something he has to do and sees that it was the hand of destiny pushing him towards the accomplishment of that purpose, which inspired him to go to the North. Or a mystic will tell a person to do or not to do a thing. If that person asks the reason he cannot tell him. His feeling comes by intuition, a knowledge which comes from the world unseen, and according to that knowledge he acts. Therefore the mystic's impulse is a divine impulse, and one can judge neither his action nor his attitude. One will find that there are various aspects of the mystic temperament.

But there is a knowledge which a mystic attains by means of the head and which prepares him to find his way to the truth. Reasoning is a faculty which the mystic uses, and which he may develop like any man of common sense, any practical man; the difference is only that the mystic does not stop at the first reason but wishes to see the reason behind all reasons. Thus in everything, whether right or wrong, the mystic seeks for the reason. The immediate answer, however, will be a reason which does not satisfy him, for he sees that behind that reason there is yet another reason. And so he progresses in the knowledge of all things, which is far greater than the knowledge gained by one thing. This is why neither wrong nor right, good nor evil, excites the mystic very much, neither does it greatly shock or surprise him. For everything seems to him to have its own nature, and it is understanding this which makes him feel at one with all that exists. And what can one wish for more in life than understanding? It is understanding that gives one harmony in the home with those near and dear to one, and peace outside the home with so many different natures and characters. If one lacks understanding one is poor, in spite of all that one may possess of the goods of this world, for it is understanding which gives a man riches.

If life could be pictured, one would say that it reminds one of the sea in a storm, the waves coming and going—such is life. And it is the understanding of this which gives man the weight which enables him to endure through rain and storm and all vicissitudes. Without understanding he is like a jolly-boat on the sea which cannot weather the storm. Through understanding a mystic learns. He learns tact; he is tactful under all circumstances; and his tact is like a heavily laden ship, which the wind cannot capsize and which rides steady in the midst of the storm.

The nature of life is such that it easily excites the mind and makes man unhappy in an instant. It makes man so confused that he does not know where to take the next step. In contrast with this the mystic stands still and inquires of life its secret; and from every experience, from every failure or success, the mystic learns a lesson; thus both failure and success are profitable to him.

The ideal of a mystic is never to think of disagreeable things. What one does not want to happen one should not think of. A mystic erases from his mind all the disagreeable things of the past. He collects and keeps his happy experiences, and out of them he makes a paradise. Are there not many unhappy people who keep part of the past before them, which causes them pain in their heart? Past is past; it is gone. There is eternity before us. If we want to make our life as we wish it to be, we should not think disagreeable thoughts and ponder over painful experiences and memories that make us unhappy.

It is for this reason that to some extent life becomes easy for a mystic to deal with. For he knows every heart, every nature, whereas those who are untouched by the mystic's secret suffer from their difficulties both at home and outside. They dread the presence of people they do not understand; they want to run away from them, and if they cannot escape they feel as if they are in the mouth of a dragon; and perhaps they are placed in a situation which cannot easily be changed. The consequence is that they heap confusion upon confusion. And how very often one sees that when two people do not understand one another, a third

c

comes and helps them to do so, and the light thrown upon them causes greater harmony! The mystic says: whether it be agreeable or disagreeable, if you are in a certain situation, make the best of it; try to understand how to deal with such a situation. Therefore a life without such understanding is like a dark room which contains everything you wish: it is all there, but there is no light.

The world is after all a wonderful place, in spite of so many souls wishing to leave it. For there is nothing which cannot be obtained in this world; everything is there, all things good and beautiful, all things precious and worth while; they are all there, if only one knows their nature, their character, and how to obtain them.

If you ask some people what is the nature of life, they will say, 'The further we go in striving for happiness, the further we are removed from it.' This is true. But the one who does not know that unhappiness does not really exist, takes the wrong way. Besides happiness is more natural than unhappiness, as good is more natural than evil, and health than illness. And yet man is so pessimistic. If we tell him how good someone is he cannot believe this to be true, but if we tell him how bad a person is he will readily believe it.

The work of a mystic, therefore, is to study life. To the mystic life is not a stage-play or an entertainment. For the mystic it is a school in which to learn, every moment of one's life; it is a continual study. And the scripture of the mystic is human nature; every morning he turns a new page of this scripture. And the books of the great ones who have brought the Message to the world from time to time, and which became sacred scriptures and were read for thousands of years, generations of people taking their spiritual food from them, are the interpretations that they gave of this scripture which is human nature. That is why all the sacred scriptures always have the same sacred feeling.

The mystic respects all religions and he understands all the different and contradictory ideas, for he understands everyone's language. The mystic can agree, without having to dispute, with both the wise and the foolish. For he sees that the nature of facts is such that they are true in their own place; he understands every aspect of their nature. The mystic sees from every point of view.

He sees from the point of view of each person and that is why he is harmonious with all. A man comes to a mystic and says, 'I cannot believe in a personal God, it means nothing to me.' Then the mystic answers, 'You are quite right.' Another man says, 'The only way of making God intelligible is in the form of man.' The mystic says, 'You are right.' And another person says, 'How foolish of these people to make of this man a God; God is above comprehension.' And the mystic will agree with him too. For a mystic understands the reason behind all the opposing arguments.

Once a missionary came to a Sufi in Persia, desiring to have a discussion and to prove his opinion on some Sufi teaching to be the right one. The Sufi was sitting there, in his silent, quiet attitude, with two or three of his pupils at his side. The missionary brought up some arguments, and the mystic answered, 'You are right.' Then the man went on to dispute but the Sufi only said, 'That is quite true.' The man was very disappointed as there was no opportunity for argument. The Sufi saw the truth in all.

The truth is like a piano: the notes may be high or low, one may strike a C or an E, but they are all notes. So the difference between ideas is like that between notes, and it is the same in daily life with the right and the wrong attitude. If we have the wrong attitude all things are wrong, if we have the right attitude all things are right. The man who mistrusts himself will mistrust even his best friend; the man who trusts himself will trust everyone.

Things which seem to be apart, such as right and wrong, light and darkness, form and shadow, to the mystic appear so close that only a hair's breadth divides right and wrong. Before the mystic there opens an outlook on life, an outlook which discloses the purpose of life. The question which the mystic puts to himself is, 'Which is my being? My body? No. This body is my possession. I cannot be that which I possess.' He asks himself, 'Is it my mind?' The answer comes, 'No. The mind is something I possess, it is something I witness. There must be a difference between the knower and the known.' By this method the Sufi eventually comes to an understanding of the illusory character of all he possesses. It is like a man who has a coat made: it is his coat, it is not himself.

Then the mystic begins to think, 'It is not myself that thinks, it is the mind. It is the body which suffers, it is not myself." It is a kind of liberation for him to know, 'I am not my mind.' For an ordinary man wonders why one moment he has a good thought, another moment a bad thought, one moment an earthly thought, the next moment a thought of heaven. Life for him is like a moving picture in which it is he who sees and it is he who is dancing there.

By seeing this the mystic liberates his real self, which owing to his illusion was buried under mind and body, what people call a lost soul, a soul which was not aware of the mystical truth that body and mind are the vehicles by which to experience life. And it is in this way that the mystic begins his journey towards immortality.

CHAPTER V

THE SECRET OF THE SPIRIT

THERE ARE four different explanations of the word 'spirit'. One meaning is essence. Spirit of camphor means the essence of camphor. The second meaning of spirit is what is understood by those who call the soul spirit when it has left the body on earth and has passed to the other side. The third meaning of spirit is that of the soul and mind working together. It is used in this sense when one says that a man seems to be in low spirits; this means that both his mind and soul are depressed, although one may not always define it in this way. And the fourth meaning of spirit is the soul of all souls, the source and goal of all things and all beings, from which all comes and to which all returns.

The first meaning of the word spirit is, as I have said, essence. The essence of flowers is honey, the essence of milk is butter, the essence of grapes is wine, and the essence of learning is wisdom. Therefore wisdom is as sweet as honey, as nourishing as butter, and as exalting as wine.

To rise above things in life one must try to get to the essence. In other words, there is one way of listening to a musician and that is to consider the form, the technique; and the other way is to grasp the feeling, the sense that the music suggests. So it is with life; we can look at life in one way and see it in different forms and make a rigid conception of it, or we can see it so that we get the suggestion of its essence. For instance a person may come to us and express a thousand false feelings. And then we go over it in our mind and realize it was all false because it could not reasonably be true; this is one way. The other way is to see immediately that it is false from first to last, without going into details. This is quite sufficient, and because we have immediately seen it we have saved our mind a great deal of trouble.

Sometimes a person says to another, 'You say you are my friend; all right, I am going to find out what you are like, how you work.' That is one way of looking at it. But the other way is to look only once at that person and, by that one glance, to know what he is worth; that is all. If one can do this it will make one brave, venturesome, and will bring one nearer to the essence. It will impart generosity and liberality; otherwise one remains narrow and small and confused and in this way thousands and millions of souls are buffeted along on the sea of life, not knowing where they are going, because they are not sure of themselves. If a person says, 'I don't know you, but perhaps I will know you some day,' that person will never know anyone, for all his life he will be unsure.

As to the second meaning of the word spirit, this mechanism of the physical body, which works from morning till evening without winding like a machine, and which stands up to all the turmoil of life, encounters all difficulties, and endures everything that comes to it, one day falls flat; it is just like when the steam or electricity, or whatever it was that kept the machine going, suddenly gives out. A physician says that the man's heart failed, or his blood pressure was too high, or something like that as an explanation of death. It means that a person who was active and sensitive is no longer active nor sensitive. That which was most important in him has left. So much the physician can tell you; but what was there he does not know.

From the point of view of a mystic, however, what has left the body is the person. This body was not the person. This body was a mask which covered that person; and when this mask is cast off that visible person becomes invisible. Not he himself but only the mask has been thrown away. He is what he already was. If death comes it is the removing of the mask.

A question arises: how does this take place; how does it happen? And the answer is that there is a magnetic action between the person and the mask. It is the strength of the physical body which holds the spirit, and it is the strength of the spirit which holds the body. The physical body holds on to the spirit because it only lives by the life of the spirit, and without the spirit it is dead. And as every being, however small, struggles for life, this physical body tries to hold on to the spirit; and it does so to the last, as someone who is on the point of losing his gold might hold it tightly in his hand until his hand is paralysed, and he can no longer hold it and so lets it drop. It does not mean he does not want it; it only means he cannot hold it any longer. And so it is with the spirit: as long as the spirit is interested in the physical body it holds it, permeates it, and embraces it. But as soon as it feels that it does not want it any more, that it no longer has any use for the body, it drops it.

Both these tendencies can be seen in people when they are studied by those who understand. There are people who have reached old age and who are no longer doing anything in the world, yet each atom of their body is consciously or unconsciously holding on to the spirit in order to live every moment they can possibly prolong their life. And as long as their strength allows them to hold on to the spirit they live; and they may live to a very great age. But one can also notice another tendency, and that is that there are some who are tired of life. They no longer attach any importance to this life on earth. The value of things has diminished in their eyes; they are disappointed by these transitory and changeable conditions. In their spirit they are feeling something quite different from the other type of person. Their tendency is to give up the physical bondage of the body, and they would be glad if the spirit were separated from it; and yet their body unconsciously clings to the spirit just the same and keeps them alive as long as it can hold on. Thus the unwilling spirit is held by the body.

In conclusion, death means a separation from the body which is nothing but a garb covering the spirit. And what follows after the separation? The body which is left on the earth by the spirit is no longer living in the sense we understand life; yet it is living. It is as if there had been a fire in the stove, and even after the fire was extinguished the warmth remained there. There is only the smallest degree of spirit, but there is life in it. Where there is no life, life cannot be created; life must come out of life. Life cannot come out of death. Living creatures such as worms and germs come out of a dead body, and how could life come out if there were no life there? There is life; not in the sense we generally understand it, but it is living just the same. There is nothing in this world of which we can say that it is without life, or dead. Everything, every object that seems without life, has some life somewhere. And even after it is destroyed it is still living. When germs and worms manifest out of the dead body we think that it means it is finished. On the contrary it goes on, life is continued in various forms. It has never ended; what has ended is this imprisonment which we recognized as such and such a person; but the existence is still going on, even the mortal existence, even the mask which in reality was nothing.

The living part was the spirit and it goes on living. When we say, 'He has gone to the other world', the other world is only our conception, though it is a beautiful conception. If one says, for instance, that a great revolution is taking place in the scientific world, it does not mean that the scientific world is outside the earth. When we have experienced a great development in the mystical world, this does not mean that we live outside this planet. It is a conception; it is a beautiful way of putting it, and it is the best we can find. 'In the other world' means in a world which is veiled from our eyes, our physical eyes; but it does not mean a world far away from us beyond our reach. Both the living and the dead inhabit the same space; we all live together. Only a veil separates us, the veil of this physical body. Separation means being unable to see one another; there is no other separation.

One need not attain to the seventh heaven in order to reach those who have passed. When one really cares for them, that bond of love and sympathy in itself makes us close to them. Two people may be living in the same house, working together, seeing each other every day, every hour, and yet they may be as far apart as the North Pole from the South Pole. There are people thrown miles apart by destiny so that they cannot reach one another because of life's difficult circumstances; and yet they can be closer to each other than anyone else. If this is true, it proves that those united in spirit may be thrown far apart in the world and yet be so close together that nothing stands between them. Therefore if those who have departed from this earth have a connection with someone on earth, they are close to him just the same. Nearness means nearness of the spirit, not of the physical body.

In India there used to be a custom called *Sati*, by which a wife who was devoted to her husband was cremated with him. Some people felt great horror at the idea, but others thought differently. I would say in regard to this question that when two souls have become one, whether they are both on earth or whether one of them has gone to another plane, they are still united. If one of them remains living, then that living person is as though dead here, for he only lives there where there is real unity. There is no separation. Nothing can separate two souls if they are really united.

The third meaning of the spirit is that it is the mind and the soul together. One might ask if the mind and soul together, that is to say the spirit, is that part of one's being which lives. It is not a part, but all. Our overcoat is not a part of our being; it is something extraneous. It becomes temporarily a part, but it is not essentially a part. The real being is the spirit, the mind and the soul together.

One might think it uninteresting to live as spirit and not as body. It might seem uninteresting to one who has not experienced on this earth how to be able to live independently of the physical body. All mysticism has been based on this: how to be able to live independently of the physical body, how to live on earth as spirit, even for five minutes a day. This gives a conviction of being able to live and yet be independent of the physical body. It is an experience in life, an education in the highest knowledge. Once a person has realized how he can exist without the physical body it produces a faith that gives an ultimate conviction which nothing can change.

It is not only a matter of existing, but of existing completely, fully. The soul is not dependent upon the eyes to see. It sees more than the physical eyes can see. It is not dependent upon the ears; it hears more than the ears can hear. Therefore he who knows spirit receives far greater inspiration from being able to exist independently of the physical body. It is very easy for a person with material knowledge to call those people fanatics who retire to the mountains or wander about thinking of spiritual things, who seem to live in a dream. They might appear to do so, but actually they only do not conform to what everyone else does. They left the life of business and profession and politics, all social life, for the sake of deeper experience. It is not necessary for everyone to follow their example, but one may benefit by what they have brought to us.

At this time West and East are coming closer together. What is needed now is that we should awaken and benefit by the fruits of the lives of people in both East and West. There is much that the West can give to the East. It has laboured along certain lines, and the fruits of this work can be of use to the East, while there are fruits which Eastern people have gathered for years and years which will be of great use to the West once people have realized this. And the particular lesson which can be learned from the experience of those in the East who have investigated life's secret, is the way of becoming conscious of one's spirit, of realizing spirit. No doubt those who wish to mystify others make complexities out of simple things. But those who wish to serve the world in the path of truth reduce complex things to simple ones. It is in a simple form that we have to realize the truth.

The fourth meaning of spirit is the source and the goal of all things; something towards which all are bound, to which all will return. It is that spirit which in religion is called God. And the best way of explaining this meaning of spirit is that it is like the sun, the centre of all life, the divine spark in us. But the sun is not as small as it appears to be. Then what is the sun? The sun is all. The part of the sun that we recognize as the sun is the centre of it, but the sun is in reality as large as its light reaches. The real sun is light itself. But as there is a point which is the central focus of light, we call that point the sun.

The light has centralized itself there; but the sun has other aspects such as rays, which are not different from the sun but which are the sun itself. And what are we? Our souls are the rays of the sun. In our inner being we are both source and goal itself. It is only our ignorance of this which keeps us ignorant of our own being.

Every atom of the universe, having come from the sun, from the divine sun, makes every effort to return to it. The tendency of the waves is to reach upward, of the mountains to point upward, of the birds to fly upward. The tendency of animals is to stand on their hind-legs. The tendency of man is to stand upright, ready to soar upward. An angel is pictured as a man with two wings ready to fly upward. Science has discovered the law of gravitation, but the mystic knows the other law, which is also a law of gravitation but in the opposite direction.

Thus not only is every soul attracted in that direction, but also every atom of this world, going through all the different processes known to biology in order to reach that state, to return to the spirit. Therefore it is not necessary to be frightened by going towards God, or by trying to attain the spirit by losing one's identity, one's individuality. A fear like this is the same as the experience of someone on the top of a mountain. A kind of terror overwhelms a person when he is looking at the immensity of the view; and in the same way a soul is frightened of spiritual attainment because of the immensity, of the largeness and depth it has. It frightens the soul which fears to lose itself, because it has this false conception of its smaller self. The mystic says, 'Try to die before death,' and to die before death is to play death; that means to get above this fright which only comes from the false conception of self.

The one who has died before death has no longer desire; he is above desire. This is shown by the picture of the God Vishnu sitting upon the lotus. The lotus represents desire: every petal is a desire. Sitting upon the lotus means that the desire is under him instead of being above his head. To some extent there is a relationship between life in the spiritual world and life on earth, for that which is collected here on earth indicates the task one has to perform here. The only condition is that the one who has stayed a shorter while here must work more for his spiritual accomplishment than the one who has stayed longer on earth. When someone has achieved spirituality here, it is not necessary for him to stay longer unless it is his desire. And the day the false conception of self is removed from his eyes he begins to see the immensity of God's majesty.

CHAPTER VI

THE MYSTICAL HEART

WHEN ONE asks, 'What is the heart? Where is the heart?' the answer usually is that the heart is in the breast. This is true; there is a nerve centre in the breast of man which is so sensitive to our feelings that it is always regarded as the heart. When a person feels a great joy it is in that centre that he feels something lighting up, and through the lighting up of that centre his whole being seems light. He feels as if he were flying. And again, if depression or despair has come into his life this has an effect upon that centre. A man feels his throat choked and his breath is laden as with a heavy load.

But the heart is not only that. To understand this one should picture a mirror standing before the heart, focused upon the heart, so that every thing and every feeling is reflected in this mirror which is in the physical being of man. Just as man is ignorant of his soul, so he does not know where his heart is nor where the centre is where his feelings are reflected. It is a fact known to scientists, that when a child is formed it begins from the heart, but a mystic's conception is that the heart, which is the beginning of form, is also the beginning of the spirit which makes man an individual. The depth of that spirit is in reality what we call the heart. Through this we understand that there is such a thing as a heart which is the deepest depth of man's being.

In these days people attribute less importance to sentiment and rely more upon the intellect. The reason for this is that when they meet the two kinds of people, the intellectual and the sentimental, they find greater balance in an intellectual man than in the one with much sentiment. This is no doubt true, but the very reason for the lack of balance is that there is a greater power than the intellect, and this power is sentiment. The earth is fruitful, but not as powerful as the water. The intellect is creative, yet not as powerful as the heart and the sentiment. In reality the intellectual man will also prove unbalanced in the end if he has no sentimental side to his being.

Are there not many people of whom one can say, 'I like him, love him, admire him, but he closes his heart'? The one who closes his heart neither loves others completely nor allows others to love him fully. Besides a man who is only intellectual in time becomes sceptical, doubting, unbelieving, and destructive, since there is no power of the heart to balance it. The Sufi considers the devotion of the heart to be the best thing to cultivate for spiritual realization. Many people may not agree, but it is a fact that the one who closes his heart to his fellow-man, closes his heart to God. Jesus Christ did not say, 'God is the intellect'; He said, 'God is love', and therefore if the peace of God can be found anywhere it is not in any church on earth, nor in heaven above, but in the heart of man. The place where one is most certain to find God is in the loving heart of a kind man.

Many people believe that by the help of reason man will act according to a certain standard of morals, but it is not reason that makes people good; and even if they seem good or righteous, they are only made so artificially. The prisoners in gaol can all be righteous, but if natural goodness and righteousness can be found anywhere, it is in the spring of the heart from which life rises, and every drop of this spring is a living virtue. This proves that goodness is not man-made; it is man's very being; and if he lacks goodness it is not through lack of training, although training is often most desirable, but because he has not yet found his true self. Goodness is natural; for a normal person is necessarily good. No one needs teaching in order to live a good or a righteous life. If love is the torch on his path, it shows him what fairness means, and the honour of his word, charity of heart, and righteousness. Do we not sometimes see a young man, who with all his boisterous tendencies suddenly finds a girl whom he begins to love, and who when he really loves her begins to show a change in his life? He becomes gentle, for he must train himself for her sake; he does without things he was never before willing to give up. And in the same way, where there is love forgiveness is not very difficult. A child comes to its mother, even after having offended a thousand times, and asks her forgiveness. There is no one else to go to, and it does not take a moment for the mother's heart to forgive. Forgiveness was waiting there to manifest itself. One cannot help being kind when there is feeling. Someone whose feeling goes out to another person, sees when that person needs his feeling, and he strikes a note of sympathy in everyone he meets, finding the point of contact in every soul, because he has love.

There are people who say, 'But is it not unwise to give oneself to everyone in unrestrained tenderness, as people in general are not trustworthy?' But if a person is good and kind, this goodness ought to become manifest to everyone, and the doors of the heart should be closed to nobody.

Jesus Christ not only told us to love our friends; he went as far as to say we should love our enemies; and the Sufi treads the same path. He considers his charity of heart towards his fellow-men to be love for God, and in showing love to everyone, he feels he is giving his love to God. Here the Sufi and the Yogi differ. The Yogi is not unkind, but he says, 'I love you all, but I had better keep away from you, for your souls are always groping in darkness, and my soul is in the light. Your friendship will harm my soul, so I had better keep away and love you from afar.' The Sufi says, 'It is a trial, but it should be tried. I shall take up my everyday duties as they come along.' Although he knows how unimportant the things of the world are, and does not overvalue these things, he attends to his responsibilities towards those who love him, like him, depend upon him, follow him; and he tries to find the best way of coming to terms with all those who dislike and despise him. He lives in the world and yet he is not of the world. In this way the Sufi considers that the main principle in the fulfilment of the purpose of his life is to love man.

Those who love their enemies and yet lack patience are like a burning lantern with little oil. It cannot keep alight, and in the end the flame fades away. The oil in the path of love is patience, and besides this it is unselfishness and self-sacrifice from beginning to end.

Some say, 'I have loved dearly once, but I was disappointed.' It is as if a man were to say, 'I dug in the earth, but when the mud came I was disappointed.' It is true that mud came, but with patience he would have reached the water one day. Only patience can endure. Only endurance produces greatness.

Imitation gold can be as beautiful as real gold, the imitation diamond as bright as a real diamond. The difference is that the one fails in the test of endurance, and the other stands up to it. Yet man should not be compared with objects. Man has something divine in him, and he can prove this by his endurance in the path of love.

Whom then should one love, and how should one love? Whatever a person loves, whether duty, human beings, art, friends, an ideal, or his fellow-creatures, he has assuredly opened the door through which he must pass in order to reach that love which is God. The beginning of love is an excuse; it leads to that ideal of love which is God alone. Some say that they can love God, but not human beings. But this is like saying to God, 'I love Thee, but not Thine image.' Can one hate the human creatures in which God's image is to be found and yet claim to love God? If one is not tolerant, not willing to sacrifice, can one then claim the love of the Lord? The first lesson is the widening of the heart and the awakening of the inner feeling of the heart. The sign of saintliness is not in the power of words, not in the high position, either spiritual or intellectual, not magnetism; the saintly spirit only expresses itself in the love of all creatures; it is the continuous springing of love from that divine fountain in the heart of man. When once that fountain is turned on it purifies the heart, it makes the heart transparent to reveal both the outer and the inner world. The heart becomes the vehicle for the soul to see all that is within and without, and then a man not only communicates with another person, but also with God.

CHAPTER VII

REPOSE

WHEN THE lips are closed, then the heart begins to speak; when the heart is silent, then the soul blazes up, bursting into flame, and this illuminates the whole of life. It is this idea which demonstrates to the mystic the great importance of silence, and this silence is gained by repose. Most people do not know what repose means, because it is something they feel they need when they are tired, while if they were not tired they would never see the necessity for it.

Repose has many aspects. It is one kind of repose when a person retires from the activity of everyday life and finds himself alone in his room. He draws a breath of thankfulness as he feels, after all his interesting or tiresome experiences, 'At last I am by myself'. It is not an ordinary feeling, for there is a far deeper feeling behind it; it expresses the certainty that there is nothing to distract his mind and nothing which demands his action. At that moment his soul has a glimpse of relief, the pleasure of which is inexpressible; but the intoxication of life from which every man suffers is such that he cannot fully appreciate that moment of relief, which everyone expects, when it is time to retire after the activities of his daily life, whether he be rich or poor, tired or not.

Does this not teach us that there is a great mystery in repose, a mystery of which people are very often ignorant? Besides we always find that a thoughtful person has repose by nature, and one who has repose is naturally thoughtful. It is repose which makes one more thoughtful, and it is continual action which takes away thoughtfulness even from a sensible person. People working in the telephone, telegraph, or post offices, upon whose mind there is a continual demand, often in time develop impertinence, insolence, and lack of patience. They do not become less sensible; it only means that lack of repose, which weakens their sense of control, makes them give way to such things. This shows that repose is necessary not only for a person on the spiritual path, but for every soul living on the earth, whatever be his grade of evolution or his standing in life. It is the most important thing to be developed in anyone's nature; not only in a grown-up person, but it is something which should be taught from childhood. Nowadays in education people think so much about the different intellectual attainments the child will need in life, and so little about the repose which is so very necessary for a child.

Sometimes cats and dogs prove more intuitive than mankind. Although man is more capable than the animals he does not give himself time to become more intuitive. It often amused me in New York, where one easily becomes exhausted by the noise of trains and trams and elevators and factories, to see that when a person had a little leisure to sit in the train or subway, he at once began looking at the newspapers. All that action was not enough; is it not in the body, then there must be action in the brain! What is it? It is nervousness, a common disease which today has almost become normal health. If everybody suffers from the same disease then this disease may be called normal. But self-control, self-discipline, only comes from the practice of repose, which is helpful not only on the spiritual path but also in one's practical life, in being kind and considerate.

The mystic therefore adopts the method of repose, and by this he tries to prepare himself to tread the spiritual path. This path is not an outer path; it is an inner path one has to tread, and therefore the spiritual laws and the journey on the spiritual path are quite contrary to the earthly laws and the journey on the outer path. To explain in simple words what the spiritual path is, I would say that it begins by living in communication with oneself, for it is in the innermost self of man that the life of God is to be found. This does not mean that the voice of the inner self does not come to everyone. It always comes, but not everyone hears it. That is why the Sufi, when he starts his efforts on this path, begins by communicating with his true self within; and when once he has addressed the soul, then from the soul comes a kind of reproduction, like that which the singer can hear on a record which has been made of his own voice.

Having done this, when he has listened to what this process reproduces, he has taken the first step in the direction within;

and this process will have awakened a kind of echo in his being. Either peace or happiness, light or form, whatever he has wished to produce, is produced as soon as he begins to communicate with himself. When we compare the man who says, 'I cannot help being active, or sad, or worried, as it is the condition of my mind and soul,' with the one who communicates with himself, it is not long before we, too, begin to realize the value of this communication.

This is what the Sufis have taught for thousands of years. The path of the Sufi is not to communicate with fairies nor even with God; it is to communicate with one's deepest, innermost self, as if one were blowing one's inner spark into a divine fire. But the Sufi does not stop there, he goes still further. He then remains in a state of repose, and that repose can be brought about by a certain way of sitting and breathing, and also by a certain attitude of mind. Then he begins to become conscious of that part of his being which is not the physical body, but which is above it. The more he becomes conscious of this, the more he begins to realize the truth of the life hereafter. Then it is no longer a matter of his imagination or of his belief; it is his actual realization of the experience which is independent of physical life, and it is in this state that he is capable of experiencing the phenomena of life. The Sufi therefore does not dabble in different wonder-workings and phenomena, for once he realizes this the whole of life becomes a phenomenon, and every moment, every experience, brings to him a realization of that life which he has found in his meditation.

The being of man is a mechanism of body and mind. When this mechanism is in order there is happiness, fullness of life; and when anything is wrong with the mechanism, the body is ill and peace is gone. This mechanism depends upon winding; it is just like a clock which is wound and it then goes for twenty-four hours. So it is in meditation; when a person sits in a restful attitude and puts his mind in a condition of repose, regulating the action of this mechanism by the process of meditation, it is like the winding of a clock. And its effect continues to be felt because the mechanism was put in order.

Thus the belief of a mystic is not an outward belief in a deity he

D

has not seen; the mystic's worship is not only an outer form—by saying prayers and then his worship is finished. Certainly he makes the best use of the outer things and his pursuit is logical and scientific; he will if possible unite them with the mystical conception; but mysticism includes the scientific explanation as well as the realization of the things taught by religion, things which would have no meaning to an ordinary person. When an ordinary person reads about the kingdom of God and heaven, he reads these names but he does not know where heaven is; he feels that there is a God but there is no evidence for it. And therefore a large number of intellectual people who really are seeking the truth, are turning away from the outer religion, because they cannot find its explanation, and consequently they become materialistic. To the mystic the explanation of the whole of religion is the investigation of the self. The more one explores oneself, the more one will understand all religions in the fullest light and all will become clear. Sufism is only a light thrown upon one's own religion like a light brought into a room where everything one wants is to be found, and where the only thing that was needed was light.

Of course the mystic is not always ready to give an answer to everyone who asks. Can parents always answer their children's questions? There are some questions which can be answered, and others which should wait for an answer until those who ask them are able to understand. I used to be fond of a poem which yet I did not understand; I could not find a satisfactory explanation. After ten years, all of a sudden, in one second, a light was thrown upon it, and I understood. There was no end to my joy. Does it not show that everything has its appointed time? When people become impatient and ask for an answer, something can be answered, something else cannot be answered; but the answer will come in its own time. One has to wait. Has anyone in the world been able to explain fully what God is, have even the scriptures and the prophets succeeded in this? God is an ideal too high and too great for words to explain. Can anyone explain such a word as love, can anyone say what truth is?

If truth is to be attained it is only when truth itself has begun to speak, which happens in revelation. Truth reveals itself, therefore the Persian word for both God and truth is *Khuda*, which means self-revealing, thus uniting God with truth. One cannot explain either of these words. The only help the mystic can give is by indicating how to arrive at this revelation. No one can teach or learn this; one has to learn oneself. The teacher is only there to guide one towards this revelation. There is only one teacher: God; and the great masters of the world were the greatest pupils; they each knew how to become a pupil.

How is this all taught or brought to the consciousness of those who tread the path of truth? By Bayat, by initiation. It is the trust of someone who guides, given to someone who is treading the path. The one who treads the path must be willing to risk the difficulties of the path; to be sincere, faithful, truthful, undoubting, not pessimistic or sceptical, otherwise with all his efforts he will not reach his aim. He must come whole-heartedly, or else he should not come at all. Half-heartedness is of no value. And what is necessary, too, is some intellectual understanding of the metaphysical aspect of life, which some have, but not all; besides this the qualities of the heart are needed, with the divinity of love as a first principle. Then one needs action, but such action as will not hinder on the path of truth, such action as creates greater and greater harmony. And finally one needs repose, which makes it possible to learn by one day of silence what would otherwise take a year of study; but no doubt only if one knows the real way of silence.

CHAPTER VIII

ACTION

VERY OFTEN a man is apt to think that it is study and meditation and prayer which alone can bring him to the way leading to the goal; but it must be understood that action also plays an important part. Few indeed know what effect every action has upon one's life, what power a right action can give, and what effect a wrong action can have. Man is only on the look-out for what others think of his actions, instead of being concerned with what God thinks of them. If man knew what effect an action produces upon himself, he would understand that though a murderer may escape the hands of the policeman, he has not escaped from the fault he has committed. For he cannot escape his self; the greatest judge is sitting in his own heart. He cannot hide his acts from himself. No doubt it is difficult, almost impossible, for a man to judge the acts of other people, for he does not know what their conditions are. Man can best judge himself; however wicked he may be, he will not be really pleased with his wrong actions, or if he is pleased for a moment, this pleasure will not last.

But what is right and what is wrong? No one can stamp a deed as right or wrong. But there is a natural sense in man which distinguishes between right and wrong, just or unjust, a sense which is to be found even in a child. The child also sees the line and colour in art or decoration; it notices when the tablecloth is not laid straight on the table, when a line that should be straight is not straight. Even a child knows when things should be harmonious, and a child normally loves harmony. There is a natural tendency in the heart of man, the same natural instinct which masons use when building a house.

Different religions have taught different morals which were right for the people at that time. No doubt the law of the masses must be respected, but the real conception of right and wrong lies in one's deepest self. The soul is not pleased with that which is not right. The soul's satisfaction lies always in something which gives it complete happiness. The whole of Sufism is based on the practice not only of thought but of action, as all religions have been based not only on truth but on action. Things both material and spiritual have been accomplished by action. To the mystic, therefore, action is most important. During my travels from place to place, when I have come in contact with different people and have had the opportunity of staying with them, I have met some who had perhaps never in their lives read a book on theology or studied mysticism, their whole life having been spent in work, business, and industry; and yet I felt a spiritual advancement made naturally by their right actions in life. They had come to a state of purity which perhaps someone else might find by means of study or meditation.

One might ask, what is the best way to take in everyday life to lead one to life's ideal? The best way is to consider harmony as the first principle to be observed; that in all circumstances and situations and conditions one should try to harmonize with one's fellow-creatures. It is easy to say, but most difficult to live; it is not always easy to harmonize. But if we question ourselves as to why it is so difficult, the answer is that it is not always that other people are difficult and not pliable; it is we ourselves who cannot bend. The palm-tree that grows straight up cannot harmonize with other trees whose trunks are not so straight and strong.

There are many good people, but they are not always harmonious. There are many true people, but their truth is not always comforting. They may utter a truth which is like a slap in the face to someone. They are just like the palm-tree, straight and righteous, yet at the same time not in harmony. A harmonious person can bend, is pliable; he can meet others. There is no doubt that in order to harmonize one has to make sacrifices, one has to bend to people one does not want to bend to; one has to be more pliable than one is by nature, one has to be more clever than one really is; and all these attempts will not succeed unless one makes a great effort, unless one realizes that harmony is the most essential thing in life.

Why does a mystic attribute such great importance to harmony? Because to a mystic his whole life is one continuous symphony, a playing of music, each soul contributing his particular part to the symphony. A person's success therefore depends upon the idea he has of harmony. Very few people in the world pay attention to harmony; they do not know that without it there is no chance of happiness. It is only the harmonious ones who can make others happy and partake of that happiness themselves, and apart from them it is hard to find happiness in the world. The fighter has no peace, as his battles will be ever increasing; it is the peacemaker who is blessed. No doubt in order to make peace he will have to fight with himself, and in that way he will be able to make peace with others. Whatever a person's education or position in life, he may possess all he wants, but if that one thing is lacking in his life and heart nothing can bring him peace.

Therefore if a man does not show in his actions some of the characteristics of a human being, characteristics which are not to be found in animals, then he has not awakened to human nature. There are certain actions such as eating, drinking, sitting, and walking, which are not different from those of the animals, yet these very same actions can become specially characteristic of human nature when they have a guiding light behind them. For instance when a man thinks he must not return a push when he is pushed by somebody while walking, and instead says, 'I am sorry,' he shows a tendency which is different from that of an animal, for animals will fight one another and will lower their horns instead of bowing to one another, while their greeting will be a howl. Man can be different.

The special characteristics of man are consideration, refinement, patience, and thoughtfulness. And when once he has practised these, it leads to another action: to the practice of self-sacrifice which in turn leads to a divine action. When man sacrifices his time and his advantages in life for the sake of another whom he loves, respects, or admires, this sacrifice raises him higher than the ordinary standard of human beings; his is then a divine nature, not human any more. Then a human being begins to think as God thinks, and his actions become more and more divine; they become the actions of God, and that makes him greater than the person who merely believes in God.

The awakened soul sees all the doings of grown-up people as the doings of the children of one father. He looks upon them as the Father would look upon all human beings on the earth, without thinking that they are Germans or Englishmen or Frenchmen. They are all equally dear to him. He looks upon all full of forgiveness, not only upon those who deserve it, but also upon the others, for he understands the reason behind it all. By seeing good in everybody and everything, he begins to develop that divine light which expands itself, illuminating the greater part of life and revealing it as a scene of divine sublimity.

The mystic develops a wider outlook on life, and this wider outlook changes his actions. He develops a point of view which may be called a divine point of view. Then he rises to the state in which he feels that all that is done to him comes from God, and when he himself does right or wrong he feels that he does right or wrong to God. To arrive at such a stage is true religion. There can be no better religion than this, the true religion of God on earth. This is the point of view which makes a person God-like, divine. He is resigned when badly treated, but for his own short-comings he will take himself to task, for all his actions are directed towards God.

The conception that the mystic has of the Deity is not only that of a King or a Judge or a Creator; the mystical conception of God is that of the Beloved, the only Beloved there is. To Him all the love of this world is like that of little girls playing with their dolls, loving them. In that way they learn the lessons they have to practise later in life when taking care of the home. The mystic learns the same lessons by proving sincere and devoted to all kinds of creatures, and this he must do in order to awaken himself to the Beloved, the only Beloved there is, to whom all love is due.

THE PATH OF INITIATION AND DISCIPLESHIP

CONTENTS

CHAPTER I

THE PATH OF INITIATION

VERY MUCH has been written and very much has been said about the path of initiation, and people who have been in contact with various schools of occultism have understood it in different ways, and thus have different ideas as to what initiation means. But in point of fact initiation only means a step forward, a step which should be taken with hope and courage, for without courage and hope it would be most difficult to take any forward step.

If I were asked to explain the meaning of initiation in plain words, I would say that it is like the experience of a person who has never learnt how to swim, and he steps into the river or into the sea for the first time, without knowing whether he will be able to float or whether he will be swept away and drowned. Every person has had an initiation in the worldly sense in some form or other. When a business man begins an entirely new enterprise, and there is nothing to support him at this moment except the thought, 'No matter whether I lose or gain, I will take a step forward, I will go into this enterprise although I do not know what will happen later', he undergoes a worldly initiation. And the first attempt of a man who wants to learn to ride, if he has never been on horseback before nor driven a horse, so that he does not know where the horse will take him—this also is an initiation.

But initiation in the real sense of the word, as it is used on the spiritual path, takes place when a person, in spite of having a religion and belief, an opinion and ideas about spiritual things, feels that he should take a step in a direction which he does not know; when he takes the first step, that is an initiation. Ghazali, a great Sufi writer of Persia, has said that entering the spiritual path is just like shooting an arrow at a point one cannot see, so that one does not know what the arrow is going to hit; one only knows one's own action, and one does not see the point aimed at. This is why the path of initiation is difficult for a worldly man. Human nature is such that a man born into this world, who has become acquainted with the life of names and forms, wants to know everything by name and form; he wants to touch something in order to be sure that it exists. It must make an appeal to his physical senses before he thinks that it exists; without this he does not believe that anything can exist. Therefore it is difficult for him to undergo an initiation on a path which does not touch any of his senses. He does not know where he is going.

Besides man has been taught from his childhood a certain faith or belief, and he feels himself so bound to that particular faith or religion that he trembles at every step he may have to take in a direction which perhaps for a moment seems different or even opposite to what he has been taught. Therefore to take the first step on the path of initiation is difficult for a thoughtful person. No doubt a person who is driven by curiosity may jump into anything, but it is all the same to him whether he has initiation or not. However, for the one who takes initiation seriously the first step is the most difficult.

Initiations, according to the mystics, are twelve in number, divided into four stages; just like the semitones in the octave, or the twelve bones in the ear. The first three initiations are the first three steps, taken with the help of a guide whom one calls in Sufi terms a Murshid, a teacher. In Vedantic terms he is called Guru. He will be someone who is walking this earth, a human being placed in the same conditions as everyone else, in the midst of active life, and subject to all trials and troubles and difficulties. The help of such a friend is the first and most important step in these first three stages of the path.

In the East one will rarely find people taking the spiritual path without the guidance of a teacher, for there it is an accepted fact that these first three steps at least must be taken with the help of someone living a human life on earth. We can trace in the traditions that all the prophets, masters, saints, and sages, however great, had an initiator. In the life of Jesus Christ one reads that he was baptized by John the Baptist; and in the lives of all the other prophets and seers there was always someone, however humble or modest or human, and very often not at all comparable in greatness to those prophets, who took these first three steps with them.

But the mother is really the first initiator of all the prophets and teachers in the world; no prophet or teacher, no saint, however great, was ever born who first walked alone without the help of the mother; she had to show him how to walk.

Then there arises the question of how to find the real guru. Very often people are in doubt, they do not know whether the guru they see is a true or a false guru. Frequently a person comes into contact with a false guru in this world where there is so much falsehood. But at the same time a real seeker, one who is not false to himself, will always meet with the truth, with the real, because it is his own real faith, his own sincerity in earnest seeking that will become his torch. The real teacher is within, that lover of reality is one's own sincere self, and if one is really seeking truth sooner or later one will certainly find a true teacher. And supposing one came into contact with a false teacher, what then? Then the real One will turn the false teacher also into a real teacher, because reality is greater than falsehood.

There is a story told of a dervish, a simple man, who was initiated by a teacher, and after that teacher has passed away this man came into contact with some clairvoyant who asked him if he had guidance on his path. The man replied, 'Yes, my master, who passed from this earth. When he was still alive I enjoyed his guidance for some time, so the only thing I would want now is just your blessing.' But the clairvoyant said, 'I see by my clairvoyant power that the teacher who has passed away was not a true teacher.' When the simple man heard this he would not allow himself to be angry with the other, but he said gently, 'This teacher of mine may be false, but my faith is not false, and that is sufficient.'

As there is water in the depths of the earth so there is truth at the bottom of all things, false or true. In some places one has to dig deep, in other places only a short distance, that is the only difference, but there is no place where there is no water. One may have to dig very, very deep in order to get it, but in the depths of the earth there is water, and in the depths of all this falsehood which is on the surface there is truth. If we are really seeking for the truth we shall always find it at some time or other.

The one who wants to protect himself from being misguided

shows a certain tendency, a kind of weakness, which comes from thinking deep in himself that there is no right guidance. If he realizes that right guidance is to be found in himself, he will always be rightly guided; and his power will become so great that if his guide is going wrong, the power of the pupil will help him to go right, because the real Teacher is in the heart of man. The outward teacher is only a sign. A Persian poet has said that he who is a lost soul, even if he is in the presence of a Saviour, will be lost just the same, because his own clouds are surrounding him. It is not a question of a guide or teacher; the obscurity which his own mind creates surrounds him and keeps him blind. What then can a teacher do?

According to a story about the Prophet Mohammad, there lived next door to him a man who was very much opposed to the Prophet and spoke against him; and this man saw that the people to whom he spoke had belief in the Prophet, while nobody believed in him. Then years passed, and many believed and many gave their life for the message of the Prophet; and it so happened that eventually a great many people came from afar, thousands and thousands from different countries, to visit the Prophet. The same man still lived in the neighbourhood, but he had never altered his opinion. And one day someone asked the Prophet, 'Why does this man, who has known the day when nobody listened, when nobody followed you, but who now sees that thousands of people who come here are benefited and filled with bliss and joy and blessing, still continue to criticize you and to oppose you?' And the Prophet said, 'His heart has become a fountain of obscurity; he produces from his own self the clouds which surround him; he cannot see.' And he was sorry for him. The perception of the light shows the thinning of the veil that covers the heart, and the thinner the veil becomes, the greater is the power of the light within.

The next step, the second step in initiation, is to go through the tests that the teacher gives. In this initiation there is a great deal that is amusing, if one thinks about it. It is like looping the loop; sometimes the teacher gives the pupil such tests that he does not know where he is, or whether a thing is true or false. There was a great Sufi teacher in India who had a thousand adherents who were most devoted pupils. One day he said to them, 'I have changed my mind.' And the words 'changed my mind' surprised them greatly; they asked him, 'What is the matter, how can it be that you have changed your mind?' He said, 'I have the feeling that I must go and bow before the Goddess Kali.' And these people, among whom were doctors and professors, well qualified people, could not understand this whim, that their great teacher in whom they had such faith, wished to go into the temple of Kali and bow before the Goddess of the hideous face, he, a God-realized man in whom they had such confidence! And the thousand disciples left him at once, thinking 'What is this? It is against the religion of the formless God, against the teaching of this great Sufi himself, that he wants to worship the Goddess Kali!' And there remained only one pupil, a youth who was very devoted to his teacher, and he followed him when he went to the temple of Kali. The teacher was very glad to get rid of these thousand pupils, who were full of knowledge, full of their learning, but who did not really know him; it was just as well that they should leave. And as they were going towards the temple, he spoke three times to this young man, saying 'Why do you not go away? Look at these thousand people, who had such faith and such admiration, and now I have said just one word, and they have left me. Why do you not go with them? The majority is right.' The pupil, how-ever, would not go, but continued to follow him. And through all this the teacher received great inspiration and a revelation of how strange human nature is, how soon people are attracted and how soon they can fly away. It was such an interesting pheno-menon for him to see the play of human nature that his heart was full of feeling, and when they arrived at the temple of Kali he experienced such ecstasy that he fell down and bowed his head low. And the young man who had followed him did the same.

When he got up he asked this young man again, 'Why do you not leave me when you have seen a thousand people go away? Why do you follow me?' The young man answered, 'There is nothing in what you have done that is against my convictions, because the first lesson you have taught me was that nothing exists save God. If that is true, then that image is not Kali; it too is God. What does it matter whether you bow to the East or to

E

the West or to the earth or to heaven? Since nothing exists except God, there is nobody else except God before whom to bow, even in bowing before Kali. It was the first lesson you taught me.' All these learned men were given the same lesson, they were students and very clever, but they could not conceive of that main thought which was the centre of all the teaching. It was this same young man who later became the greatest Sufi teacher in India, Khwaja Moin-ud-Din Chishti. Every year thousands of people of all religions make pilgrimages to his tomb at Ajmer, Hindus, Mohammedans, Jews, and Christians. To the Sufi all religions are one.

There are tests of many kinds that the teacher may give to his pupil to test his faith, his sincerity, his patience. Before a ship puts to sea the captain goes and makes sure that everything is in order for the voyage; and such is the duty of the teacher. Of course it is a very interesting duty. Besides the path of the mystic is a very complex path. What he says may perhaps have two meanings: the outer meaning is one and the inner meaning is another. What he does may also have two meanings, an outer and an inner meaning, and a person who only sees things outwardly cannot perceive the inner meaning. Because he only sees their outer aspect, he cannot understand his own teacher's action, thought, speech, or movement. It is in this way that the pupil is tested.

Thus to the pupil the teacher may often appear to be very unreasonable, very odd, very meaningless, very unkind and cold and unjust. And during these tests, if the faith and the trust of the pupil do not endure he will step back from this second initiation, but if he endures through all this then comes the third step, the third initiation.

The third initiation consists of three stages: receiving the knowledge attentively; meditating upon all one has received patiently; assimilating all the outcome of it intelligently. Thereby the mission of the teacher in this world is completed. Gratitude still remains, but the principal work is finished.

The fourth initiation the seeker gets from his ideal. And who is this ideal, who can give this initiation? No living creature on earth, however great, can prove to be the ideal of anyone else; he may for a certain time, but not for ever. The great ones like

Buddha, Zoroaster, Christ, and Krishna, who have been the ideal of humanity for thousands of years, when did they become the ideal? During their lifetime? During their lifetime they gave a sense of being the ideal, they left impressions which afterwards proved them to be the ideal, but during their lifetime they could not prove it. Why is this? The reason is that even perfect man is limited in the imperfect garb of humanity. The human limitation covers perfection. However great, however deep, however spiritual a person is, with all his goodness, with all his inspiration and power, he remains limited. His thought, speech, word, and action are all limited. A man cannot make himself as his pupil imagines him. Imagination goes further than the progress of man; the imagination of every person is his own, and therefore one can only make one's ideal oneself. No one has the power to make the ideal of another person, and therefore it is the impression of the great saviours of humanity, it is their goodness, it is whatever little grain of an ideal they have left behind them that becomes just like a seed, and that seed put into the soil of the devotee's heart develops into a plant and bears fruit and flowers as it is reared. So in this fourth initiation there is this ideal of man's imagination. He may call it Christ or Buddha, he may call it Mohammad or Moses or Zoroaster; it is his ideal; it is he who has made it; it is his saviour, and certainly it will save him if he considers it to be his saviour. But he has to make it; if he does not make it, the saviour will not save him. When once he has made his saviour, then he is face to face with that perfection which his heart has created; then this impression of Christ or Buddha with which he has impressed himself flowers and grows into a tree, and bears the flowers and fruit which he has desired. No doubt this initiation is a phenomenon in itself. Once this initiation is received man begins to radiate, to radiate his initiator who is within him as his ideal.

Then there is the second stage which is the fifth initiation. And in the fifth initiation man does not imagine his ideal, but finds his ideal a living entity within himself, a friend who is always close to him, within him; he can just bow his head and see his friend—he is there. To the real devotees of Christ, Christ is near, as near as they are to themselves to their own self. In times of trouble, in difficulties, he is always there.

The third stage, which is the sixth initiation, is the one where Christ speaks, where Christ acts; the acts of the initiate become the actions of Christ, his speech becomes the speech of Christ. And when one has arrived at that initiation one need not declare before humanity how greatly one loves one's Lord or Saviour or Master; the initiate himself becomes a proof, his life, his word, his action, his feeling, his attitude, his outlook.

Life is such that no falsehood, no pretence can endure, nothing false can go far; it will only go a step and then it will tumble down; it is only the real which will go on. And the more real something is, the less it expresses itself. It is lack of reality that makes a person say: he is so and so, he has such great love for God; or he is so spiritual or pious or clairvoyant, or he has such psychic power. When one sees one does not need to say that one sees, everybody will notice that one is not blind.

But how different it is today, when so many people ask, 'Are you clairvoyant, can you see?' And if they say they do, what do they see? They have perhaps seen some colour or some light here and there, or something peculiar, which means nothing. Perhaps it is their imagination. And then there are others who encourage them and make them still more crazy; and people feed their pride by telling others how much they see. But when one begins to see one cannot speak about it, it is something which cannot be told. How could one? When one sees with the eyes of Christ one can only see, when one hears with the ears of Christ one can only hear; there is nothing to be said.

The further initiation, which is the seventh, is the initiation in God. There is an account in the story of Rabia, a great Sufi. Once in her vision she saw the Prophet, and the Prophet asked her, 'Rabia, to whom have you given your devotion?' And Rabia said, 'To God.' And the Prophet said, 'Not to me?' And Rabia said, 'Yes, Prophet, you include God, but it is God I gave my devotion to.' There comes a stage where a person even rises above the ideal he has made. He rises to that perfect Ideal which is beyond the human personality, which is the perfect Being. In this initiation one rises to the spheres where one sees no other than God.

In the second stage, which is the eighth initiation, one communicates with God, so that God becomes to the initiate a living entity; God is then no longer an ideal or an imagination, no longer one whom he has made; the One whom he once made has now become alive—a living God. Before this there was belief in God, there was worship of Him; perhaps He was made in the imagination; but in this stage God becomes living. And what a phenomenon this is! This stage is a miracle in itself. The God-realized person need not speak of or discuss the name of God; his presence will inspire the sense of God in every being, and charge the atmosphere with it. Everyone that meets him, whether he is spiritual or moral or religious or without religion, will feel God in some form or other.

The prophets and the holy ones who have come from time to time to give the world a religion, an ideal, have not brought any new ideas; they have not brought a new belief in God, because belief in God has always existed in some form or other. What they brought was a living God. When there remained no more than God's name in the scripture or in the people's imagination or on the lips of the followers of a certain religion, and when that name began to become a profane name, a vain repetition, then such souls were born on the earth and brought with them a living God. If they gave anything else to humanity, either law, ethics, or morals, these were secondary. The principal thing that they gave to the world was a living God.

The ninth initiation is what is called in Sufi terms *Akhlak-e Allah*, which means the Manner of God. The one who touches that plane or that realization expresses in his manner the manner of God; his outlook on life is God's outlook; his action, his thought, and his word are God's action, thought, and word. Therefore what the prophets spoke was *Kalam-ullah*, the Word of God, as for instance the Bhaghavat Gita which means the Song Celestial. Why? Because at this stage God himself speaks. These holy ones became that perfect Spirit and were moved by it. They became actors, for their action was no longer their own action; it was the action of God. Their word was no longer a human word; it was the word of God.

Very few arrive at the last three initiations in their lifetime, for after the first nine initiations begins what is called the phase of self-realization. When those who have not arrived at this stage begin to utter affirmations such as 'I am God', they utter nothing but vain repetitions, and this obscures the God-ideal. They do not know what they are saying. If people only knew to what an extent they should be authorized before speaking about such things, they would be very careful about what they say.

When after having gone through all the other stages of consciousness one arrives at this stage, one can speak very little; for it is beyond the stage of religion and even beyond the notion of God; it is the stage of self-expression. This stage of self-expression is reached when a person has thoroughly dug his self out, so that nothing of the self is left but only that divine substance; and only then is he authorized to express himself. Thus the tenth initiation is the awakening of the real self, the real ego, and this awakening is brought about by meditation, the meditation which makes one forget one's false or limited self. The more one is able to forget it, the more the real self awakens.

In the next stages one experiences a sensation of splendour, which in Persian is called *Hairat*. It is like when a child is born and begins to see everything new: this old world is seen by the child as a new world. As soon as the point of view is changed by the help of meditation, one sees the whole world, which is before everybody and which everybody is seeing, quite differently. One begins to see reason behind reason, cause behind cause, and one's point of view also changes in regard to religion. It changes because where the average man would want to accuse or punish or blame a person for a certain action, the one who has risen to this stage can neither judge nor blame; he only sees; but he sees the cause behind the cause. Whom then shall he accuse? Whom shall he blame? How can he refrain from forgiving, whatever be the fault, when he sees all that is behind the fault, when he sees the reason behind it, perhaps a more valid reason than even the one who committed the fault can see himself. Therefore naturally the manner of continually sacrificing, the manner of spontaneous love and sympathy, the manner of respect both for the wise and foolish, for the deserving and the undeserving, arises and expresses itself as divine life. It is at this stage that the human soul touches perfection and becomes divine, and that it fulfills its real purpose in life.

CHAPTER II

THE MEANING OF INITIATION

THE MEANING of the word 'initiation' can be understood from its association with 'initiative'. It is a fact that every child which is born on earth is born with initiative; but then, as it grows, that spirit more or less dies away, because the knowledge it gathers in its lifetime makes it doubt. This doubt, increasing more and more, very often makes a man lose the power of initiative, and then he does not want to take another step until he is sure whether there is land or water in front of him, and very often water looks like land, and land looks like water. According to the mystics life is an illusion, and thus man bases his reason upon illusion. Nevertheless, the reasoning power which he acquires helps him in his life in the world, although it is very often just this reasoning which holds him back from taking what is called the initiative.

It is through this spirit of initiative that anyone in the world who has accomplished something great, has been able to do so. At the beginning of his efforts people call such a person mad or fanatical, or crazy, or devoid of reason, but when they see the result they think that he is most wise. Great prophets, the builders of nations, famous inventors, and great discoverers have all proved this. One may ask then if they do not see what is before them in the same way that a reasoning person does. They do, but with different eyes. Their point of view is different; it does not always agree with the point of view of the average person, and so it is natural that people should call them fanatical, although they see perhaps more than do all those around them. Those who have helped themselves to achieve success after complete failure, or to get over an illness after great suffering, have only succeeded in this by the spirit of initiative.

There are different kinds of initiation that souls experience. One is natural initiation. A kind of natural unfoldment for which the soul cannot give any cause or reason, comes to a soul, although no effort or attempt has been made by that soul to experience it. Sometimes this initiation comes after great illness, pain, or suffering. It comes as an opening up of the horizon, it comes as a flash of light, and in a moment the world seems transformed. It is not that the world has changed; it is that that person has become tuned to a different pitch. He begins to think differently, feel differently, see and act differently; his whole condition begins to change. One might say of him that from that moment he begins to live. It may come as a vision, as a dream, as a phenomenon—in any of these forms; one cannot determine the manner in which it will manifest.

Another initiation known to the mystics is the initiation that one receives from a person living on the earth. Every mystical school has its own initiation. In the Orient, where mystical ideas are prevalent and are regarded as most sacred, any person who wishes to tread the spiritual path considers initiation to be the most important thing. If a soul such as Jesus Christ had to be baptized by John the Baptist, no soul on earth can say, 'I have risen above initiation.' Is that then impossible? Nothing is impossible. It may be possible for a person to jump into the water with the intention of swimming to the port of New York, but his life will be more secure if he books his passage with the normal shipping lines. And the difference between these two souls is the same, or even greater—between the one who wishes to journey on the spiritual path by taking initiation, and the other who refuses to do so.

Initiation by a spiritual teacher means both a trust given by the teacher to the pupil, and a trust given by the pupil to the teacher. And the progress of the one who is initiated depends upon how much he gives himself to the teacher's guidance. One might give only a finger, another even a part of a finger, while a third would give his whole hand. That makes a great difference, for if a pupil says, 'Well, I will give a certain amount of my time and thought to your guidance, will that be enough?' the teacher will say, 'Yes, if you think it is enough;' but in reality it is never enough. Then one might wonder if one would not be giving up one's own point of view in order to follow someone else's point of view; but actually if one has a point of view, one never loses it. The point of view which one loses is not one's own. And by looking at a thing from another person's point of view one only enlarges one's own: then one has two points of view instead of one. If the thought of the pupil happens to be different from that of the teacher, by taking the teacher's thought his own is doubled; the pupil keeps his own point of view just the same, only now he has something for his vision from which to make his choice; the horizon of his thought is expanded. But the pupil who closes himself and says, 'I will guard my point of view or it will escape me,' will never derive any benefit from this attitude.

The mystical path is the most subtle path to tread. The relationship between teacher and pupil is too subtle for words to express. Besides the language of a mystical teacher is always elusive; you cannot, so to speak, pin him down as to his words; you cannot ask him to say clearly that something is so and so, or such and such. And if a mystic does so he is not a mystic, for a mystic cannot do this. The mystic may seem to be standing on the earth, but he is flying in the air. The air cannot be made into a rock, nor can the mystic be made into a gross entity. His 'yes' does not mean the same as the 'yes' of another, nor does his 'no' mean the same as the 'no' of others. The language of the mystic is not the language of words; it is the language of meaning. It is the greatest distress for a mystic to have to use the words of everyday language, which are not his words. He cannot express himself in these words. And we find the same in the action of the mystic. His outward actions will not express to everybody the meaning which is behind them, and that meaning may be much more important inwardly than the action is outwardly.

The teacher therefore tests his pupil continually. He tells him and he does not tell him, for everything must come in its right time. Divine knowledge has never been taught in words, nor will it ever be so taught. The work of a mystical teacher is not to teach but to tune, to tune the pupil so that he may become the instrument of God. For the mystical teacher is not the player of the instrument; he is the tuner. When he has tuned it, he gives it into the hands of the Player whose instrument it is to play. The duty of the mystical teacher is his service as a tuner.

Dispute with a spiritual teacher is never any good. For the pupil may be speaking one language while the teacher speaks another, and when there is no common language, how can the dispute be profitable? Therefore in the path of mysticism there is no dispute.

Also, there are no fixed rules to follow on this path. For every person there is a special rule. But there is one law which applies to everything in life: sincerity, which is the only thing that is asked by a teacher of a pupil, for truth is not the portion of the insincere.

Several initiations may be given to the pupil whom the teacher has taken in hand, but his progress depends upon the pupil himself. Just as parents are anxious, so the spiritual teacher is naturally anxious to see the advancement of his pupil. There is no reason for the teacher to keep any pupil back from success; for as the happiness of the parents lies in the happiness of the child, so the satisfaction of the teacher lies in the advancement of the pupil.

But then there is another kind of initiation which comes afterwards, and this initiation is also an unfoldment of the soul. It comes as an after-effect of the initiation that one had from the teacher. It comes as a kind of expansion of consciousness, and the greatness of this initiation depends upon the distance and width of the horizon of the consciousness. Many may claim it, but few realize it. Those who realize do not claim. As the more fruitful a tree is the more it bends, so the more divine his spiritual realization is the more humble a person becomes. It is the one who is less fruitful who becomes more pretentious. The really initiated ones hardly ever mention the word initiation; they find no profit in convincing others that they are initiated. They possess their real inner gains so they do not want an outer gain; it is the one who has not got any who wants recognition from outside. And if we ask what profit we derive from initiation, the answer is that religion, mysticism, or philosophy—all that we gain—should help us to achieve one result, and that is to be best fitted for serving our fellow-men.

It may be asked whether it is desirable for every soul to take initiation. The word 'initiation' and the associated word 'initiative' suggest going forward, so the answer is that progress is life and standing still is death. Whatever be our grade of evolution, it is always advisable to try to go forward, be it in business or in a profession, in society or in political life, in religion or in spiritual advancement. No doubt there is a danger in being too enthusiastic.

The nature that is too enthusiastic may, instead of benefiting, perhaps harm itself in whatever line it may have taken up, worldly or spiritual. For everything there is a time, and patience is necessary in all striving. A cook may burn food by applying more heat in order to cook more quickly, and this rule applies to all things. With little children the parents are often anxious and enthusiastic; they think their children should learn and understand every good and interesting thing on earth. Too much enthusiasm is not right. We must give time to all things; the first and most important lesson in life is patience; we must begin all things with patience.

The Sufi Order is mainly an esoteric school. There are three principal esoteric schools known in the East: the Buddhist school, the Vedantic school, and the Sufi school. The two former use asceticism as their principal means of spiritual advancement; the peculiarity of the Sufi school is that it uses humanity as its chief means to the same end. In the realization of truth the Sufi school is no different from the Vedantic or the Buddhist, but the Sufi presents truth in a different manner. It is the same frame in which Jesus Christ has given his teaching.

No doubt the method of helping spiritual development by contemplation and meditation is used in all three schools, the science of breath being the foundation of each; but the Sufi thinks that man was not created as man to live the life of an angel, neither was he created to live the life of an animal. For the life of an angel, angels are created, and for the life of an animal there are animals. The Sufi thinks that the first thing which is necessary for man in life is to prove to his own conscience to what extent he can be human. It is not only a spiritual development, it is the culture of humanity: in what relation man stands to his neighbour or friend, to those who depend upon him and those who look up to him, to strangers unknown to him; how he stands with those younger than himself and with older people, with those who like him and others who dislike him and criticize him; how he should feel and think and act through life, and yet keep on progressing towards the goal which is the goal for every soul in the world. It is not necessary for the Sufi to seek the wilderness for his meditation, since he can perform part of his work in the midst of worldly life. The Sufi need not prove himself a Sufi by extraordinary power, by wonder-working or by an exceptional spiritual manifestation or claim. A Sufi can prove to his own conscience that he is a Sufi by watching his own life amidst the strife of this world.

There are some who are content with a belief taught at home or in church. They are contented, and they may just as well rest in that stage of realization where they are contented until another impulse is born in their hearts to rise higher. The Sufi does not force his belief or his thoughts upon such souls. In the East there is a saying that it is a great sin to awaken anyone who is fast asleep. This saying can be symbolically understood: that there are many in this world who work and do things and are yet asleep; they seem awake externally, but inwardly they are asleep. The Sufi considers it a crime to awaken them, for some sleep is good for their health. The work of the Sufi is to give a helping hand to those who have had sufficient sleep and who now begin to stir in their sleep, to turn over. And it is that kind of help which is the real initiation.

No doubt there are things which pass the ordinary comprehension of man. There are things one can teach only by speaking or by acting, but there is a way of teaching which is called *Tawajoh* and this way of teaching is without words. It is not external teaching; it is teaching in silence. For instance, how can man explain the spirit of sincerity, or the spirit of gratefulness? How can man explain the ultimate truth, the idea of God? Whenever it has been attempted it has failed; it has made some confused, and it has made others give up their belief. It is not that the one who tried to explain did not understand, but that words are inadequate to explain the idea of God.

In the East there are great sages and saints who sit quite still, with lips closed, for years. They are called *Muni*, which means 'he who takes the vow of silence'. The man of today may think, 'What a life, to be silent and do nothing!' But he does not know that some by their silence can do more than others can accomplish by talking for ten years. A person may argue for months about a problem and not be able to explain it, while another, with inner radiance, may be able to answer the same thing in one moment. But the answer that comes without words explains still more. That is initiation.

However, no one can give spiritual knowledge to another, for this is something which is within every heart. What the teacher can do is to kindle the light which is hidden in the heart of the disciple. If the light is not there, it is not the fault of the teacher.

There is a verse by Hafiz in which he says, 'However great be the teacher, he is helpless with the one whose heart is closed.' Therefore initiation means initiation on the part of the disciple and on the part of the teacher, a step forward on the part of both. On the part of the teacher, a step forward with the disciple in order that the pupil may be trusted and raised from his present condition. A step forward for the pupil, because he opens his heart; he has no barrier any more, nothing to hinder the teaching in whatever form it comes, in silence or in words, or in the observation of some deed or action on the part of the teacher.

In ancient times the disciples of the great teachers learned by a quite different method, not an academic method or way of study. The way was that with open heart, with perfect confidence and trust, they watched every attitude of the teacher both towards friends and towards people who looked at him with contempt; they watched their teacher in times of trouble and pain, how he endured it all; they say how patient and wise he had been in discussing with those who did not understand, answering everyone gently in his own language; he showed the mother-spirit, the father-spirit, the brother-spirit, the child-spirit, the friend-spirit, forgiving kindness, an ever tolerant nature, respect for the aged, compassion for all, the thorough understanding of human nature. This also the disciples learnt: that no discussion or books on metaphysics can ever teach all the thoughts and philosophy that arise in the heart of man. A person may either study for a thousand years, or he may get to the source and see if he can touch the root of all wisdom and all knowledge. In the centre of the emblem of the Sufis there is a heart; it is the sign that from the heart a stream rises, the stream of divine knowledge.

On the path of initiation two things are necessary: contemplation, and the living of a life such as a Sufi ought to live; and they depend upon each other. Contemplation helps one to live the life of a Sufi, and the life of a Sufi helps contemplation. In the West, where life is so busy and where there is no end to one's responsibilities, one wonders if to undertake contemplation, even for only ten minutes in the evening, is not too much when one is tired. But for that very reason contemplation is required more in the West than in the East where everything, even the surroundings, is helpful to contemplation. Besides a beginning must be made on the path. If contemplation does not develop in such a form that everything one does in life becomes a contemplation, then the contemplation does not do a person any good. It would be like going to church once a week and forgetting all about religion on the other days. To a man who gives ten or twenty minutes every evening to contemplation and forgets it all the rest of the day, contemplation will not do any good. We take our food at certain times every day; yet all the time, even when we are sleeping, the food nourishes our body. It is not the Sufi's idea to retire in seclusion or to sit silent all day. His idea is that by contemplation he becomes so inspired that in study, in every aspiration, in every aspect of life, progress is made. In this way he proves his contemplation to be a force helping him to withstand all the difficulties that come to him.

The life that the Sufi ought to live may be explained in a few words. There are many things in the life of a Sufi, but the greatest is to have a tendency to friendship; this is expressed in the form of tolerance and forgiveness, in the form of service and trust. In whatever form he may express it this is the central theme: the constant desire to prove one's love for humanity, to be the friend of all.

CHAPTER III

WHAT IS NEEDED ON THE PATH

INITIATION needs courage and the tendency to advance spiritually, although it may not seem to be the way of life for everyone. Therefore the first duty of a mureed is not to be shaken in his faith by any opposing influence or by anything said against the path he has taken. He should not allow himself to be discouraged by anybody. The mureed must be so firm in his path that if the whole world says it is a wrong path, he will say it is the right path. And if anybody says that it will take a thousand years or perhaps more, the mureed must be able to say that even if it should take a thousand years, he will have the patience to go through with it. As it is said in Persian, it is the work of the *Baz*, the wayfarer of the heavens.

In this mystical path courage, steadfastness, and patience are what is most necessary, but also trust in the teacher at whose hand initiation is taken, and the understanding of the idea of discipline. In the East, where for thousands of years the path of discipleship has been understood, these things are regarded as most important and acceptable from the hand of the teacher. How few in the world know trust! What is necessary is not trusting another, even the teacher, but oneself, and one is not capable of trusting oneself fully when one has not experienced in life how to trust another. Some will ask, 'But if we trusted and our trust was in vain, should we not be disappointed?' The answer is, that we must trust for the sake of the trust, and not for the sake of a return and to see what fruit it brings. The utmost trust is the greatest power in the world. Lack of trust is weakness. Even if we have lost something by trusting, our power will be greater than if we had gained something without developing trust.

Patience is very necessary on the path. After my initiation into the Order of the Sufis I was for six months continually in the presence of my murshid before he said a word on the subject of Sufism; and as soon as I took out my notebook he went on to another subject; it was finished! One sentence after six months! A person would think that it is a long time, six months sitting before one's teacher without being taught anything; but it is not words, it is something else. If words were sufficient, there are libraries full of occult and mystical books. It is life itself, it is living that is important. The one who lives the life of initiation not only lives himself, but also makes others who come in contact with him alive. Therefore one is initiated into the Sufi Order not especially for study, but to understand and follow what real discipleship means.

With regard to the subject of discipline, anybody without a

sense of discipline is without the power of self-control. It is discipline which teaches the ideal, and the ideal is self-discipline. It is the disciplined soldier who can become a good captain. In ancient times the kings used to send the princes out as soldiers, to learn what discipline means. The path of initiation is the training of the ego, and it is self-discipline which is learned on the path of discipleship.

One may ask what one should think of the path of initiation: what must be our goal, what must we expect from it? Should we expect to be good, or healthy, or magnetic, or powerful, or developed psychically, or clairvoyant? None of these does one need to be, although in time one will cultivate them all naturally, but one should not strive for these things.

Suppose a person develops power, and he does not know how to use it, the outcome will be disastrous. Suppose he develops magnetism, and by his power he attracts all, both good and bad; then it will be difficult to get rid of what he has attracted by his power. Or perhaps a person is very good, so good that everyone seems bad to him; he is too good to live in the world, and in that way he will become a burden to himself. These things are not to be sought for through initiation. The aim is to find God within ourselves, to dive deep into ourselves, so that we may touch the unity of the whole Being. It is towards this end that we are working by the power of initiation, in order that we may get all the inspiration and blessing in our life from within.

For this two things are necessary: one is to do the exercises that are given regularly and to do them with heart and soul; the second is to undertake the studies that are given, not considering them to be only for superficial reading, but for every word to be pondered upon. The more one thinks about it, the more it will have the effect of opening the heart. Reading is one thing, contemplating is another. The lessons must be meditated upon; one should not take even the simplest word or sentence for granted. Think of the Hindus, Chinese, Parsis, who for thousands of years have always meditated upon the readings which they held sacred and yet never tired of them.

Initiation is a sacred trust, a trust given by the murshid to his mureed and a trust given by the mureed to the murshid. There should no longer be a wall from the moment of this initiation; for if there is a wall, then the initiation is not an initiation any more. And when the wall between the mureed and the murshid has been removed, then the next step will be for the wall to be removed that stands between God and the worshipper. Besides the Sufi Order is an order of mysticism, and there are certain thoughts and considerations which should be observed. One of these is that when once a secret has been entrusted to one, it must be kept as one's most sacred trust. One must also accept all the teaching that may be given to one; whether it is bitter medicine or sweet, the patient takes it. There is a time for everything, and so illumination has its time. But progress, the real progress, depends upon the patience of the pupil, together with his eagerness to go forward.

The path of initiation is also a path of tests: tests from the initiator, tests from God, tests from the self, and tests from the world; and to go through these tests is the sign of real progress in the mureed, while the one who does not undertake these tests will be wasting his time.

The Order, and this is apparent from the word 'order' itself, means that there is a certain formal hierarchy of the initiators and of the Pir-o-Murshid, and that they should be regarded and respected as those who have gone further in that chosen direction. This law is in no way different from the law of nature and of life: when a child who has been disrespectful to its parents itself becomes a parent, it will find the same attitude in its own children. A soldier who does not observe discipline under his captain or colonel will experience the same from his subordinates when later he holds that position. But the question is whether he will ever arrive at that rank, not having considered and observed that which should have been observed; for those who have advanced in any line, whether in music, in poetry, in thought, or in philosophy, have always done so in a humble way, at every step greeting those who have gone further.

Then there are three stages for the pupil, the mureed, who treads the spiritual path. The first stage is receptivity, taking all that is given without saying, 'This teaching I will accept and that I will not accept.' The next stage is assimilating the teachings. And the third stage is fixing them in the mind and letting the mind see the reason of things; but this comes after assimilation. Thus the one who considers these three stages and goes through them carefully, securely—the stage of receptivity, the stage of assimilation, and the stage of consideration—will be the successful mureed on the path.

Although the outer form might appear to be a hierarchy, yet the Sufi message leads to true democracy, for it holds the promise of that goal which is the yearning of every soul. This itself is the principal thing in democracy, because it is this which makes democracy; and the reason, according to the Sufi belief, is that the divine spark is in every soul. It is with trust and confidence in God, in the murshid, and in that divine spark which is in one's own heart that one is assured of success in life if one will only step forward.

CHAPTER IV

THE DIFFERENT STEPS ON THE PATH

THE WORD initiation is interpreted by different people in different ways. By some it is considered to be a kind of attachment to a certain secret order, but what I mean by initiation is taking a step forward on a path unknown to oneself.

Initiations are of three different kinds. One initiation comes from within oneself, and this initiation is a person's intention to proceed on a path which is not generally taken by his fellow-creatures. If this does not come from within he will always be afraid to take a step further on a path which others around him do not take, for the conception of the generality is not that of an individual. The nature of most people is like that of sheep; wherever sheep are taken, there all the other sheep will follow. One should realize that although it is the nature of sheep to move in a flock this is not the real nature of man. He will always deny that he has this tendency and he will disapprove of it, and yet he will do the very thing without knowing that he does it. If you want to see it, just stand in the street and look up with surprise, acting as if you were absorbed in what you see, and soon twenty persons will be standing by your side, not only foolish people but wise ones too! Therefore he who is initiated, who walks on the path of initiation, is someone who has risen above the crowd, and goes his individual way forward, independent of those who are around him.

When a man begins to feel that there is something behind the veil, when he begins to feel that there is something which he can attain by effort, then he takes the first step on the path which as yet he does not know. One should not be surprised if one notices this initiation in a five-year-old child, neither need one be surprised if one does not see any sign of it in a man of sixty years; he has had no tendency towards it and all his life he has not thought about it. But the one who has received this initiation will go on; even in childhood he will show the tendency to take a step forward on a path which others do not take.

One will find this initiation in all the different aspects of life. A child taking a slate and pencil and drawing a picture, while not being an artist yet has a tendency to draw something, perhaps an idea which is not a child's idea but is very wonderful. One will find a child humming or singing a piece of music which a composer will be surprised to hear. He is doing something which is not ordinary, something which comes spontaneously from his soul and which shows his initiation in that path. One will also hear a child speak on certain subjects, and express ideas which are quite different from what one would expect from a child, ideas which are perhaps even beyond the comprehension of a grown man. Yet the child speaks about it; it is his initiation. I have known a child to ask me, 'Why must one kneel down, why must one prostrate oneself when they say that God is above?' and another to say, 'Why must there be one direction in which a person should look in order to worship, why should not all directions be equally good for worship?'

Many grown-up people have the fixed idea that they must perform their worship in a certain direction and not in any other, and never once in their lives have they asked themselves why. One will find grown-up people who have perhaps worshipped kneeling down all their life, and have never asked themselves why they should kneel down on the earth when they are supposed to worship God in the heavens. Therefore to believe, to worship, to be pious, to be good is quite different from the idea of being initiated. Initiation means emerging from the ordinary, it is rising above the conditions which are common; and this shows the maturity of the soul.

The second stage is the materialization of this initiation; and this materialization is possible with someone living on the earth. For the condition of being initiated completely is to become initiated on this plane of earth, on the physical plane where one is living and moving and through which one is experiencing life.

People make a great many mysteries out of the name initiation, but the simple explanation of initiation is trust on the part of the pupil and confidence on the part of the initiator. I heard from my murshid, from my initiator, something which I shall never forget, 'This friendship, this relationship which is brought about by initiation between two persons is something which cannot be broken, it is something which cannot be separated, it is something which cannot be compared with anything else in the world; it belongs to eternity.'

When this initiation takes place it then becomes the responsibility of the initiator to think of the welfare and well-being of his pupil; and it becomes the responsibility of the initiated to be faithful and true and steady and unshaken through all tests and trials. There are some who will go to one person and be initiated, and then afterwards they go to another to be initiated, and then to a third. They might go to a hundred persons, but they will become a hundred times less instead of a hundred times more blessed. For the object of friendship is not the making of many friends, the object is to keep friendship steady, unchanged, whole. And of all kinds of friendship, the friendship that is established by initiation is the most sacred, a friendship which must be considered beyond all other relationships in the world.

There is a story of a peasant in India, a young peasant who used to take a great interest in spiritual things. And someone with a great name happened to come to his town, about whom it was said, as it was always said among simple peasants, that he was so great that by coming into his presence one would be sure to enter the heavens. The whole town went to see him and to get from him that guarantee of entering the heavens, except that peasant who had once been initiated. The great man having heard about his refusal went to his house and asked him, 'How is it that you who take such interest in holy subjects did not come, while everyone else came to see me?' He said, 'There was no ill-feeling on my part, there was only one simple reason. My teacher who initiated me has passed from this earth, and since he was a man with limitations I do not know whether he has gone to heaven or to the other place. And if through the blessing of your presence I were sent to heaven, I might be most unhappy there; heaven would become another place for me if my teacher were not there.'

It is this oneness, this connection, it is this relationship between the initiator and the initiated which gives them the necessary strength, power, and wisdom to journey on this path. For it is the devotion of the initiated which supplies all that is lacking in the initiator, and it is the trust of the initiator which supplies all that is lacking in the initiated.

There is no ceremony that a Sufi considers really necessary, but Sufis never regard ceremonies or dogmas as undesirable, so they are not prejudiced against ceremonies. They have even adopted ceremonies for themselves at different times.

Sufis have various paths of attainment, for instance the paths of Salik and Rind; and among those who tread the path of Salik, of righteousness, there are many whose method of spiritual attainment is devotion. Devotion requires an ideal; and the ideal of the Sufis is the God-ideal. They attain to this ideal by a gradual process. They first take Bayat, initiation, from the hand of one whose presence gives them confidence that he will be a worthy counsellor in life and a guide on the path as yet untrodden, and who at the same time shows them in life the image of the Rasul personality, the personality of the ideal man. He is called Pir-o-Murshid.

There are several steps on the path. This is a vast subject, but condensing it I would say that there are five principal steps. The first is responsiveness to beauty of all kinds, in music, in poetry, in colour or line. The second is one's exaltation by beauty, the feeling of ecstasy. The third step is tolerance and forgiveness, when these come naturally without striving for them. The fourth is that one accepts as if they were a pleasure things one dislikes and cannot stand: in the place of a bowl of wine, the bowl of poison. And the fifth step is taken when one feels the rein of one's mind in one's hand; for then one begins to feel tranquillity and peace at will. This is just like riding on a very vigorous and lively horse, yet holding the reins firmly and making it walk at the speed one desires. When this step is taken the mureed becomes a master.

The time of initiation is meant to be a time for clearing away all the sins of the past. The cleansing of sins is like a bathe in the Ganges. It is the bath of the spirit in the light of knowledge. From this day the page is turned. The mureed makes his vow to the murshid that he will treasure the teachings of the masters in the past and keep them secret, that he will make good use of the teachings and of the powers gained by them, and that he will try to crush his Nafs, his ego. He vows that he will respect all the masters of humanity as the one embodiment of the ideal man, and will consider himself the brother not only of all the Sufis in the Order to which he belongs, but also outside that order of all those who are Sufis in spirit although they may call themselves differently, and of all mankind, without distinction of caste, creed, race, nation, or religion. Sufis engage in *Halka*, a circle of Sufis sitting and practising *Zikr* and *Fikr* so that the power of the one helps the other. Furthermore they practise *Tawajoh*, a method of receiving knowledge and power from the teacher in silence. This way is considered by Sufis to be the most essential and desirable.

Sometimes a receptive mureed attains in a moment greater perfection than he might attain in many years by study or practice, because it is not only his own knowledge and power that the murshid imparts, but sometimes it is the knowledge and power of Rasul; and sometimes even of God. It all depends upon the time and upon how the expressive and receptive souls are focused.

The task of the Sufi teacher is not to force a belief on a mureed, but to train him so that he may become illuminated enough to receive revelations himself.

CHAPTER V

INNER STUDY

WHY DO Sufis study esoteric subjects? Is it for the acquisition of spiritual powers or inspiration, to bring about phenomena, or out of curiosity? If this were so it would be wrong. Is it in order to accomplish something material or for worldly success? That is not desirable. Self-realization, to know what we are, should be the Sufi's aim.

Some people who admire piety and goodness want everyone to be an angel, and discovering that this is impossible they are full of criticism. Man has in him both a devil and an angel; he is at once human and animal. It is the devil in man that drives him to do harm without a motive, by instinct, and the first step should be to abandon this attitude. Although nowadays hardly anyone believes that his particular demon can be a manifestation of the devil, who can say that he is free from such an evil spirit? We can be under the power of a spell, but we must overcome such a power; we must liberate ourselves from evil. Everyone can fight.

We must discover at which times we have manifested our devil or our animal spirit. We want a human spirit, and self-realization is the search for this human spirit; everything must become human in us. But how should we accomplish this? Read the Bible and other holy scriptures? All these books tell us what we should do, but we must also find the store of goodness that is within us, in our heart. As we cultivate our heart it rises. By asceticism one can develop one's soul and reach ecstasy, but what is the use of Samadhi if we are not first human? If we want to live in this world we must be human. The ascetic should live in the forest.

How should we cultivate the heart, the feeling? There is no doubt that harmlessness, devotion, and kindness are necessary; but there is something besides these. It is the awakening of certain centres which make one sensitive, not only externally but also mentally.

There are two kinds of people: one will be struck by the beauty of music or other manifestations of beauty; another is as dull as a stone to all this. Why? Because something in his heart and mind is not awakened. We have five senses, but we also have inner senses, and these can enjoy life much more keenly. Some people will say that they need no inner senses, that the outer senses satisfy them completely. They would speak differently if, for instance, they lost their eyesight or another of their five senses. In order to be complete a human being must also develop his inner senses; but first of all he should develop his inner feeling.

Intellectual study may last the whole of one's life; there is no end to it, and this is why the teacher does not encourage speculation. A doctrine means a separation from other doctrines. The Sufi belongs to every religion, and thus he has no special beliefs and speculations. There can for instance be one Sufi who believes in reincarnation, and another who realizes heaven and hell. The work of the Sufi is personal development. It is what one practises that is important rather than what the teacher says, though the teacher can give protection.

Initiation contains several degrees. It is a trust given to one by the teacher, but the real initiation is the work of God. No teacher can or will judge. The real pupil is he whom the teacher knows he can trust, though all are welcome to him. Spiritually he is both father and mother to the pupil. The life of the teacher is often a sacrifice; he is often persecuted and suffers much, but what little help he can give, he will give.

No special qualification is needed in order to become a pupil. The teacher gives; the pupil can take it or leave it. The teaching is like a precious jewel hidden in a stone; it is for the pupil to break the stone and find the jewel. In the East this inner teaching is part of religion, whereas in the West it is often looked upon merely as a form of education. It ought to be a sacred education. In the East the murshid gives the lesson and the pupil practises it for a month or a year; he cannot have a different practice every week. My grandfather practised one meditation for forty years, then a miracle happened to him. One should not be ambitious to do other exercises before having had a result from the first one.

There are different degrees, but they are not to be discussed on this path. Because, after all, different stages are the conceptions, the speculations of some wise people. It is just the same as with music: there are seven notes of music, because the musician has accepted that there are seven, but a scale can be made to contain more notes or less notes if the musician wishes to make it so. We distinguish stages, although in reality it is impossible to do so. It is a spontaneous development on the spiritual path which may be called treading the path of initiation.

How can one explain spiritual progress? What is it? What is it like? Spiritual progress is the changing of the point of view. There is only one way to recognize this progress, and that is to see the progress in one's own outlook on life, to ask oneself the question, 'How do I look at life?' This one can do by not judging others, but by being only concerned with one's own outlook; as long as a person is concerned with the faults of others, as long as he criticizes others, he is not yet ready to make his sight clear enough to see if his outlook on life is right.

What in reality are the different initiations? Is one better than the other, or higher than the other? In what way are they to be distinguished? By knowing some more mysteries, or by knowing some secrets, or by studying something very wonderful, or by communicating with something unseen? Nothing whatever of this kind, not one of these things, can assure one of a higher initiation, of greater progress in the spiritual life. In the first place we need not strive for mystery, for life itself is a mystery. All that seems simple to us, all that presents no mystery, becomes mysterious as soon as the outlook on life is changed. Secrecy is to be found in simplicity; it is the simple life which is full of secrets. A person may study a whole library, may write fifty books and may read a thousand, yet all this leads him nowhere. If any study is required we need not go anywhere else; our life itself is study, if we will only study it. For one who studies, life offers every opportunity; from morning to evening, every moment of the day, in the home, outside, at work, in leisure, in all things there is something to study. No book can give the joy and the pleasure that human nature itself can give.

The wise, the foolish, the good, the weak, whom we meet every day with their tendencies and their attitude, are all the greatest material for study. Besides, there is so much to study in success and failure, in sorrows and pleasures, and in all things in life whether unfavourable or favourable. All that we do right, all that we do wrong, everything is a lesson, everything is a study if we take it as such. But the important thing is this, that the one who is life's student, the one who is really initiated, studies himself before studying others. Does an initiator teach the truth? No man has the power to teach another the truth; man must discover it himself. What the initiator can do from his side is to say, 'This is the path, do not go astray.' The initiator will put his pupil on that path where the further he goes the more he will receive at every step; it is like a hand raising him upward. But the first step is the most difficult, and that step is taken by the help of an initiator on the earth.

What is it that the initiator teaches the initiated one? He tells the initiated one the truth of his own being. He does not tell him something new or something different. He tells him something which his soul already knows but which his mind has forgotten. There is a fable which illustrates this. A lion walking through the desert found a little lion-cub playing with some sheep. It happened that the little lion had been reared with the sheep, and so it had never had a chance or an occasion to realize what it was. The lion was greatly surprised to see a lion-cub running away and being just as afraid of a lion as sheep are. The lion jumped in among the flock of sheep and said, 'Halt, halt!' But the sheep ran away and the little lion ran too. The lion only pursued the lion-cub, not the sheep, and when it caught up with it the lion said, 'I wish to speak to you.' The cub said, 'I tremble, I am afraid, I cannot stand before you.' The lion said, 'Why are you running about with the sheep? you yourself are a little lion!' 'No,' said the little one. 'I am a sheep; let me go, let me go with the sheep.' 'Come along,' said the lion, 'come with me and I will show you what you are before I let you go.' Trembling and yet helpless, the cub followed the lion to a pool of water. Pointing at their reflections in the pool the lion said, 'Look at me and look at yourself. Do we not resemble each other closely? You are not like the sheep, you are like me!'

This lion is symbolical of the souls who become God-conscious, the souls who have realized the truth. And when they see the same divine spirit in another soul, their first thought is to take that soul by the hand and to show it that in it also there is the same divine spark which they possess. Therefore although outwardly it is an aristocratic picture, inwardly it is leading to democracy. The command of the lion to that lion-cub is apparently aristocratic, but what is the intention of the lion? It is democracy, it wants to make the little lion conscious of the same grandeur that the lion has. And that is the path of spirituality. Its outward appearance may not seem so, but its inner intention and its culmination are democracy.

The initiations beyond those I have spoken of are greater still. Some people, although not all, will tell you of their experiences, and how at different times in their life a sudden change of outlook came to them. It is not our usual experience to wake up suddenly one day from sleep and find that our point of view has changed; but it is no exaggeration to say that it takes but one moment to change one's outlook on life entirely. This is what an initiation is, an initiation which is above the initiations of the earth as we know them. One thing leads to another, and so we go on in life from one initiation to the next; and each step on the ladder that seems to be standing before us, for us to climb, becomes an initiation. And each step on that ladder changes our point of view if only we hold on to the ladder and do not drop down; for there is always the possibility of going either forward or backward. Nevertheless, the one anxious to go forward will never go backward. Even if the whole world pulled him back by a chain attached to his feet, he would still go forward, because his desire to go forward is more powerful than all the forces of the world.

CHAPTER VI

THREE ASPECTS OF INITIATION

AS BIRDS gather in flocks and animals in herds, so there are human beings who move in groups in this or that direction drawn by the power of others; and yet if one asked a person if this is the case with him too, he would say, 'No; not with me, but with all others.' It is difficult for anyone to realize to what extent he can unconsciously move with the crowd to the right or the left. And when a person takes a step in a different direction, dissatisfied with being held and swayed by the crowd, by his friends and relations, by those who surround him, then he shows initiative. So the real meaning of the word initiation, which is related to initiative, is that a man takes his own direction instead of that in which the crowd is pulling him. And when this happens the religious people will say that he has become a heathen, his friends will say that he has become foolish, and his relations will say that he has gone crazy.

Initiation has three different aspects: one is natural initiation, another is advanced initiation, and the third is higher initiation.

The natural initiation may come to a person at any time of his life. It does not come to everyone, but only to some. And for this initiation one need not go to a teacher; it comes when it is time for it to come. It comes in the form of a sudden change of outlook on life; a person feels that he has suddenly awakened to quite another world; although he remains in the same world it has become totally different to him. Things which seemed important become less important; colours pale and the brightness of things disappears. Things show themselves to have different values. The value of everything changes the moment the outlook is changed. It is a change like looking through a telescope; through a telescope one sees things quite differently.

A person may be young and have that experience; it may come at any time in one's life. To some it comes gradually, but then it is a long process, while to others something suddenly happens in their lives and in the twinkling of an eye the world has become different; everything suddenly has a different value. This is natural initiation.

How is this initiation brought about? What is its metaphysical process? The soul is veiled by covers, one cover over the other, and the rending of these covers allows the soul to emerge or to rise higher. Naturally with the next step the horizon of its outlook becomes wider, and the soul reaches further while life becomes more clear. A person may not be conscious of such a change; he may ignore it or not know about it, yet it is there, even though among a hundred people perhaps only one is really conscious of it.

At every step forward that the soul takes on the path it naturally comes closer to God, and coming closer to God means inheriting or drawing towards oneself the qualities of God. In other words the soul sees more, hears more, comprehends more, and enjoys more, because it lives a greater, a higher life.

The teachers and prophets who had to give a message to humanity, who had to render a service to humanity, had such initiations even in their childhood. There is a symbolical story that the heart of the Prophet Mohammad was opened and some substance was taken out of it. People take this literally; but the real meaning is that a cover was torn away, and the soul was allowed to reach upward and go further on the path. There may be many such initiations, perhaps one or two or six or seven according to the state of evolution of the initiate.

Life as we live it today is very difficult for a person whose outlook is thus suddenly changed, for the world lives nowadays at a certain pitch and it cannot tolerate someone whose pitch is below or above the ordinary pitch of life. People dislike such a one, they make difficulties for him, they disapprove of him and of his ideas; and if he does not have any friend or guide on the path, then he may linger on in the same plane of thought till nature helps him, for everything else pulls him backwards.

Some people think that saints, masters, or sages have no need for initiation, but they forget that no soul can go further on the path without initiation.

What is the result of this natural initiation? Bewilderment, extreme bewilderment. But this bewilderment is not the same as confusion; there is a vast difference between the two. In confusion there is an element of doubt, but when a person is bewildered he says, 'How wonderful, how marvellous; words cannot explain it; it is a miracle!' It may appear quite simple to someone else, but to an advanced person it is a miracle. And there may be others who say, 'How foolish, I do not see anything in what you have seen!' But what one has perceived is so marvellous that it cannot be explained.

Such is life; it is a difference of outlook. One person sees a wonder, a splendour, and another says, 'What of it? It is quite simple; it is nothing.' And the one who says this thinks that he is superior because to his mind it is simple, while the one who wonders has the outlook of a child, for a child wonders at everything. No doubt it is childlike, but it is the child's soul that sees; it sees more than the soul of a grown-up which has become covered by a thousand veils. In infancy the child can see the angelic world, it can talk with unseen entities, it can see wonderful things belonging to the different planes. It is easy to say of something that it is childlike, innocent, or ignorant; yet it is the most wonderful thing to be childlike and to have the innocence of an infant. There is nothing better to wish for, as in this all happiness and beauty are to be found.

This bewilderment produces a kind of pessimism in a person, but a pessimism which cannot be compared with what we ordinarily call pessimism. For we regard pessimism as a kind of wretchedness, but this is something different. A hint of this is to be found in Omar Khayyám's verse, 'O, my Beloved, fill the cup that clears today of past regret and future fears; tomorrow, why, tomorrow I may be myself with yesterday's sev'n thousand years!' This pessimism comes as an upliftment, it makes a person see life from a different angle. The very life which seemed before to be towering over his head suddenly appears to be beneath his feet.

What is it then? Besides calling it pessimism one could also call it indifference, or independence, and yet it is none of these three things. There is no word for it in English; in Sanskrit it is called *Vairagya*, an emotion, a feeling quite different from all other ways of looking at life, an outlook which brings one into an entirely different world of thought. The values of things and conditions seem to change completely.

One might think that it would be an uninteresting life to be indifferent, but that is not so; it is most interesting; it gives one a feeling as if the burden of life was lightened. What a wonderful feeling this is! Think what a little relaxation after a day's toil can do, when one can just rest for a moment; what upliftment comes, what soothing vibrations, and how the mind feels refreshed! If then the spirit has the same experience, feeling that the load it is continually carrying day and night is lifted, then it too feels widened for a moment. What a blessing this is! It cannot be spoken of in words, but the one who has had even a slight experience of it can comprehend its value.

No doubt there comes a time in a man's life when even if he were initiated a thousand times by nature he still seeks for a guide walking on earth. Many will say, 'Why is God not sufficient? Why must there be someone between God and man? Why must it be a man who is just as limited as we are? Why can we not reach the spirit of God directly?' But in a man who is your enemy and who has tortured you throughout your life, in another who is your greatest friend, and in your teacher who inspires and guides you, in all these is to be seen the hand of God. They have all three guided you on the path of inspiration; they are all three needed in order that you may go further in life. The one who has disappointed you, who has harmed you, is also your initiator, for he has taught you something, he has put you on the road, even if not in the right way. And he who is your friend is your initiator too, for he gives you the evidence of truth, the sign of reality; only love can give you a proof that there is something living, something real. And then there is the inspiring teacher, be he a humble man, an illiterate person, or a meditative soul, a great teacher or a humble one, he is what you think him to be, as everyone is to us what we think them to be.

If it were not necessary that man should guide his fellow-men, Jesus Christ would not have been placed among those fishermen who could not understand him; and yet he proved to be their guidance. The presence on earth of personalities such as Buddha and all the other teachers—many of them not even known to humanity though they have done so much, but who always are and always will be under whatever name and in whatever guise they may work—gives guidance to individuals and to humanity. God never reaches so directly and so fully as when He reaches through His teachers. The best way for God to reach human beings is through a human being; not through an angel but through man who is subject to birth and death and to all the faults that everyone has.

The way of the teacher with his initiate is strange. The greater

the teacher the stranger may be the way. The teacher may test
and the teacher may give trials; and the attitude of the teacher
can never be understood, for a real teacher never commits himself. Neither his yes nor his no can be understood, for their meaning will be symbolical and very subtle. Perhaps he will speak in
parables, perhaps he will teach without teaching, perhaps he will
teach more just by a glance than by speaking a hundred words.
Perhaps the presence of the teacher is of greater blessing in the life
of the pupil than a hundred books he has read. Neither the
indifference nor the sympathy of the teacher may be taken for
what they appear to be, for in both there is something else. The
more one studies the personality of the teacher, the more puzzled
one becomes. The teacher is the initiator of life, he is the example
of the subtlety of the whole of life.

Some people affirm that they have been initiated by a teacher
on the other side. Well, perhaps they have; but are they not then
in two worlds, the teacher in one and the initiate in the other?
The initiate neither belongs to the teacher's world, nor does the
teacher belong to his. This surely gives one less trouble than
having to regard the pleasure of a living being; it is easier to feel
that one has someone at one's back who is always whispering in
one's ear and who speaks to one in dream or vision. It is not
wrong and in some cases it is even true; there are souls, there are
teachers who have perhaps not given on earth what they had to
give, what they had to impart to others. But that is not the normal
process. If it were a normal process then all the teachings would
have been sent from the other side, but neither Buddha nor Jesus
Christ nor Mohammad gave their teachings from there.

Today the prevailing thought is that no man should guide his
fellow-men and that there is no virtue in such guidance. This
thought is so widespread that it is preventing people from seeking
guidance from someone who is facing the same struggles, the same
troubles, and who has the same experiences as everyone else. They
go on rejecting such a man, as Jesus Christ was rejected, and at the
same time they are looking for someone on the other plane.
Many societies and groups have puzzled their heads so much over
this subject that they have deprived themselves of that living
water which follows its natural course through the world of man.

The work of the teacher is most subtle. It is like that of a jeweller who has to melt the gold first in order to make an ornament out of it. It has first to be melted, but once it is melted, once it is not hard metal any more but has become liquid, then it can be made into a crown or a ring or an ornament; then one can make a beautiful thing out of it.

And after this there is a further step. When the pupil has received the initiations that the teacher has to give, then the teacher's task is over, and he sends him on. The teacher does not hold the pupil indefinitely; he has his part to perform during the journey on the path, but then comes the inner initiation. This comes to the disciple who has become meditative, whose interest has become keen, whose outlook has widened, who sees life differently, whose conscience has acquired the habit of reasoning, of expanding.

No doubt in this experience also there is always help to be had. As help comes on earth so in the unseen world too that help then comes. It is as if we were in the street in some kind of difficulty; naturally others would come up to see if they could be of any assistance. So as one goes further one attracts the sympathy of beings who are always busy helping humanity from all planes of existence. The sympathy of those who are close to the one who is travelling on the path is attracted, giving him a hand to go forward. It is that giving of a hand which is called initiation. There are so many different initiations: they are all steps by which to go upward.

In conclusion I shall mention what is attained through initiation. What one attains is that realization for which we are born, which is our life's purpose. Unless we approach life's purpose, nothing we do will help us sufficiently; it will only help us perhaps in a certain need of ours, but not any further. There is only one thing which gives complete satisfaction, and that is to arrive at self-realization. It is not simple and it needs more than just meditation and concentration, although these are of great help in the attainment of self-realization. And those who believe that by reading a book on Yoga they can get to that realization are mistaken. They are mistaken because it is a phenomenon; and it is by this phenomenon that one proceeds further.

G

Some people think that by straightforward study, by purely scientific study, they can come to realization, but in order to attain self-realization a certain way of life is necessary. Is it the life that religious people teach, that one should live in such and such a way? Is it a life according to certain principles, certain dogmas? No, nothing of that kind. It is the continual process of effacing the self; it is just like grinding something which is very hard; it is a continual grinding of the self. And the more that self is softened, the more highly a person evolves and the greater his personality becomes. No matter what power and inspiration a person may have acquired, if there is no self-effacement nothing is accomplished. The result brought about by initiation is self-effacement, and it is self-effacement which is needed in order to arrive at true wisdom.

CHAPTER VII

DISCIPLESHIP

ONE WONDERS, especially in the Western part of the world, what the path of discipleship may really be. Although the path of discipleship was the path of those who followed Christ and all the other teachers, the modern trend of thought has taken away much of the ideal that existed in the past. It is not only that the ideal of discipleship seems to be little known, but even the ideal attitude towards motherhood and fatherhood, as well as towards the aged, seems to be less understood. This change in the ideal of the world has worked unwittingly to such an extent that world-conflicts have been the result in our times. The troubles between nations and classes, in social and domestic life, all arise for one and the same reason. If someone were to ask me what is the cause of today's world unrest, I would answer that it is the lack of idealism.

In ancient times the path of discipleship was a lesson to be applied in every direction of life. Man is not only his body; he is his soul. When a child is born on earth, that is not the time that the soul is born; the soul is born from the moment that consideration is born. This birth of consideration is in reality the birth of the soul; man shows his soul in his consideration. Some become considerate as children, others perhaps do not awaken to consideration throughout their whole life. Love is called a divine element, but love's divine expression is nothing but consideration; and it would not be very wrong to say that love without consideration is not fully divine. Love that has no consideration loses its fragrance. Moreover intelligence is not consideration. It is the balance of love and intelligence, it is the action and reaction of love and intelligence upon each other that produce consideration. Children who are considerate are more precious than jewels to their parents. The man who is considerate, the friend who has consideration, all those with whom we come in contact who are considerate, we value most.

Thus it is the lesson of consideration given by the spiritual teachers which may be called the path of discipleship. This does not mean that the great teachers have wanted the discipleship, devotion, or respect of the pupils for themselves. If any teacher expects that, he cannot be a teacher. How could he then be a spiritual teacher, as he must be above all this in order to be above them? But respect, devotion, and consideration are taught for the disciple's own advantage, as an attribute that must be cultivated. Until now there has been a custom in India, which I myself experienced when young, that the first things the parents taught their children were respect for the teacher, consideration, and a kindly inclination. A modern child going to school has not the same idea. He thinks the teacher is appointed to perform a certain duty; he hardly knows the teacher nor does the teacher know him well. When he comes home he has the same tendency towards his parents as at school. Most children grow up thinking that all the attention their parents give them is only part of their duty; at most they will think, 'Perhaps one day if I am able I shall repay it.' The ancient idea was different. For instance the Prophet Mohammad taught his disciples that the greatest debt every man had to pay was to his mother, and if he wished his sins to be forgiven he must so act through life that at the end his mother before

passing from this earth would say, 'I have forgiven you the debt.'
There was nothing a man could give or do, neither money nor
service, which would enable him to say, 'I have paid my debt'; no,
his mother must say, 'I have forgiven you that debt.' What does
this teach? It teaches the value of that unselfish love which is
above all earthly passion.

If we inquire of our self within for what purpose we have come
on earth and why we have become human beings, wondering
whether it would perhaps have been better to remain angels, the
answer will certainly come to the wise, from his own heart, that
we are here to experience a fuller life, to become fully human.
For it is through being considerate that we become fully human.
Every action done with consideration is valuable, every word
said with consideration is precious. The whole teaching of Christ
—'Blessed are the meek . . . the poor in spirit'—teaches one thing:
consideration. Although it seems simple, yet it is a hard lesson to
learn. The more we wish to act according to this ideal, the more
we realize that we fail. The further we go on the path of consideration, the more delicate do the eyes of our perception
become; we feel and regret the slightest mistake.

It is not every soul that takes the trouble to tread this path.
Everyone is not a plant; there are many who are rocks, and these
do not want to be considerate, they think it is too much trouble.
Of course the stone has no pain, it is the one who feels who has
pain. Still, it is in feeling that there is life; life's joy is so great that
even with pain one would rather be a living being than a rock,
for there is a joy in living, in feeling alive, which cannot be
expressed in words. After how many millions of years has the
life buried in stones and rocks risen to the human being! Even so
if a person wishes to stay a rock, he had better stay so, though the
natural inclination in every person should be to develop the
human qualities fully.

The first lesson that the pupil learns on the path of discipleship
is what is called *Yaqin* in Sufi terms, which means confidence.
This confidence he first gives to the one whom he considers his
teacher, his spiritual guide.

In the giving of confidence, three kinds of people can be distinguished. One gives a part of his confidence and cannot give

another part. He is wobbling and thinking, 'Yes, I believe I have confidence; perhaps I have, perhaps I have not.' And this sort of confidence puts him in a very difficult position. It would be better not to have it at all. It is like lukewarm water, neither hot nor cold. In all things this person will do the same, in business, in his profession. He trusts and doubts, he trusts and fears. He is not walking in the sky, he is not walking on the earth; he is in between the two. Then there is another kind, the one who gives his confidence to the teacher, but he is not sure about himself, he is not inwardly sure if he has given it. This person has no confidence in himself, he is not sure of himself; therefore his confidence is of no value. And the third kind of person is the one who gives confidence because he feels confident. This confidence alone can rightfully be called Yaqin.

Jesus Christ had people of all these categories around him. Thousands of people of the first category came, thronged round the Master, then left him. It did not take one moment for them to be attracted, nor one moment for them to leave the Master. In the second category are those who go on for some time, just as a drunken man goes on and on; but when they are sober again things become clear to them and they ask themselves, 'Where am I going? Not in the right direction.' Thousands and thousands in this category followed the masters and prophets, but those who stayed to the end of the test were those who before giving their confidence to the teacher first had confidence in their own heart. It is they who, if the earth turned to water and the water turned to earth, if the sky came down and the earth rose up, would remain unshaken, firm in the belief they have once gained. It is by discipleship that a person learns the moral that in whatever position he is, as husband or wife, son or daughter, servant or friend, he will follow with confidence, firm and steady wherever he goes.

After acquiring Yaqin there comes a test, and that is sacrifice. That is the ideal on the path of God. The most precious possession there is, is not too valuable, nothing is too great to sacrifice. Not one of the disciples of the Prophet—the real disciples— thought even their life too great a sacrifice if it was needed. The story of Ali is very well known: a plot was discovered, that one night some enemies wanted to kill the Prophet, and Ali learnt about it. He did not tell the Prophet, but persuaded him to leave home. He himself stayed, for he knew that if he went too the assassins would follow him and find out where the Prophet was. He slept in the same bed in place of the Prophet, so that the assassins might find him, though at the same time he did not intend to lose his life if he could fight them off. The consequence was that the plot failed and the enemies could not touch either the Prophet or Ali.

This is only one instance, but there are thousands of instances which show that the friendship formed in God and truth between the teacher and the disciple is for always, and that nothing in the world is able to break it. If the spiritual link cannot hold, how can a material link keep intact? It will wear out, being only a worldly link. If spiritual thought cannot form a link between two souls, what else can constitute such a strong tie that it can last both here and in the hereafter?

The third lesson on the path of discipleship is imitation; this means imitating the teacher in his every attitude, his attitude towards the friend, towards the enemy, towards the foolish, and towards the wise. If the pupil acts as he wishes and the teacher acts as he wishes, then there is no benefit, however great the sacrifice and devotion. No teaching or meditation is as great or valuable as the imitation of the teacher in the path of truth. In the imitation of the teacher the whole secret of the spiritual life is hidden. No doubt it is not only the imitation of his outward action, but also of his inner tendency.

The fourth lesson that the disciple learns is different again. This lesson is to turn the inward thought of the teacher outward, until he grows to see his teacher in everyone and everything, in the wise, in the foolish, and in all forms.

Finally, by the fifth lesson the disciple learns to give everything that he has so far given to his teacher—devotion, sacrifice, service, respect—to all, because he has learnt to see his teacher in all.

One person will perhaps learn nothing all his life, whereas another will learn all five lessons in a short time. There is a story of a person who went to a teacher and said to him, 'I would like to be your pupil, your disciple.' The teacher said, 'Yes; I shall be very glad.' This man, conscious of so many faults, was surprised that the teacher was willing to accept him as a disciple. He said, 'But I wonder if you know how many faults I have?' The teacher said, 'Yes, I already know your faults, yet I accept you as my pupil.'—'But I have very bad faults,' he said, 'I am fond of gambling.' The teacher said, 'That does not matter much.'—'I am inclined to drink sometimes,' he said. The teacher said, 'That does not matter much.'—'Well,' he said, 'there are many other faults.' The teacher said, 'I do not mind. But now that I have accepted all your faults, you must accept one condition from your teacher.'—'Yes, most willingly,' he said. 'What is it?' The teacher said, 'You may indulge in your faults, but not in my presence; only that much respect you must reserve for your teacher.' The teacher knew that all five attributes of discipleship were natural to him, and he made him an initiate. And as soon as he went out and had an inclination to gamble or to drink he saw the face of his murshid before him. When after some time he returned to the teacher, the teacher smilingly asked, 'Did you commit any faults?' He answered, 'O no, the great difficulty is that whenever I want to commit any of my usual faults my murshid pursues me!'

Do not think that this spirit is only cultivated; this spirit may be found in an innocent child. When I once asked a little child of four years, 'Have you been naughty?' it answered, 'I would like to be naughty, but my goodness will not let me.' This shows us that the spirit of discipleship is in us. But we should always remember that he who is a teacher is a disciple himself.

In reality there is no such thing as a teacher; God alone is Teacher, we are all disciples. The lesson we all have to learn is that of discipleship; it is the first and the last lesson.

CHAPTER VIII

FOUR KINDS OF DISCIPLESHIP

THERE ARE four kinds of disciples, of whom only one can be described as a real disciple. One kind is the disciple of modern times who comes and says to his teacher, 'We will study this book together,' or 'Have you read that book? It is most interesting,' or 'I have learnt from someone else before, and now I would like to learn what I can from you and then I will pass on to something which is still more interesting.' Such a person may be called a student, but not yet a disciple. His spirit is not that of a disciple; it is the spirit of a student who goes from one university, from one college, to another; from one professor he passes into the hands of another. He may be well suited for such intellectual pursuits, but the spirit of the disciple is different.

Then there is another type who thinks, 'What I can get out of him I will get. And when I have collected it, then I shall use it in the way I think best.' Well, his way is that of a thief who says, 'I will take what I can from the purse of this person, and then I shall spend it for my own purpose.' This is a wrong attitude, because spiritual inspiration and power cannot be stolen; a thief cannot take them; and if he has this attitude such a disciple may remain with a teacher for a hundred years and still leave empty-handed. There are many in this world today who make intellectual theft their occupation; anything intellectual they find, they take it and use it. But they do not know what harm they do by this attitude. They paralyse their minds and they close their own spirit.

Then there is a third wrong tendency of a disciple: to keep back something which is most essential, namely confidence. He will say, 'Tell me all you can teach me, all I can learn, give me all that you have,' but in his mind he says, 'I will not give you my confidence, for I do not yet know if this road is right or wrong for me. When you have taught me I shall judge, then I shall see what it is. But until then I do not give you my confidence, though my ears are tuned to your words.' This is the third wrong tendency. As long as a disciple will not give his confidence to his spiritual guide, he will not get the full benefit of his teaching.

The fourth kind is the right kind of discipleship. And this does not come by just thinking that one would like to go on the spiritual path, or that one would like to be a disciple, a mureed, a chela, but there comes a time in every person's life when circumstances have tried him so much that he begins to feel the wish to find a word of enlightenment, some counsel, some guidance, a direction on the path of truth. When the values of all things and beings are changing in his eyes, that is the time he begins to feel hungry for spiritual guidance. Bread is meant for the hungry, not for those who are quite satisfied. If a person like this goes in search of a teacher, he takes the right step; but there is a difficulty, and this is that if he wants to test the teacher first, then there is no end to the testing. He can go from one teacher to another, from the earthly being to the heavenly being, testing everyone, and in the end what will he find? Imperfection. He is looking for it, and he will find it. Man is an imperfect being, a human being, a limited being. If he wants to find perfection in a limited being, he will always end by being disappointed whoever he meets, whether it is an angel or a human being. If he were simple enough to accept any teacher that came his way and said, 'I will be your mureed,' it would be easier, though this is perhaps not always practicable.

Someone asked a Brahmin, 'Why do you worship a god of rock, an idol of stone? Look, here I am, a worshipper of the God who is in heaven. This rock does not listen to you, it has no ears.' And the Brahmin said, 'If you have no faith, even the God in heaven will not hear you; and if you have faith this rock will have ears to hear.'

The middle way and the best way is to consult one's own intuition and inspiration. If one's intuition says, 'I will seek guidance from this teacher, whether he is raised high by the whole of humanity or whether he is looked at with contempt and pre-judice by thousands, I do not care,' then one follows the principle of constancy in adhering to that one teacher. But if a person is not constant on the spiritual path he will naturally have difficulty in the end. For what is constancy? Constancy is the reflection of eternity. And what is truth? Truth is eternity, and so in seeking for truth one must learn the principle of constancy.

The disciple has to have full confidence in the teacher's guid-ance, in the direction that is given to him by the teacher. The Buddhists who regard a spiritual teacher with great reverence say, 'We do not care whether he is well-known or not; and even if he is we do not know if he will accept our reverence; and if he receives it we are not sure he needs it.' Worship can only be given to those of whose presence we are conscious; and it is especially intended for the spiritual teacher, for he shows us the only path that frees us from all the pains of which this life is full. That is why among all other obligations involving earthly gain and benefit the obligation to the spiritual teacher is the greatest, for it is concerned with the liberation of the soul on its journey towards Nirvana, which is the only desire of every soul.

The teacher does not always teach in plain words. The spiritual teacher has a thousand ways. It may be that by his prayers he can guide his disciple; it may be by his thought, his feeling, or his sympathy, so that even at a distance he may guide him. And therefore when a disciple thinks that he can be taught only by words or teachings, by practices or exercises, it is a great mistake.

In order to get the right disciples and the right people to come to him, a Sufi who lived in Hyderabad made a wonderful arrangement. He got a grumpy woman to sit just near his house; and to anyone who came to see the great teacher, she would say all kinds of things against the teacher: how unkind he was, how cruel, how neglectful, how lazy; there was nothing she would leave unsaid. And as a result out of a hundred, ninety-five would turn back; they would not dare to come near him. Perhaps only five would come, wanting to form their own opinion about him. And the teacher was very pleased that the ninety-five went away, for what they had come to find was not there; it was somewhere else.

There is another side to this question. The first thing the teacher does is to find out what is the pressing need of his disciple. Certainly, the disciple has come to seek after truth and to be guided to the path of God, but at the same time it is the psychological task of the teacher to give his thought first to the pressing need of his disciple, whether the disciple speaks of it or not. And the teacher's effort is directed towards removing that first difficulty, because he knows it to be an obstacle in the disciple's way. It is easy for a soul to tread the spiritual path because it is the spiritual path that the soul is looking for. God is the seeking of every soul, and every soul will make its way naturally, providing there is nothing to obstruct it, and so the most pressing need is the removal of any obstruction. Thus a desire can be fulfilled, it can be conquered, or it can be removed. If it is fulfilled so much the better. If it is not right to fulfil it then it should be conquered or removed in order to clear the way. The teacher never thinks that he is concerned with his disciple only in his spiritual progress, in his attainment of God, for if there is something blocking the way of the disciple it will not be easy for the teacher to help him.

There are three faculties which the teacher considers essential to develop in the disciple: deepening the sympathy, showing the way to harmony, and awakening the spirit of beauty. One often sees that without being taught any particular formula, or receiving any particular lesson on these three subjects, the soul of a sincere disciple will grow under the guidance of the right teacher like a plant which is carefully reared and watered every day and every month and every year. And without knowing it himself he will begin to show these three qualities, the ever-growing sympathy, the harmonizing quality increasing every day more and more, and the expression and understanding and appreciation of beauty in all its forms.

One may ask, is there no going backward? Well, sometimes there is a sensation of going backward; just as when one is at sea, the ship may move in such a way that one sometimes has the feeling that one is going backward although one is really going forward; one can have the same sensation when riding on an elephant or a camel. When in the lives of some disciples this sensation is felt, it is nothing but a proof of life. Nevertheless a disciple will often feel that since he became a disciple he finds many more faults in himself than he had ever seen before. This may be so, but it does not mean that his faults have increased; it only means that now his eyes have become wider open so that every day he sees many more faults than before.

There is always a great danger on the spiritual path that the disciple has to overcome: he may develop a feeling of being exalted, of knowing more than other people, of being better than other people. As soon as a person thinks, 'I am more', the doors of knowledge are closed. He will no more be able to widen his knowledge, because automatically the doors of his heart are closed the moment he says, 'I know'. Spiritual knowledge, the knowledge of life, is so intoxicating, so exalting, it gives such a great joy, that one begins to pour out one's knowledge before anyone who comes along as soon as this knowledge springs up.

But if at that time the disciple could realize that he should conserve that kindling of the light, reserve it, keep it within himself, and let it deepen, then his words would not be necessary, his presence would enlighten people; but as soon as the spring rises, and he pours forth what comes out of that spring in words, although on the one side his vanity will be satisfied yet on the other his energy will be exhausted. The little spring that had risen he has poured out before others, and he remains without power. This is why reserve is taught to the true disciple, the conserving of inspiration and power. The one who speaks is not always wise; it is the one who listens who is wise.

During discipleship the first period may be called the period of observation; in this the disciple with a respectful attitude observes everything good and bad and right and wrong, without expressing any opinion about them. And every day this reveals to the disciple a new idea on the subject. Today he thinks it is wrong, but does not say so; tomorrow he wonders how it can be wrong. The day after tomorrow he thinks, 'But can this really be wrong?', while on the fourth day he may think that it is not wrong, and on the fifth day that it is right. And he may follow the same process with what is right, if only he does not express himself on the first day. It is the foolish who always readily express their opinion; the wise keep it back. By keeping their opinion back they become wiser every day; by expressing their opinion they continually become less wise.

The second thing that is most important for the disciple is learning. And how is he to learn? Every word the disciple hears coming from the lips of the teacher is a whole sacred book. Instead of reading a sacred book of any religion from beginning to end, he has taken in one word of the teacher, and that is the same. By meditating upon it, by thinking about it, by pondering upon it, he makes that word a plant from which fruit and flowers come. A book is one thing and a living word is another. Perhaps a whole book could be written by the inspiration of one living word of the teacher. Besides the disciple practises all the meditations given to him, and by these exercises he develops within him that inspiration, that power which is meant to be developed in the disciple.

And the third step forward for the disciple lies in testing the inspiration, the power that he has received. One might ask, how can one test it? Life can give a thousand examples of every idea that one has thought about. If one has learnt from within that a certain idea is wrong or right, then life itself is an example which shows why it is wrong or why it is right.

If a person does not become enlightened, one can find the explanation by watching the rain: it falls upon all trees, but it is according to the response of those trees that they grow and bear fruit. The sun shines upon all the trees; it makes no distinction between them, but it is according to the response that the trees give to the sun that they profit by its sunshine. At the same time a mureed is very often an inspiration to the murshid. It is not the murshid who teaches; it is God who teaches. The murshid is only a medium, and as high as the response of the mureed reaches, so strongly does it attract the message of God.

The mureed can inspire, but he can also cease to inspire. If there is no response on his side or if there is antagonism or lack of interest, then the inspiration of the murshid is shut off; just like the clouds which cannot produce a shower when they are above the desert. The desert affects them, but when the same clouds are above the forest the trees attract them and the rain falls.

The attributes of the disciple are reserve, thoughtfulness, consideration, balance, and sincerity. Special care should be taken that during the time of discipleship one does not become a teacher, for very often a growing soul is so eager to become a teacher that before he has finished the period of discipleship he becomes impatient. It should be remembered that all the great teachers of humanity such as Jesus Christ, Buddha, Mohammad, and Zarathushtra, have been great pupils; they have learned from the innocent child, they have learned from everyone, from every person that came near them. They have learned from every situation and every condition of the world; they have understood and they have learned. It is the desire to learn continually that makes one a teacher, and not the desire to become a teacher. As soon as a person thinks, 'I am something of a teacher', he has lost ground. For there is only one teacher: God alone is the Teacher, and all others are His pupils. We all learn from life what life teaches us; and the day when a soul begins to think that he has learned all he had to learn, and that now he is a teacher, he is very much mistaken. The greatest teachers of humanity have learned from humanity more than they have taught.

CHAPTER IX

THE ATTITUDE OF A DISCIPLE

A MUREED'S attitude towards life must be hopeful; towards his motives courageous; towards his murshid faithful; towards the cause sincere; towards that object which he has to accomplish earnest without the slightest doubt. In every aspect of life it is our attitude which counts and which in the end proves to be creative of all kinds of phenomena. Both success and failure depend upon it, as in the Hindu saying, 'If the attitude is right, all will come right'.

There is a natural tendency in the seeker on the spiritual path to wonder if he is really progressing. And very often he begins to wonder from the day he sets foot on the path. It is like asking 'Shall I be able to digest?' while one is still eating. The spiritual path leads to selflessness. The more we worry about ourselves, the less progress we make, because our whole striving should be to forget the self; it is mostly the self which obstructs the path. The path is made for the soul, and it is natural and easy for the soul to find it. Therefore when a person is wondering about his progress he is wasting his time; it is like standing still on the path on which one must go forward.

Can anyone distinguish how his face and body change day by day? No, for one cannot point out distinct signs of change from one day to another; and if one cannot properly distinguish any change in the external self, then how can one expect to distinguish change in the inner process? It is not something that can be weighed on the scales as one weighs oneself on coming back from a holiday and sees that one has gained or lost several pounds. There is no such gain in spiritual progress.

Then there are some who imagine that they have progressed for a certain time but are then going backward. They are discouraged and say, 'I thought I had arrived somewhere, but surely it must have been an illusion.' But life is like the sea, and the sea is not always calm. There are times when the sea is rough and then the boat naturally moves up and down, and to think while the boat is moving downward that it will sink is a mistake. It is going down in order to go up; it is its movement; it is natural. A mureed is subject to such experiences in the path of life. Life will take its own course. The one who sails will have many times to meet a rough sea; he has to be prepared for this and not be frightened or discouraged. He still has to go on through life. If life's journey were soft and smooth there would be no need for spiritual development. He has to have control of the rudder to be able to go through both calm seas and storms.

Sometimes the mureed wonders what others are saying and if they are displeased or pleased; if they are displeased he thinks he is not progressing. But this has nothing to do with progress. Those who are displeased would be displeased even with Jesus Christ, and at the same time they might be pleased with the worst person. The displeasure of others does not mean that one is not progressing.

Then if conditions are adverse the mureed thinks that he is not on the right path. But does it mean that the ship is not on its right course if a storm meets it? Neither the murshid nor God are responsible if the conditions are adverse, and the best thing is to meet them, to be more brave and courageous and to make one's way through them. Ghazali, the great Sufi writer of Persia, says that spiritual progress is like shooting at a target in the dark. We do not know where the target is, we do not see it, but we shoot just the same.

The true ideal of the spiritual person is not great power nor a great amount of knowledge. His true ideal stands beyond power and knowledge; it is that which is limitless, incomprehensible, nameless, and formless. There are no milestones to count; one cannot say, 'I have gone so many miles and there are so many still before me.' This does not belong to a spiritual journey. The pursuit of the limitless is limitless, of the formless, formless; one cannot make it tangible. But then what is it that assures progress, what evidence have we to go on? There is only one evidence and that is our belief; there is one assurance and that is our faith. If we believe we can go on, if we are convinced we will, we must, reach our goal.

There are innumerable outer signs of one's progress, but one need not think in the absence of these signs that one is not progressing. What are these signs of progress? The first is that one feels inspiration, and that things which one could not understand yesterday are easy today. Yet if there are things which one is not ready to understand one should have patience till tomorrow. Agitating against lack of inspiration means closing the doors to inspiration. Agitation is not allowed on this path; agitation disturbs our rhythm and paralyses us, and then we prove in the end to be our own enemy. But people will generally not admit this and blame others instead; or if they have kind feelings towards others then they blame the circumstances, although very often it is their own lack of patience rather than other people or the conditions.

The next sign of progress is that one begins to feel power. To some extent it may manifest physically and also mentally; and later the power may manifest in one's affairs in life. As spiritual pursuit is endless, so power has no end.

The third sign of progress is that one begins to feel a joy, a happiness. But in spite of that feeling it is possible that clouds of depression and despair may come from without, and one might think at that moment that all the happiness and joy which one had gained spiritually was snatched away. But that is not so. If spiritual joy could be snatched away it would not be spiritual joy. It is not like material comforts; when these are taken away from us we have lost them; but spiritual joy is ours, it is our property; no death nor decay can take it away from us. Changing clouds like those which surround the sun, might surround our joy, but when they are scattered we will find our property still there in our own heart. It is something we can depend upon, something nobody can take away from us.

There is another sign of progress, and that is that one becomes fearless. Whatever be the situation in life, nothing seems to frighten one any more, even death. Then one becomes fearless in all that might seem frightening, and a brave spirit develops, a spirit which gives one patience and strength to struggle against all adverse conditions however terrible they seem to be. It can even develop to such an extent that one would like to fight with death. To such a person nothing seems so horrible that he would feel helpless before it.

Still another sign of progress is that at times one begins to feel peaceful. This may increase so much that a restful feeling comes in the heart. One might be in the solitude, but even if one is in a crowd one still feels restful. Life in the world is most exciting; it has a tiring effect upon a sensitive person. When one is restless the conditions in life can make one experience the greatest discomfort, for there is no greater pain than restlessness. And if there is any remedy for the lack of peace, it is spiritual progress. Once peace is developed in a soul, that soul feels such a great power and has such a great influence upon those who approach it and upon all upsetting conditions and jarring influences coming from all sides, that just as water makes the dust settle down, so all jarring influences settle down under the feet of the peaceful. What do we learn from the story told in the Bible of Daniel who was thrown into the lions' den, what does this story suggest? Was it Daniel's hypnotism which calmed the lions? If it was hypnotism, let the hypnotizers of today go to the lions and try the experience! No, it was his inner peace. The influence of that peace acts so powerfully upon all passions, that it even calms lions and makes them sleep.

One may make the excuse that one's surroundings are worrying one, that one's friends are troublesome or that one's enemies are horrible; but nothing can withstand that peace which is awakened in the heart. All must calm down, all must settle down like dust after water has been sprinkled on it.

But if this power does not come immediately to a mureed, let him not be disappointed. Can one expect this whole journey to be made in a week? I would not be surprised if many mureeds do expect this, but it is a lifelong journey and those who have really accomplished it are the ones who have never doubted that they would progress. They have never allowed this doubt to enter

H

their minds to hinder them. They do not even concern themselves with this question. They only know that they must reach the goal, that they will reach it, and that if they do not reach it today they will reach it tomorrow. The right attitude is never to let one's mind feel, after one has taken some steps, that one must go to the right or to the left. If a man has that one strength which is faith, that is all the power he needs on the path. He can go forward and nothing will hinder him, and in the end he will accomplish his purpose.

SUFI POETRY

CONTENTS

CHAPTER I

THE POET AND THE PROPHET

THERE IS a saying that a poet is a prophet, and this saying
has a great significance and a hidden meaning. There is no doubt
that though poetry is not necessarily prophecy, prophecy is born
in poetry. If one were to say that poetry is a body which is
adopted by the spirit of prophecy, it would not be wrong.
Wagner has said that noise is not necessarily music, and the same
thing can be said in connection with poetry: that a verse written
in rhyme and metre is not necessarily true poetry. Poetry is an
art, a music expressed in the beauty and harmony of words. No
doubt much of the poetry one reads is meant either as a pastime
or for amusement, but real poetry comes from the dancing of the
soul. And no one can make the soul dance unless the soul itself is
inclined to dance. Also, no soul can dance which is not alive.

In the Bible it is said that no one will enter the kingdom of God
whose soul is not born again, and being born means being alive. It
is not only a gay disposition or an external inclination to merriment
and pleasure that is the sign of a living soul; for external joy and
amusement may come simply through the external being of man,
although even in this outer joy and happiness there is a glimpse
of the inner joy and happiness which is the sign of the soul having
been born again. What makes it alive? It makes itself alive when it
strikes its depths instead of reaching outward. The soul, after
coming up against the iron wall of this life of falsehood, turns
back within itself, it encounters itself, and this is how it becomes
living.

In order to make this idea more clear I should like to take as
an example a man who goes out into the world; a man with
thought, with feeling, with energy, with desire, with ambition,
with enthusiasm to live and work in life. And because of the actual
nature of life, his experience will make him feel constantly up
against an iron wall in whatever direction he strikes out. And the
nature of man is such that when he meets with an obstacle then he

struggles; he lives in the outer life, and he goes on struggling. He does not know any other part of life, for he lives only on the surface. But then there is another man who is sensitive because he has a sympathetic and tender heart, and every blow coming from the outer world, instead of making him want to hit back outwardly, makes him want to strike at himself inwardly. And the consequence of this is that his soul, which after being born on this earth seems to be living but in reality is in a grave, becomes awakened by that action; and when once the soul is awakened in this way it expresses itself outwardly, whether in music, in art, in poetry, in action, or in whatever way it wishes to express itself.

In this way a poet is born. There are two signs which reveal the poet: one sign is imagination, the other is feeling, and both are essential on the spiritual path. A man, however learned and good, who yet lacks these two qualities, can never arrive at a satisfactory result, especially on the spiritual path.

The sacred scriptures of all ages, whether of the Hindus or the Parsis, the race of Ben Israel or of others, were all given in poetry or in poetic prose. No spiritual person however great, however pious and spiritually advanced, has ever been able to give a scripture to the world unless he was blessed with the gift of poetry. One may ask if this would still be possible nowadays, when sentiment takes second place in life's affairs and people wish everything to be expressed plainly, 'cut and dried' as the saying is, and when one has become so accustomed to having everything, especially in science, explained in clear words. But it must be understood that facts about the names and forms of this world may be scientifically explained in plain words, but when one wishes to interpret the sensation one gets when looking at life, it cannot be explained except in the way that the prophets did in poetry. No one has ever explained nor can anyone ever explain the truth in words. Language exists only for the convenience of everyday affairs; the deepest sentiments cannot be explained in words. The message that the prophets have given to the world at different times is an interpretation in their own words of the idea of life that they have received.

Inspiration begins in poetry and culminates in prophecy. One can picture the poet as a soul which has so to speak risen from its grave and is beginning to make graceful movements; but when the same soul begins to move and to dance in all directions and to touch heaven and earth in its dance, expressing all the beauty it sees—that is prophecy. The poet when he is developed reads the mind of the universe, although it very often happens that the poet himself does not know the real meaning of what he has said. Very often one finds that a poet has said something, and after many years there comes a moment when he realizes the true meaning of what he said. And this shows that behind all these different activities the divine Spirit is hidden, and the divine Spirit often manifests through an individual without his realizing that it is divine.

In the East the prophet is called *Payghambar*, which means the Messenger, the one who carries somebody's word to someone else. In reality every individual in this world is the medium of an impulse which is hidden behind him, and that impulse he gives out, mostly without knowing it. This is not only so with living beings, but one can see it even in objects; for every object has its purpose, and by fulfilling its purpose that object is fulfilling the scheme of nature. Therefore whatever be the line or activity of a man, whether it is business or science or music or art or poetry, he is a medium in some way or other. There are mediums of living beings, there are mediums of those who have passed to the other side, and there are mediums who represent their country, their nation, their race. Every individual is acting in his own way as a medium.

When the prophet or the poet dives deep into himself he touches that perfection which is the source and goal of all beings. And as an electric wire connected with a battery receives the force or energy of the battery, so the poet who has touched the innermost depths of his being has touched the perfect God, and from there he derives that wisdom, that beauty, and that power which belong to the perfect Self of God. There is no doubt that in all things there is the real and the false and there is the raw and the ripe. Poetry comes from the tendency to contemplation. A man with imagination cannot retain the imagination, cannot mould it, cannot build it up unless he has this contemplative tendency within him. The more one contemplates the more one is able to conceive of what one receives. Not only this, but after contemplation a person is able to realize a certain idea more clearly than if that idea had only passed through his mind.

The process of contemplation is like the work of the camera: when the camera is put before a certain object and has been properly focused, then only that object is received by the camera. And therefore when an object before one is limited, then one can see that object more clearly. What constitutes the appeal of the poet is that he tells his readers of something he has seen behind these generally recognized ideas. The prophet goes still further. He not only contemplates one idea, but he can contemplate on any idea. There comes a time in the life of the prophet or of anyone who contemplates, when whatever object he casts his glance upon opens up and reveals to him what it has in its heart. In the history of the world we see that besides their great imagination, their great dreams, their ecstasy and their joy in the divine life, the prophets have often been great reformers, scientists, medical men or even statesmen.

This in itself shows their balance; it shows that theirs is not a one-sided development; they do not merely become dreamers or go into trances, but both sides of their personality are equally developed. It is an example of God in man that the prophets manifest. We can see this in the life of Joseph: we are told that he was so innocent, so simple that he went with his brothers, yielding to them, and that this led to his betrayal. In his relationship with Zuleikha we see the human being, the tendency to beauty. And at the same time there is the question he continually asks: What am I doing? What shall I do? Later in his life we see him as one who knows the secret of dreams, as the mystic who interprets the dream of the king. And still later in his life we see that he became a minister, with the administration of the country in his hands, able to carry out the work of the state.

Spirituality has become far removed from material life, and so God is far removed from humanity. Therefore one cannot any more conceive of God speaking through a man, through someone like oneself. Even a religious man who reads the Bible every day will have great difficulty in understanding the verse,. 'Be ye perfect, even as your Father in heaven is perfect.' The Sufi message and its mission are to bring this truth to the consciousness of the world: that man can dive so deep within himself that he can touch the depths where he is united with the whole of life, with all souls, and that he can derive from that source harmony, beauty, peace, and power.

CHAPTER II

SUFI POETIC IMAGERY

SUFI POETIC imagery stands by itself, distinct and peculiar in its character. It is both admired and criticized for its peculiarity. Why it is different from the expressions of other poets born in various countries, is because of its Persian origin and the particular qualities of Persia—the fine climate, the ancient traditions, its being the place where, it is said, wine was tasted for the first time; a land of luxury, a land of beauty, a land of art and imagination. It was natural that with Persian thinkers of all periods, who thought deeply on life, its nature and character, their expressions should become subtle, artistic, fine, and picturesque. In short, it is the dancing of the soul. In all other living beings, the soul is lying asleep, but when once the soul has awakened, called by beauty, it leaps up dancing, and its every movement makes a picture, whether in writing, poetry, music or whatever it may be. A dancing soul will always express the most subtle and intricate harmonies in the realm of music or poetry.

When we read the works of Hafiz and of many other Sufi poets, we shall find that they are full of the same imagery and this is partly because that was the time of Islam. The mission of Islam had a particular object in view, and in order to attain that object it had strict rules about life. A free-thinker had difficulty in expressing his thoughts without being accused of having done a great wrong towards the religion and the State. And these free-thinkers of Persia, with their dancing soul and continual enthusiasm, began to express their soul in this particular imagery, using words such as 'the beloved', 'wine', wine-press', and 'tavern'. And this poetry became so popular that not only the wise derived benefit from it, but also the simple ones enjoyed the beauty of its wonderful expressions which make an immediate appeal to every soul. There is no doubt that the souls which were already awakened and those on the point of awakening were inspired by these poems. Souls which were opening their eyes after the deep slumber of many years began to rise up and dance; as Hafiz says, 'If those pious ones of long robes listen to my verse, my song, they will immediately begin to get up and dance'. And then he says at the end of the poem, 'Forgive me, O pious ones, for I am drunk just now!'

This concept of drinking is used in various connections and conveys many different meanings. In the first place, imagine that there is a magic tavern where there are many different kinds of wine. Each wine has a different effect upon the person who drinks it. One drinks a wine which makes him light-hearted, frivolous, humorous; another drinks a wine which makes him sympathetic, kind, tender, gentle. Someone else drinks one which makes him bewildered at everything he sees. Another drinks and finds his way into the ditch. One becomes angry after drinking while another becomes passionate. One drinks and is drowned in despair. Another drinks and begins to feel loving and affectionate; yet another drinks a wine that makes him discouraged with everything. Imagine how interested we should all be to see that tavern! In point of fact we live in that tavern and we see it every day; only, we do not take proper notice of it.

Once I saw a Madzub, a man who pretends to be insane, who though living in the world does not wish to be of the world, standing in the street of a large city, laughing. I stood there, feeling curious to know what made him laugh at that moment. And I understood that it was the sight of so many drunken men, each one having had his particular wine.

It is most amusing when we look at it in this way. There is not one single being on earth who does not drink wine; only, the wine of one is different from the wine of the other. A man does not only drink during the day but the whole night long, and he awakens in the morning intoxicated by whatever wine he has been drinking. He awakens with fear or with anger, he awakens with joy, or with love and affection; and the moment he awakens from sleep he shows what wine he has been drinking.

One might ask why the great Sufi teachers have taken such a great interest in the particular imagery of these poets. The reason is that they found the solution to the problem of life by looking upon the world as a tavern, with many wines and each person drinking a different one. They discovered the alchemy, the chemical process, by which to change the wine that a person drinks, and give him another wine to see how this works. The work of the Sufi teacher with his pupil is of that kind. He first finds out which blend of wine his mureed drinks, and then he finds out which blend he must have.

But, one will ask, is there then no place for soberness in life? There is, but when that soberness is properly interpreted, one sees that it too is wine. Amir, the Hindustani poet, has expressed it in verse, 'The eyes of the sober one spoke to the eyes of the drunken one: "You have no place here, for your intoxication is different from mine." ' The awakened person seems to be asleep to the sleeping one, and so the one who has become sober also appears to be still drunk; for the condition of life is such that no one appears to be sober. It is this soberness which is called *Nirvana* by Buddhists and *Mukti* by Hindus. But if I were asked if it is then desirable for us to be sober, my reply would be, no. What is desirable is for us to know what soberness is, and after knowing what soberness is, then to take any wine we may choose. The tavern is there; wines are there. There are two men: one who is the master of wine, the other who is the slave of wine; the first drinks wine, but wine drinks up the other. The one whom wine drinks up is mortal; he who drinks wine becomes immortal. What is the love of God? What is divine knowledge? Is it not a wine? Its experience is different, its intoxication is different, for there is ordinary wine and there is most costly champagne. The difference is in the wine.

In the imagery of the Sufi poets this tavern is the world, and the Saki is God. In whatever form the wine-giver comes and gives a wine, it is God who comes. In this way, by recognizing the Saki, the wine-giver, in all forms, the Sufi worships God; for he recognizes Him in friend and foe as the wine-giver. And wine is that influence which we receive from life, an harmonious influence or a depressing influence, a beautiful influence or one that lacks beauty. When we have given in to it then we become drunk, then we become addicted to it, then we are under its influence; but when we have sought soberness then we have risen above it all, and then all wines are ours.

CHAPTER III

THE PERSIAN POETS

AT ALL TIMES Persia has had great poets and it has been called the land of poetry; in the first place because the Persian language is so well adapted to poetry, but also because all Persian poetry contains a mystical touch. The literary value of the poetry only makes it poetry; but when a mystical value is added this makes the poetry prophecy. The climate and atmosphere of Persia have also been most helpful to poetry, and the very imaginative nature of the people has made their poetry rich. At all times and in all countries, when the imagination has no scope for expansion, poetry dies and materialism increases.

There is no poet in the world who is not a mystic. A poet is a mystic whether consciously or unconsciously, for no one can write poetry without inspiration, and when a poet touches the profound depths of the spirit, struck by some aspect of life, he brings forth a poem as a diver brings forth a pearl.

In this age of materialism and ever-growing commercialism man seems to have lost the way of inspiration. During my travels I was asked by a well-known writer whether it is really true that there is such a thing as inspiration. This gave me an idea of how far nowadays some writers and poets are removed from inspiration. It is the materialism of the age which is responsible for this; if a person has a tendency towards poetry or music, as soon as he begins to write something his first thought is, 'Will it catch on or not? What will be its practical value?' And generally what catches on is that which appeals to the average man. In this way culture is going downward instead of upward.

When the soul of the poet is intoxicated by the beauty of nature and the harmony of life, it is moved to dance; and the expression of the dance is poetry. The difference between inspired poetry and mechanical writing is as great as the difference between true and false. For long ages the poets of Persia have left a wonderful treasure of thought for humanity. Jelal-ud-Din Rumi has revealed in his Masnavi the mystery of profound revelation. In the East his works are considered as sacred as holy scriptures. They have illuminated numberless souls and the study of his work can be considered to belong to the highest standard of culture.

The poet is a creator, and he creates in spite of all that confronts him; he creates a world of his own. And by doing so he rises naturally above that plane where only what is visible and touchable is regarded as real. When he sings to the sun, when he smiles to the moon, when he prays to the sea, and when he looks at the plants, at the forests, and at life in the desert, he communicates with nature. In the eyes of the ordinary person he is imaginative, dreamy, visionary; his thoughts seem to be in the air. But if one asked the poet what he thinks of these others, he would say that it is those who cannot fly who remain on the ground. It is natural that creatures which walk on the earth are not always able to fly; those which fly in the air must have wings, and among human beings one will find that same difference, for in human beings there are all things.

There are souls like germs and worms, there are souls like animals and birds, and again there are souls like jinns and angels. Among human beings all can be found: those who belong to the earth, those who dwell in heaven, and those who dwell in the very depths.

Those who were able to soar upward by the power of their imagination have been living poets. What they said was not only a statement, it was music itself; it not only had a rhythm, but it had also a tone in it. It made their souls dance and it would make anyone dance who heard their poetry. Thus Hafiz of Shiraz gives a challenge to the dignified, pious men of his country when he says, 'Pious friends, you would forget your dignity if you would hear the song which came from my glowing heart.' And it is such souls who have touched the highest summits of life, so that they have been able to contribute some truth, giving an interpretation of human nature and the inner law of life.

It is another thing with poets who have made poetry for the sake of fame or name or popularity, or so that it might be appreciated by others; for that is business and not poetry. Poetry is an art, an art of the highest degree. The poet's communication with nature brings him in the end to communicate with himself, and by that communication he delves deeper and deeper, within and without, communicating with life everywhere. This communication brings him into a state of ecstasy, and in his ecstasy his whole being is filled with joy; he forgets the worries and anxieties of life, he rises above the praise and blame of this earth, and the things of this world become of less importance to him. He stands on the earth but gazes into the heavens; his outlook on life becomes broadened and his sight keen. He sees things that no one else is interested in, that no one else sees.

This teaches us that what may be called heaven or paradise is not very far from man. It is always near him, if only he would look at it. Our life is what we look at. If we look at the right thing then it is right; if we look at the wrong thing then it is wrong. Our life is made according to our own attitude, and that is why the poet proves to be self-sufficient, and also indifferent and independent; these qualities become as wings, for him to fly upward. The poet is in the same position as anyone else in regard to the fears and worries that life brings, the troubles and difficulties that everyone feels in the midst of the world, and yet he rises above these things so that they do not touch him.

No doubt the poet is much more sensitive to the troubles and difficulties of life than an ordinary person. If he took to heart everything that came to him, all the jarring influences that disturbed his peace of mind, all the rough edges of life that everyone has to rub against, he would not be able to go on; but on the other hand if he hardened his heart and made it less sensitive, then he would also close his heart to the inspiration which comes as poetry. Therefore in order to open the doors of his heart, to keep its sensitiveness, the one who communicates with life within and without is open to all influences whether agreeable or disagreeable and is without any protection; and his only escape from all the disturbances of life is through rising above them.

The prophetic message which was given by Zarathushtra to the people of Persia was poetic from beginning to end. It is most interesting to see that Zarathushtra showed in his scriptures and all through his life how a poet rises from earth to heaven. It suggests to us how Zarathushtra communicated with nature, with its beauty, and how at every step he took he touched deeper and deeper the depths of life. Zarathushtra formed his religion by praising the beauty in nature and by finding the source of his art which is creation itself in the Artist who is behind it all.

What form of worship did he teach? He taught the same worship with which he began his poetry and with which he finished it. He said to his pupils, 'Stand before the sea, look at the vastness of it, bow before it, before its source and goal.' He said to them, 'Look at the sun, and see what joy it brings. What is at the back of it? Where does it come from? Think of its source and goal, and how you are heading towards it.' People then thought that it was sun-worship, but it was not; it was the worship of light which is the source and goal of all. That communication within and without sometimes extended the range of a poet's vision so much that it was beyond the comprehension of the average man.

When the Shah of Persia said that he would like to have the history of his country written, for one did not exist at that time, Firdausi, a poet who was inspired and intuitive said, 'I will write it and bring it to you.' He began to meditate, throwing his search-light as far back into the past as possible, and before the appointed time he was able to prepare that book and bring it to the court. It is said that the spiritual power of that poet was so great that when someone at the court sneered at the idea of a man being able to look so far back into the past, he went up to him and put his hand on his forehead and said, 'Now see!' And the man saw with his own eyes that which was written in the book.

This is human; it is not superhuman, although examples of it are rarely to be found; for in the life of every human being, especially of one who is pure-hearted, loving, sympathetic, and good, the past, present, and future are manifested to a certain extent. If one's inner light were thrown back as a searchlight it could go much further than man can comprehend. Some have to develop this gift, but others are born with it; and among those who are born with it we find some who perhaps know ten or twelve years beforehand what is going to happen. Therefore a poet is someone who can focus his soul on the past, and also throw his light on the future, and make that clear which has not yet happened but which has been planned beforehand and which already exists in the abstract.

It is such poetry that becomes inspirational poetry. It is through such poetry that the intricate aspects of metaphysics can be taught. All the Upanishads of the Vedas are written in poetry; the suras of the Qu'ran and Zarathushtra's scriptures are all in poetry. All these prophets, whenever they came, brought the message in poetry.

The development of poetry in Persia occurred at a time when there was a great conflict between the orthodox and the free-thinkers. At that time the law of the nation was a religious law and no one was at liberty to express his free thoughts which might be in conflict with the religious ideas. And there were great thinkers such as Firdausi, Farid-ud-Din-Attar, Jelal-ud-Din Rumi, Sa'di, Hafiz, Jami, Omar Khayyám, who were not only poets, but who were poetry itself. They were living in another world although they appeared to be on earth. Their outlook on life, their keen sight, were different to those of everyone else. The words which arose from their hearts were not brought forth with effort, they were natural flames rising up out of the heart. And these words remain as flames enlightening souls of all times, whatever soul they have touched.

Sufism has been the wisdom of these poets. There has never been a poet of note in Persia who was not a Sufi, and every one of them has added a certain aspect to the Sufi ideas, but they took great care not to affront the minds of orthodox people. Therefore a new terminology had to be invented in Persian poetry; the poets had to use words such as 'wine' and 'bowl' and 'beloved' and 'rose', words which would not offend the orthodox mind and would yet at the same time serve as symbolical expressions to explain the divine law.

It belongs to the work of the Sufi Movement to interpret the ideas of these poets, to express their ideas in words that can be understood by modern people, for the value of those ideas is as great today as it ever was.

CHAPTER IV

FARID-UD-DIN-ATTAR

FARID-UD-DIN-ATTAR was one of the earliest Sufi-poets of Persia, and there is no doubt that the work of Attar was the inspiration of Rumi and of many other spiritual souls and poets of Persia. He showed the way to the ultimate aim of life by making a sort of picture in a poetic form. Almost all the great teachers of the world, when they have pointed out the right way to seeking souls, have had to adopt a symbolical form of expression, such as a story or legend which could give a key to the one who is ready to understand and at the same time interest the one who is not yet ready. Thus both may rejoice, the one who sleeps and the one who is already awakened. This method has been followed by the poets of Persia and India, especially the Hindustani poets, and they have told their stories in a form which would be acceptable, not only to the seekers after truth, but to those in all the different stages of evolution.

Attar's best known work is called *Mantiq-ut-Tayr,* or the Colloquy of the Birds, from which the idea of the Blue Bird has been taken today. Very few have understood the idea of the Blue Bird, or the Bird of the Sky. It contains a very ancient teaching, through the use of the Persian word for sky. This teaching points out that every soul has a capacity which may be called the sky, and this capacity can accommodate the earth or heaven, whichever it partakes of and holds within itself. When one walks in a crowd what does one see? One sees numerous faces, but one might better call them various attitudes. All that we see in individuals, all that presents itself to us, has expression, atmosphere and form. If we give it one name, it is the attitude, whatever attitude they have towards life, right or wrong, good or bad; they are themselves that attitude. Does this not show how appropriate the word sky is? In point of fact, whatever one makes of oneself, one becomes that. The source of happiness or unhappiness is all in man himself. When he is unaware of this, he is not able to arrange his life, but as he becomes more acquainted with this secret he gains mastery, and the process by which this mastery is attained is the only fulfilment of the purpose of this life. It is this process which is explained by Attar in his description of the seven valleys through which this Bird of the Sky has passed.

The first valley is the Valley of the Quest. How true it is that every child is born with the tendency to search, to know! What we call inquisitiveness or curiosity is born in each one of them, and it represents the inner feeling of quest. And as man is born with this tendency, he cannot be satisfied until by searching he has obtained the knowledge he wishes to have. There is no doubt that what prevents man from gaining that knowledge which his soul is really searching for, is himself. It is his small self, always standing in his way, that keeps him from searching for the only thing which every soul strives to find. Therefore it would be safe to say that there is no one in this world who is a worse enemy of man than man himself.

In this search some people think that one can perhaps find out from science or from art something which is behind this manifestation; and surely, whether the quest be material or spiritual, in the end one will arrive, and one must arrive, at that goal which is the same for everyone. Scientists and engineers, people who are absorbed in research into material things and hardly ever think of spiritual matters, even they, after much research, arrive very close to the same knowledge which is the ultimate knowledge. Therefore, whatever a man may seem to us, materialist, atheist, or agnostic, we cannot really call him that, because in the end his goal is the same and his attainment is the same. If he really reaches the depths of knowledge, if he goes far enough, whatever he was searching for he will arrive at the same goal.

And when he has searched enough and found something satisfying, a man still cannot enjoy that satisfaction unless there is one faculty in play, and that is the faculty of love and devotion. Do we not see in our everyday life that people of great intellect and wide interests very often seem to miss something? When it happens with a couple that one is very intellectual, the other may feel there is something lacking to make their lives complete, that intellect alone is not enough. What is it? It is the heart which balances life, and the absence of heart keeps life dry. Knowledge and heart are just like the positive and negative forces; it is these two things which make life balanced. If the heart quality is very strong and intellect is lacking then life lacks balance. Knowledge and heart quality must be developed together. And therefore according to Attar the faculty of devotion or quality of heart is the second valley, the Valley of Love; and the third valley is the Valley of Knowledge, the knowledge which illuminates and comes by the help of the love element and the intellect. That is the knowledge which is called spiritual knowledge. Without a developed love quality man is incapable of having that knowledge. There are fine lights and shades in one's life which cannot be perceived and fully understood without having touched the deeper side of life, which is the devotional side. The person who has never in his life been wholly grateful cannot know what it is. He who has not experienced humility in life does not know its beauty. The one who has not known gentleness or modesty cannot appreciate its beauty or recognize it.

No doubt a person of fine qualities is often ridiculed if he happens to be in a place where these qualities are not understood, where they are like a foreign language. This shows there is a refinement in life for which intellect alone is not sufficient. The heart must be open too. A very intellectual man went to Jami and asked him to take him as his pupil and give him initiation. Jami looked at him and said, 'Have you ever loved anybody?' This man said, 'No, I have not loved.' Then Jami said, 'Go and love first, then come to me and I will show you the way.'

Love has its time at every stage of life. As a child, as a youth, as a grown-up person, whatever stage of life one has reached, love is always asked for and love has always its part to perform; whatever situation we are placed in, among friends or foes, among those who understand us or among those who do not, in ease or in difficulty, in all places, at all times, it has its part to perform. And the one who thinks, 'I must not let the principle of love have its way, I must harden myself against it', imprisons his soul. There is only one thing in the world which shows the sign of heaven, which gives the proof of God, and that is pure unselfish love. For all the noble qualities which are hidden in the soul will spring forth and blossom when love helps them and nurtures them. Man may have a great deal of good in him and he may be very intelligent, but as long as his heart is closed he cannot show that nobleness, that goodness which is hidden in his heart; and the psychology of the heart is such that once one begins to know it one realizes that life is a continual phenomenon. Then every moment of life becomes a miracle; a searchlight is thrown upon human nature and all things become so clear that one does not ask for any greater phenomenon or miracle; it is a miracle in itself. What one calls telepathy, thought-reading, or clairvoyance, and all such things, come by themselves when the heart is open.

If a person is cold and rigid, he feels within himself as if he were in a grave; he is not living, he cannot enjoy this life, for he cannot express himself and he cannot see the light and life outside. And what keeps man back from developing the heart quality? His exacting attitude. He wants to make a business of love. He says, 'If you will love me I will love you.' As soon as a man measures and weighs his favours and his services, and all that he does for one whom he loves, he ceases to know what love is. Love sees the beloved and nothing else. As Rumi says, 'Whether you love a human being or you love God, there will come a day when all lovers, either of man or of God will be brought before the throne of love, and the presence of that only Beloved will reign there.' What does this show? In loving our friend, in loving our neighbour, even in the love that one shows to one's enemy, one is only loving God. And the one who says, 'I love God but I cannot love man,' does not love God; he cannot. It is like saying, 'I love you very much but I do not like looking at your face!'

And after this third valley, where the knowledge of human nature and of the fine feelings which are called virtues is attained, the next step is annihilation. But what we call destruction or annihilation is nothing but change. Neither substance nor form nor spirit, nothing, is absolutely destroyed; it is only changed. But man sometimes does not like to change. He does not like it but he cannot live without it. There is not one single moment of our life when there is no change; whether we accept it or not the change is there. Destruction or annihilation or death might seem a very different change, and yet there are a thousand deaths that we die in life. A great disappointment, the moment when our heart breaks, is worse than death. Often our experiences in life are worse than death, yet we go through them. At the time they seem unbearable; we think we cannot stand it, and yet we live. If after dying a thousand deaths we still live, there is nothing in the world to be afraid of. It is man's delusion, his own imagination which makes death dreadful to him. Can anyone kill life? If there is any death, it is that of death itself, for life will not die.

Someone went to a Sufi with a question; he said, 'I have been puzzling for many, many years and reading books, and I have not been able to find a definite answer; tell me what happens after death?' The Sufi said, 'Please ask this question of someone who will die. I am going to live.' The idea is that there is one sky which is our own being; in other words we can call it an accommodation. And what has taken possession of this accommodation? A deluded ego which says 'I'. It is deluded by this body and mind and it has called itself an individual. When a man has a ragged coat he says, 'I am poor'. In reality his coat is poor, not he. What this capacity or accommodation contains, is that which becomes his knowledge, his realization, and it is that which limits him; it forms that limitation which is the tragedy of every soul.

Now this capacity may either be filled with self or it may be filled with God. There is only room for one. Either we live with our limitation, or let God reign there in His unlimited Being. In other words, we take away the home which has always belonged to someone else and fill it with delusion and call it our own; and not only call it our own, but even call it our self. That is man's delusion, and all religious and philosophical teachings are given in order to rid man of this delusion which deprives him of his spiritual wealth. Spiritual wealth is the greatest wealth, spiritual happiness the only happiness; there is no other. Once a person is able to disillusion himself, he arrives at the stage described in the fourth valley, the Valley of Non-Attachment, and he is afraid. He thinks, 'How can I give my home to someone else, even if it is

God? This is my body, my mind, my home, my individuality. How can I give it away, even to God?' But in reality it is not something upon which he can rely. It is delusion from beginning to end and subject to destruction. Does anything stand above destruction? Nothing. Then why be afraid to think for the moment that it is nothing? This natural fear arises because man is unaccustomed to face reality. He is so used to dreams that he is afraid of reality. People are afraid of losing themselves, but they do not know that non-attachment is not losing one's self; it means losing illusion, and in reality it is only by losing this illusion that they can find themselves. One's soul has become lost in this illusion; and the process is to get out of it, to rise above it.

By the time the fifth valley, the Valley of Unity, is reached one has disillusioned one's self, and it is this act which is called in the Bible rebirth; when the soul has emerged from illusion it is the birth of the soul. And how does this birth of the soul express itself? What does one feel? It expresses itself first in a kind of bewilderment together with a great joy. A man's interest in life is increased; all that he sees he enjoys. He concerns himself with few things but wonders at all. This bewilderment is such that it becomes wonderfully amusing to look at life. The whole world becomes a kind of stage to him, full of players. He then begins to amuse himself with the people of this world, as one might play with children and yet not be concerned with what they do, for he expects no better. If children do something different from the parents, the parents are not much concerned; they know it is a stage of the child's life and that they cannot expect any better from them. So likes and dislikes, favours and disfavours may interest him, but they will not affect him in the least.

There is another stage, where this bewilderment brings a man to see the reflection of the One who has taken possession of his heart. This means also to see one's Beloved in everyone, even in one's enemy. The Beloved is seen in all things, and then the bowl of poison given by the Beloved is not so bitter. Those who, like Christ, have sacrificed themselves and suffered for humanity, have given an example to the world, revealing a God-conscious soul which has reached the stage where even an enemy appears as a friend, as the Beloved. And it is not an unattainable stage, for the soul is made of love and it is going towards the perfection of love. All the virtues man has learned, love has taught him. Therefore this world of good and bad, of thorns and flowers, can become a place of splendour only.

In the sixth valley, the Valley of Amazement, man recognizes and understands what is beyond all things, the reason of all reasons, the cause of all causes; for all intuition and power develop in man with this unfoldment.

And the seventh valley, the Valley of God-Realization, is the valley of that peace which every soul is looking for whether spiritually or materially, seeking from morning until night for something which will give it peace. To some souls that peace comes when asleep; but for the God-conscious that peace becomes his home. As soon as he has closed his eyes, as soon as he has relaxed his body and stilled his mind and lost the limitations of his consciousness, he begins to float in the limitless spheres.

CHAPTER V

JELAL-UD-DIN RUMI

THE POETRY of Jelal-ud-Din Rumi has made the greatest impression upon humanity. In the beginning he was inspired by Farid-ud-Din-Attar. Although Jelal-ud-Din Rumi was a highly educated man, who had the gift of speech, yet his soul was waiting for an enlightenment which came in the latter part of his life. Then Shams-e Tabrèz, a dervish, entered his life, a man in rags, showing no learned qualifications recognizable by the world, and yet he was in tune with the infinite and, to speak in religious terms, had gained the kingdom of God.

This man happened to come to the home of Rumi, who welcomed him as was his habit. Rumi was working on a manuscript, and the first thing Shams-e Tabrèz did was to throw the manuscript away. Rumi looked at him in wonder. Shams-e Tabrèz said, 'Haven't you had enough of reading and study? Now study life instead of a book!'

Rumi respectfully listened to the words of Shams-e Tabrèz who said, 'All things which seem of importance, what are they on the day when you depart? What is rank, what is power, what is position? A far greater problem is what will go with you, for the solution of that problem will lead you to eternity. The problems of this world, you may solve them and solve them, yet they are never finished. What have you understood about God, about man? What relationship have you found between man and God? If you worship God, why do you worship Him? What is limitation, what is perfection? And how can one seek for it?'

After this conversation Rumi realized that it is not learning but living the knowledge that counts. For he had read much, and he had thought much, but he suddenly saw that what is important is not saying but being. When he realized this, and after Shams-e Tabrèz had left, he wrote a verse, 'The King of the earth and of heaven, of whom people have spoken, today I have seen in the form of man.' For he saw how wide can be the heart of man, how deeply the soul of man can be touched, and how high the spirit of man can reach.

Rumi then followed this dervish. And everyone in his family and also his friends were against this, because to ordinary people a mystic is a queer individual who is not of this world and whose ideas are unusual. The language of the mystic is quite different; his ways are strange; his ideas do not correspond with the ideas of the practical man. Naturally they thought Rumi was going backward instead of forward.

Rumi had to give up his position, and wandered from place to place with Shams-e Tabrèz. After he had followed Shams-e Tabrèz for several months, everyone blaming him for this action, one day the Master disappeared. This left Rumi in very great sorrow; on the one hand he had given up his position and his work, and on the other the teacher whom he followed had left him. But this was his initiation; for Rumi this was the birth of the soul. From that moment he looked at life from quite a different point of view.

The result of this impression was that for a long period of time Jelal-ud-Din Rumi experienced a kind of ecstasy, and during this ecstasy he wrote the *Divan of Shams-e Tabrèz*. For, owing to the oneness he had achieved with the heart of his teacher, he began to see all that his teacher had thought and spoken of; and for that reason he did not call it his book, but he called it his teacher's book. And his heart which had listened to his master so attentively became a reproducing and recording machine. All that had once been spoken began to repeat itself, and Rumi experienced a wonderful upliftment, a great joy and exaltation. In order to make this exaltation complete Rumi began to write verses, and the singers used to sing them; and when Rumi heard these beautiful verses sung by the singers with their *rabab*, the Persian musical instrument, he experienced the stage known to Yogis as *Samadhi*, which in Persian is called *Wajad*.

Man today has become so material that he is afraid of any experience except that of the senses. He believes that only what he can experience through the senses is a real experience, and that which is not experienced by the senses is something unbalanced, something to be afraid of; it means going into deep waters, something abnormal, at the least an untrodden path. Very often man is afraid that he might fall into a trance, or have a feeling which is unusual, and thinks that those who experience such things are fanatics who have gone out of their minds. But it is not so. Thought belongs to the mind, feeling to the heart. Why should one believe that thought is right and feeling is wrong?

All the different experiences of meditative people are of thought and feeling, but the poet who receives inspiration experiences a joy which others cannot experience. It is a joy which belongs to inspiration, and the poet knows it. A composer after having composed his music is filled with a certain joy, a certain upliftment others do not know. Does a poet or musician lose his mind by this? On the contrary, he becomes more complete. He experiences a wider, deeper, keener, fuller life than the life which others live. A life of sensation lacks the experience of exaltation. Even religious prayers, rituals, and ceremonies were intended to produce exaltation, for it is one of the needs of life; exaltation is as necessary, or perhaps even more so, as the cultivation of thought.

Rumi had many disciples seeking guidance from him. Through his deep sorrow and bewilderment he achieved another outlook; his vision became different. At that time he wrote his most valuable work, which is studied in all the countries of the East: it is called *Masnavi-i Ma'navi*, and it is a living scripture in itself which has enlightened numberless souls. It has led the sincere seeker as far as he was able to go, and yet it is so simple; there is no complexity, there are no dogmas, no principles, no great moral teachings, no expressions of piety. What he wrote is the law of life, and he has expressed that law in a kind of word-picture.

In this work Rumi tried to show the mystic vision and to explain in verse what the prophetic mission means. In the Western world many have never even thought about the subject of the prophet and his work in the world. What they know about prophets is only what is told in the Old Testament about those who prepared the world for the message of Jesus Christ. But what Rumi wished to explain about prophethood was the meaning of Jesus' words, 'I am Alpha and Omega.' Rumi wished to express that the One who is first and last was, and is, and ever will be, and that we should not limit Him to one period of history.

Then Rumi explains that the words of the prophet are the words of God Himself; he takes as an example the flute of reed, which is open at one end while the other end is in the mouth of the musician, the player. He wished to show that at one end of the flute are the lips of the prophet, and that at the other end is to be heard the voice of God. For the Muslims have never called the message given by the Prophet the message of Mohammad; they always speak of Kalam-ullah, which means the Word of God. The person of the Prophet is not mentioned, and that is why the Muslims also never call their religion Mohammadanism, but Islam, or 'peace'. They are even offended if one calls their religion the Mohammadan religion; they say, 'The Prophet was the instrument through which God expressed Himself, God is capable of speaking through any instrument; all are His instruments. It is the spirit of God which must be brought forward.'

The original words of Rumi are so deep, so perfect, so touching, that when one man repeats them hundreds and thousands of people are moved to tears. They cannot help penetrating the heart. This shows how much Rumi himself was moved to have been able to pour out such living words. Many wanted to consider him a prophet, but he said, 'No, I am not a prophet, I am a poet.' When Hafiz wrote about Rumi he said, 'I am not capable of writing about the verses of Rumi. What I can say is that he is not a prophet, but he is the one who brought the Sacred Book.' In other words he wanted to say that in fact he was a prophet.

No poet of Persia has given such a wonderful picture of metaphysics, of the path of evolution, and of higher realization as Rumi, although the form of his poetry is not so beautiful as that of Hafiz. Explaining about the soul Rumi says, 'The melodious music that comes as a cry from the heart of the flute of reed brings to you a message: the flute wants to say, "I was taken away from the stem to which I belonged, I was cut apart from that stem, and several holes were made in my heart. And it is this that made me sad; and my cry appeals to every human being." ' By the flute he means the soul; the soul which has been cut apart from its origin, from the stem, the stem which is God. And the constant cry of the soul, whether it knows it or not, is to find again that stem from which it has been cut apart. It is this longing which those who do not understand interpret as due to lack of wealth or position or worldly ambitions; but those who understand find the real meaning of this longing, and that is to come nearer, closer to the Source, as the reed longs to find its stem.

The difference between Jelal-ud-Din Rumi's work and the work of the great Hafiz of Persia is that Hafiz has pictured the outer life, whereas Rumi has pictured the inner life. And if I were to compare the three greatest poets of Persia, I would call Sa'di the body of the poet, Hafiz the heart of the poet, and Rumi the soul of the poet.

CHAPTER VI

MUSLIH–UD–DIN SA'DI

IN THE EAST the works of Sa'di have been considered to be simple, educational, and at the same time uplifting. In India Sa'di's poem *Karima* is taught to children of nine and ten, and this work is not just a legend or an amusing story; it is like a seed sown in the heart of a child of that age, so that in time it may flourish and bring forth fruits of good thought and imagination. *Karima* is a poem of thanksgiving. In it the first lesson Sa'di gives is how to be grateful, how to express gratitude, how to appreciate; and he gives the lesson of gratefulness and appreciation for everything in the world, for the kindness and love of the mother and father, of the friend and the companion, by teaching first of all gratefulness to God for all the blessings and benefits man receives.

Sa'di was a lover of humour, and he was a very simple man. He begins his *Gulistan* with a prayer in which he says, 'Let me not show my infirmities to others but to thee, my Lord, for Thou art the Judge and Thou art the Forgiver. Thou choosest whatever Thou likest, whether to be Judge or Forgiver.' The way in which he proceeds in this prayer is wonderful and so simple, and yet it has touched thousands and thousands of people.

In *Karima* Sa'di begins by saying, 'O Lord, most merciful, I ask Thy forgiveness for I am limited, and in this life of limitation I am always apt to err.' He teaches in the first lesson that man should recognize his limited condition, and realize that this limitedness makes him subject to error; at the same time he suggests that the innermost desire of every soul is to rise above limitations and keep from error, to seek divine love and ask pardon, and to appreciate all the blessings received in life, in order to rise towards the ideal stage of the human man.

And when we look at life today, it seems this is the very thing which is lacking. When children grow up without that tendency of appreciation they often cannot understand what their mother has done for them, what their father has done, what their duty is to their friends, to older people, or to their teacher. And when they grow up without developing this gratefulness then the egoistic aspect of their nature naturally develops and becomes a menace. A boy who does not appreciate in his childhood all that his mother has done for him, cannot learn to be tender and gentle to his wife, for he should have learned his first lesson with his mother. Everything that springs up by nature has to be refined, and in its fulfilment it has to become perfect. From child-hood there is a self-asserting tendency in human beings. In the nature of the child the 'I' is most pronounced, and of everything he possesses he says 'my'. If this is not changed, if the same attitude persists when that child grows older, he becomes hard to those around him, and this 'I' and what he calls 'my' cause difficulties for them all.

The whole of religious, spiritual, and philosophical teaching leads us towards the development of the personality. There is something in man that is made by nature, but there is also something that a man himself has to make. Man is born as man, but man develops in order to become human. And if man remains only man as he was born, and the same qualities with which he was born remain undeveloped and unrefined, then he does not fulfil the object of life. With all the great ones who have come from time to time to this world and whom we recognize as saints and sages, masters, teachers, and inspired helpers, it is not always the philosophy they taught, it is not always the dogmas or the form of religion they gave that was of the greatest importance; what was most important was their personality, their person. The teachings of Buddha are held in esteem by many millions, but greater than his teachings were the life he lived and the wisdom he expressed in his life, for therein lies the fulfilment of his message.

Man is born with a purpose, and that purpose is fulfilled in the refinement of his personality. This unrefined nature of the ego, when developed through life, has an effect like the prick of a thorn. Wherever, whoever, whatever it touches, it causes some harm or disturbance, some destruction. And so when the personalities of human beings are not refined, and they are confronted with temptations, with all the things that attract them, things they like and admire and wish to possess, then they come up against the conflicting activities of life, and they rub against everything like a thorn, tearing it to pieces. And what happens? No doubt when thorns rub against thorns they crush one another and they feel it less; but when thorns rub against flowers, they tear them to pieces. If we ask individuals in all walks of life what they find to be their difficulty in life, they may tell us that they lack wealth or power or position, but mostly their complaint will be that they are in some way or other hurt by others, by a friend, a parent, a child, their life's companion, a neighbour, or a colleague; they are disturbed or troubled and in difficulty from morning till night by the influence of this thorn-life which touches and scratches them. And yet man does not seem to ponder deeply enough on this subject. Life is blinding, and it keeps him always busy and engaged in finding fault with others. He does not find the thorn in himself; he always sees the thorn in other people.

Sa'di has tried in simple language to help man towards the development in his personality of the flowerlike quality: to train his personality which was made to be a flower and not a thorn. He has called his books *Gulistan*, which means a flower-bed or a rose-garden, and *Bustan*, a place of fragrance; and his whole life's work was to explain to man how the heart can be turned into a flower and that it is made to spread its perfume. If only one can train it and tend it, it will show the delicacy and beauty and fragrance of a flower; and that is the purpose of our life.

There is no mystification in Sa'di's poetry. It is full of wit and intelligence, and at the same time it is original. And the most wonderful thing that one finds in the poetry of Sa'di is his humorous turn of mind. He is ready to look at the funny side of things and to amuse and enjoy himself. How few of us in this world know what real, true mirth means, humour that is not vulgarized, not abused! It shows the rhythm and tune of the soul. Without humour life is dull and depressing. Humour is the reflection of that divine life and sun which makes life like a day full of sunshine. And a person who reflects divine wisdom and divine joy adds to the expression of his thought when he expresses his ideas with mirth.

One day Sa'di was sitting in a bookseller's shop, where his books were sold. The bookseller was absent, and someone came in and asked for one of Sa'di's books, not knowing that he was speaking to the poet himself. Sa'di said, 'What do you like about Sa'di's books?' He replied, 'O, he is a funny fellow!' Whereupon Sa'di made him a present of the book, and when he wished to pay for it said, 'No, I am Sa'di, and when you called me a funny fellow, you gave me all the reward I could wish for!'

He wanted life to be joyous. Spirituality does not mean a long face and deep sighs. No doubt there are moments when we sympathize with the troubles of others; there are moments that move us to tears, and there are times when we must close our lips. But there are other moments when we can see the joyous side of life and enjoy its beauties. Man is not born into this world for depression and unhappiness. His very being is happiness. Depression is something unnatural. By this I do not mean to say that sorrow is a sin or that suffering is always avoidable. We all have to experience both in life, in order to accomplish the purpose of life. We cannot always be smiling, and there is no spiritual evolution in ignoring either side of life. As long as one is not bound, it is no sin to stand in the midst of life. Man need not go into the forest away from everyone to show his goodness and virtue. Of what use is his goodness and virtue if he buries himself in the forest? It is in the midst of life that we have to develop and express all that is beautiful and perfect and divine to our souls.

In the *Gulistan* Sa'di expresses a wonderful thought. He says, 'Every soul is meant for a certain purpose and the light of that purpose has been kindled in that soul.' It is one short verse, but it is a volume in itself. It suggests to us that this whole universe is like a single symphony, and that all souls are like the different notes. Their activities accord with the rhythm of this symphony, and the purpose of their life is to perfect this symphony.

People are often anxious to do a certain thing, and wait for years and years, unhappy, in despair, for the right moment to come. The soul knows subconsciously that there is a note to be struck, and at the moment when it strikes that note, this soul will be satisfied; and yet the soul does not know what note it is nor when it will be struck. What is life, and what keeps us living in this world of limitation, this world of continual changes, full of falsehood and full of suffering and trouble? If there is anything in this world that keeps us alive it is hope, the honey of life. There is not one soul in this world who will say, 'Now I am satisfied, I have no further desire.' In everyone, whatever be his position in life, very rich or very poor, full of health or ailing, in all conditions man is continually yearning and waiting for something to come; he does not know what, but he is waiting for something to come. The real explanation of life is waiting; waiting for something. And what is it that man awaits? It is the fulfilment of the purpose of life, which comes when the soul strikes that note, the note which is meant to be that soul's note; this it seeks, whether on the outer plane or the inner plane.

Man has not fulfilled his life's purpose until he has struck that

K

note which is his note, and the greatest tragedy in life is obscurity of purpose. When the purpose is not clear man suffers; he cannot breathe. He does not know what to do. This life will present him with things that will interest him for the moment, but as soon as he possesses them he will say, 'No, this is not it; it is something else.' So man goes on in illusion, constantly seeking, and yet not knowing what he seeks. Blessed is he who knows his life's purpose, for that is the first step to fulfilment.

How are we to know our life's purpose? Can anybody tell us? No; no one can tell us, for life in its very nature is self-revealing, and it is our own fault if we are not open to that revelation which life offers to us; it is not the fault of life. Man is the offspring of nature, therefore his purpose belongs to nature. But the artificiality of life brings obscurity, and this prevents him from receiving that knowledge which is the revelation of his own soul.

And if asked how one should proceed, I would advise the study of every object, whether false or true, which holds and attracts us either outwardly or inwardly; we should not be doubting and suspicious. What Christ taught from morning until night was faith, but the interpretation generally given to this word does not make it clear. People have said it means faith in a priest, in a church, or in a sect, but that is not the meaning. The true meaning of faith is trust in oneself.

The works of Sa'di from beginning to end teach the first lesson of faith, which is to understand that we are not here in this world in vain, to waste our lives. We are here for a purpose, everyone for a particular purpose. Each one of us is an atom of this universe and completes the symphony, and when we do not strike our note it means that note is lacking in the symphony of the whole. When we do not fulfil our life's purpose in the way for which we were created we are not living rightly and consequently we are not happy.

Our happiness depends on living rightly, and right living depends on striking our note; the realization of that purpose is in the book of our heart. Open that book and look at it. The aim of all meditation, concentration, and contemplation is only to open this book, to focus our mind, and to see what purpose there is in our life. And as soon as we see that our ultimate goal, our life's object and happiness, our true health and well-being, and our real wealth lie in the fulfilment of our purpose, then the whole trend of our life will change.

CHAPTER VII

SHAMS-UD-DIN MOHAMMAD HAFIZ

THE NAME of Hafiz is well known to every one interested in the poetry of Persia, because among the Persian poets Hafiz is unique in his depth of thought, and the excellence of the symbolism with which he expresses his thoughts and philosophical ideas.

There was a time when a deep and independent thinker had great difficulty in expressing his thoughts. Although this has not entirely changed, there does seem in some ways to be much more freedom of expression in this age. In ancient times, when anyone expressed his thought freely about life and its hidden law, about the soul, God, creation, and manifestation he met with great difficulties. The chief difficulty was that the government was in the hands of various religious authorities, and under their rule the principles of exoteric religion prevailed; therefore those who sought attainment through the esoteric side of philosophy always had difficulty in speaking to people about it. Many were persecuted; they were stoned, they were flayed, they were put to death in different ways; all sorts of punishments were inflicted upon them, and because of this the progress of humanity was retarded. Today we no longer see this, nevertheless the limited attitude of the human mind in regard to religious and philosophical questions is to be found in all ages. For the Sufis, who by the help of meditation found the source of knowledge in their own hearts, it was very difficult to give to the world in plain words what little they could explain of the truth. No doubt the truth cannot be spoken of in words, yet those gifted with poetic and prophetic expression have always had the inclination and tendency to express what their souls experienced.

Hafiz found a way of expressing the experiences of his soul and his philosophy in verse, for the soul enjoys expressing itself in verse. The soul itself is music, and when it is experiencing the realization of divine truth its tendency is to express itself in poetry. Hafiz therefore expressed his soul in poetry. And what poetry! Poetry full of light and shade, line and colour, poetry full of feeling. No poetry in the world can be compared to that of Hafiz in its delicacy. Only the fine soul who has a subtle perception of light and shade expressed in words, can grasp the meaning of the illumination of the soul. Nevertheless the words of Hafiz have won every heart that listens, and even those who do not wholly understand them are won by their rhythm, charm, and beauty of expression.

In the East the Persian language is considered the most delightful of all for poetry. It is soft, it is expressive, and its expression is tender. Every object has perhaps ten names for the poet to choose from, and the slightest thought can be expressed in some twenty different ways according to the poet's choice.

Hafiz, whose style resembles that of Solomon, used in his poetry symbolical terms such as the beloved's beautiful countenance, her smiles, her glance, her graceful movements; the lover's feeling heart, his deep sigh, his pearl-like tears; the nightingale, the rose, the wine, the cup and the tavern, the arrow and the bow, spring and autumn. With these terms he composed a special language in which he subtly expressed life's secret. All the other Persian poets, and also many of the poets of India, have adopted this terminology. Persian poetry is like painting; these poets painted pictures of the different aspects of life. The work of Hafiz, from beginning to end, is one series of beautiful pictures, ever-revealing and most inspiring. Once a person has studied Hafiz he has reached the top of the mountain, from whence he beholds the sublimity of the immanence of God.

The mission of Hafiz was to express to a fanatical religious world that the presence of God is not to be found only in heaven, but also here on earth. Very often religious belief in God and in the hereafter has kept man asleep, waiting for that hour and day to come when he will be face to face with his Lord; and he is certain that that day will not come before he is dead. Therefore he awaits his death in the hope that he will see God in the hereafter, for heaven is the only place where God can be found; there is no other place. And he thinks that only a certain place, that is the church, is a sacred place of worship, and that God cannot be found anywhere else. The mission of Hafiz was to destroy this idea and to make man conscious of the heaven close to him, and to tell him that all he expects as a reward in the hereafter could be had here if he lived a fuller life.

The same ideal which one finds in all religions, and which was one of the principal teachings of Jesus Christ, namely that God is love, was also the chief ideal of Hafiz, and he has expressed it constantly in his *Divan*. If there is anything divine in man it is love. If God is to be found anywhere it is in man's heart which is love. And if the love element is awakened in the heart then God is, so to speak, made alive and is born in man's self. But at the same time Hafiz has shown in his poetry what is the key to this; and that key is appreciation of beauty in all forms. Beauty is not always to be found in an object or a person; beauty depends upon one's attitude towards life, how one looks at it, and its effect depends upon our power of appreciation. The very same music or poetry or painting will touch one person so that he feels its beauty to the very depth of his being, while another person may look at it but not see it. The whole of manifestation has its beauty. Sometimes its beauty is clearly manifest to us, sometimes we have to look for it. We may meet a good person, and we are always charmed by the beauty of goodness. But we may meet another person who seems bad, and yet at the same time there is good hidden in him somewhere if we would only look for it, if we only had the desire to draw it out. The badness is not always in the objects and persons, but is often in our way of looking at them. The whole trend of the poetry of Hafiz is to awaken that appreciation and love of beauty which is the only means by which to experience that bliss which is the purpose of our life.

Someone asked a Sufi the reason for this creation, and he answered, 'God, whose being is love itself, desired to experience the nature of His own being, and in order to experience it He had to manifest Himself.' God Himself and His manifestation, the soul and God—this dual aspect—can be seen in all forms of nature, in the sun and the moon, in night and day, in male and female, in positive and negative, and in all things of opposite characteristics in order that this love principle, itself the original and the only principle behind the whole of manifestation, may have full play. That is why the fulfilment of the purpose of life lies in the full expression of the love principle.

Very often by learning philosophy and by looking at this world with pessimistic thought, people have renounced the world and have called it material and false; they have left this world and gone to the forest and desert or to a cave, and have taught the principle of self-denial and renunciation. This was not the way of Hafiz. He said life is like journeying over the sea and coming to a new port, and before landing a man becomes frightened and says, 'But perhaps I shall be attacked, or the place will attract me so much that I shall not be able to go back to where I came from.' But he does not know why he has started on that journey; he has certainly not undertaken it in order to go back again without landing somewhere. The attitude of Hafiz is to land there, to risk it. If it turns out to be an attractive place, he is ready to be won; if it will crush him, he is ready to be crushed. This is a daring attitude: not to run away from this false world, but to discover glimpses of the truth in this false world and to find God's purpose in this maze.

There is another great revelation which Hafiz has brought before humanity in a most beautiful form. Many people in this world have at one time believed in God, in His mercy and compassion, in His love and forgiveness; but after having suffered, after seeing catastrophes and·injustice, they have given up their belief, and after great sorrow they have given up their religion. The reason for this is that the religion they have followed has taught them that God is goodness, or God is Judge; and so they ask justice from that Judge, but a justice to satisfy their own ideas. They think that their standard of justice is God's, and they also look for goodness according to their understanding of it. Thus a struggle arises in their hearts. They do not see justice, because they are looking for it from their own point of view; they are looking for goodness, kindness, and mercy from their own point of view, and there are many situations which make them think that there is no justice and no such thing as an element of forgiveness. But the way of Hafiz is different. The name of God is hardly to be found in the *Divan*. He does not express belief in God as the Just and the Good. His God is his Beloved, to whom he has surrendered in perfect love and devotion, and everything coming from the Beloved is accepted by him with love and devotion, as a reward. He prefers poison coming from the hand of the Beloved to nectar from the hand of another. He prefers death to life, if it is the wish of the Beloved.

One may ask if this is fair. There is no question of fairness where there is love. Law is beneath love. Law is born of love. The mistake today is that we consider law to be higher than love. We do not see that the divine principle which is love, stands above law. Man makes of God a judge who is bound by law, who cannot do His own will, but has to do according to what is written in His book. God is not justice. Justice is His nature, but love is predominant. People attach such importance to actions and their results. They do not know that above action and result is a law which can consume the fire of hell, which can dominate even if the whole world were being drowned in the flood of destruction; they do not know that the power of love is greater than any other. Think of the hen when she takes care of her little ones. If they are threatened with danger, even if it should be a horse or an elephant, she would fight because the love principle is predominant. A kind mother is ready to forgive when her son comes with bowed head and says, 'Mother, I have been foolish, I have not listened to you, I have been insolent; I am sorry.' She is ready to understand, she is ready to forgive. So we see mercy and compassion going forth as love, a stream of love which can purify all the evil actions of years. Also, if a human being can actually forgive, why should God not forgive? Many of the dogmatic religions have taken away the love element which makes God sovereign; instead they make a God who is limited, who is bound by the book, and who cannot show His compassion. If God were so limited He could not be just; an individual would be better, because an individual can forgive.

The poetry of Hafiz has inspired the poets of Persia as well as of India. And the great Indian poet Rabindranath Tagore sometimes imparted a Persian colour to his poems, and it is that colour which has made them so popular.

Hafiz was the disciple of a master, and on one occasion he and some of the other disciples were told to meditate at a certain time of the night. And while he was in meditation the teacher called, 'Hafiz!' and Hafiz came immediately. It was at this moment that the teacher inspired him, for he had reached that stage where he could inspire anyone instantly. But there were ten other disciples whose name was Hafiz too, so the teacher called, 'Hafiz!' ten times, and each time this same Hafiz came, for the others were sleeping instead of meditating.

This is a symbolical story. The Inspirer is calling us from every direction, but we do not all respond. The voice is always there, the light is there, the guidance is there; but we are not always ready or willing to respond, and are not always open to the call. In reality this is not only the story of Hafiz, but the story of every soul on earth.

Hafiz gives a picture of human nature: hate, jealousy, love, kindness, vanity; the play of friendly impulse, the play of pride; all aspects of life. Hafiz is not only a poet, he is a painter. He has made pictures of the different aspects of life. Every verse is a picture; and in every picture, whatever be its colour—vanity, pride, conceit, love, mercy, or compassion, in all their garbs—he sees only one spirit, the spirit of the Beloved. And he shows the same devotion, appreciation, and love to all the manifestations of that one and the same Beloved.

He has insight into life and looks at life from a psychological point of view, but at the same time he sees the whole of life as the phenomenon of love, harmony, and beauty, and he recognizes all the different aspects of love, harmony, and beauty. Whatever they be, he weaves them into a form so beautiful that it makes a most wonderful picture. From beginning to end his phraseology is peculiar to himself. He uses words such as wine, the goblet, the beloved, the beautiful countenance of the beloved, the running river, the rising spring, the clear sky, the moon, the sun. Also, in these poems the lover continually reproaches the beloved. Then there is the indifference of the beloved towards all except her lover, so beautifully expressed that it almost seems as if while he was writing these poems the poet's soul was dancing. There is such musical inspiration that every line of his poetry is a strain of music.

The word 'wine' is often used, and according to the mystic, life is wine. To the mystic each person drinks a wine peculiar to himself. Hafiz pictures the whole world as a wine-press, and every person takes that wine which is in accord with his own evolution. The wine of one is not the wine of another. He wishes to express the idea that every person, whether evolved or ignorant, whether honest or dishonest, whether he realizes it or not, whether he has a great belief or no belief at all, is in every case taking a certain wine. It is the type of intoxication produced by that particular wine which is his individuality, and when a person changes, he does so by drinking another wine. Every different kind of wine changes the outlook on life, and every change in life is like taking a different wine.

Then Hafiz praises those who have come to a high realization. He says, 'Be not fooled by the patched garment of the wandering dervish, for under the patched sleeves most powerful hands are hidden.' He also says, 'The bare-headed have a crown over their head, if you only knew.' By this he means that once a person has absorbed the thought of reality, it is not only that this ennobles his soul, but it gives him a kingly spirit. It is like being crowned. It is this inspiration and power which in his poetry he calls intoxication.

There are many religions and beliefs according to which some day man will be able to communicate with God. But when will that day come? Life is so short and our hearts are so hungry! And if it does not come today, perhaps it will not come at all. Therefore the one thing that Hafiz has pointed out from beginning to end is this, 'Do not wait for that day to come tomorrow. Communicate with the Beloved now; He is before you here in the form of your friend and in the form of your enemy; with a bowl of poison or with a rose. Recognize this and know it, for this is the purpose of life.' Religions have made it seem like a journey of millions of miles, but Hafiz has brought it close at hand.

Man likes complexity. He does not want to take only one step; it is more interesting to look forward to millions of steps. The man who is seeking the truth gets into a maze, and that maze interests him. He wants to go through it a thousand times more. It is just like children: their whole interest is in running about; they do not want to see the door and go in until they are very tired. And so it is with grown-up people: they all say that they are seeking truth, but they like the maze. That is why the mystics made the greatest truths a mystery, to be given only to the few who were ready for them, letting the others play because it was the time for them to play.

According to the ideas of the Sufis and of all the prophets and sages who ever came to this world, the love principle is the first principle, and so also it is the last principle. There are different Yogas practised by people of India, which are the intellectual, scientific, philosophical, and moral paths to God; but the most desirable path to God that the Hindus have ever found, one which makes the whole of life beautiful, is Bhakta Yoga, the path of devotion, for it is the natural path. Man's inclination is love. If he is cold it is because he is longing for love; if he is warm, it is because love is alive. If he is suffering from depression, is yearning or sorrowing, it is because the love principle is not alive. The only life, the very source of inspiration, salvation, and liberation, is love.

Those great souls who have brought the message of God to humanity from time to time, like Buddha, Krishna, Jesus Christ, Moses, Abraham, or Zarathushtra, were well known as most learned men. But whatever they learned, they learned from the love principle; what they knew was compassion, forgiveness, sympathy, and tolerance, the attitude of appreciation, the opening of the heart to humanity. What they taught was love, a simple truth. If religions seem complex they have been added to. In every case what was brought by the prophet was simple, and it was expressed in his personality and his life; and it is that influence which has remained for centuries after they have passed away. It is not the literature they have left; most of the literature is from their pupils. It is the simple truth shown in their personalities, in their lives. The error of this day and age is that we cannot understand the simple truth, the truth as it is manifested everywhere. Instead we are trying to find truth covered by a shell.

At the same time Hafiz teaches one to see both the ultimate truth and the ultimate justice in God. He teaches that justice is not in related things, that perfect justice is in totality. And he shows that the power behind manifestation is the love power, and that it is by this power that the whole world was created. It is the love principle, whether it works through God or through man, and if that principle is at the back of the whole of creation then it is this same principle which helps man to fulfil the purpose of his life.

ART: YESTERDAY, TODAY, AND
TOMORROW

CONTENTS

CHAPTER I

THE ESSENCE OF ART

MANY THINK that art is something different from nature, but it would be better to say that art is the completion of nature. One may ask how man can improve upon nature which is made by God, but the fact is that God Himself, through man, finishes His creation in art. As all the different elements are God's vehicles, as all the trees and plants are His instruments through which He creates, so art is the medium of God through which God Himself completes His creation.

No doubt not all so-called art is necessarily art. By looking at true art man is able to see the realization of the prayer, 'Thy will be done, on earth as it is in heaven.' Throughout the whole of creation, from one thing to another, the Creator has worked through evolution. In man the Creator has, so to speak, completed nature; yet the creative faculty is still working through man, and thus art is the ultimate step in creation. Although in fact all that man creates, scientifically or artistically, is art, those objects which are produced with a sense of beauty and which appeal to the sense of beauty in man, are the main expression of this creative faculty.

Besides being the creative power of God, art is the expression of the soul of the artist. An artist cannot give out what he has not collected, although man ignores the way this is done. The artist's soul conceives, and the artist produces only that which his soul recognizes as having been conceived. Once it is understood that the artist not only produces but also conceives, then it is not difficult for a man whose heart is awakened to see into the soul of an artist. For art in colour, in line, is nothing but the echo of his soul. If the soul of the artist is going through torture his picture gives us the feeling of awe; if the soul of the artist is enjoying harmony we will see harmony in his colours, in the lines. What does this show? It shows that the soul works automatically through the brush of the artist. The more deeply the artist is touched by the beauty that his soul conceives from outside, the greater is the appeal of that beauty to those who see his work.

What is it in line and colour which has such an influence on man's faculties? The vibrations which the colour produces thrill the centres, the centres of the intuitive faculties which are hidden in the body. A person looks at a colour and immediately feels thrilled by it. Each degree of vibration that the various colours produce is different, and therefore their influence too is different. Yet while one person may be open to that effect and influence, another is so blocked that colours make little impression upon him. For the same reason women are more responsive to colour and line than men, for a woman is responsive by nature, a man is expressive; therefore a woman receives the impression of colour more readily than a man who is apt to repel it. But at the same time a man with fine feeling, with the intuitive faculty awakened, will respond to colour, while a man whose faculties are not yet opened does not.

Strong colours produce more distinct vibrations, their effect is more noticeable than that of soft colours, and therefore it is natural that strong colours can make an impression upon every soul; but in order to distinguish the impression made by soft colours delicacy of sense is required. For instance the simple words of everyday language are understood by anyone, but the finer shades which follow the words are not understood by everybody. Therefore colour, which is only a colour and nothing else to ordinary people, has its special value, its degrees of influence, for a person with a fine sense.

The harmony of colour is based on the same principles as the harmony of music. The reason is that music is audible vibrations while colour is the visible form of vibrations. From the metaphysical point of view, colour has a great significance in man's life. The first thing to be understood in connection with colour is that the different colours come from the essence of light. All the different colours are different degrees of light, but as there are three aspects of light this sometimes produces confusion in the mind of those who have not given thought to the subject. One aspect of light manifests through colour; it is the radiance of the colour itself. The next aspect is when the sun or something else throws its light upon the colour; the light of the colour responds to that light. And the third light is the light of the eyes which see; therefore any given colour is not the same to everybody, not only because the degree of light of every person is different, or the light which falls on the subject is different, or the degree of the colour is different, but also because the element which that particular colour represents produces a certain degree of response in an individual.

According to the mystical idea there are four principal elements which can be distinguished and one which is indistinct. The distinct elements are earth, water, fire, and air. They are not elements in the sense in which a scientist would use this word, but according to the meaning that the mystic attaches to it. The indistinct element is the ether. All these elements are in the body of man, in his mind, and in his deeper self. The whole edifice of an individual existence is built by means of these five distinct elements, and it is not necessary for a certain element which is predominant in one plane of existence, to continue to be so on all other planes. It is possible for there to be harmony between the elements which are predominant on the inner plane and those which are predominant on the outer plane. In short, it is according to the working of the different elements in one's being that one is responsive to the different colours which represent the different elements.

From the point of view of a mystic, yellow is the colour of the earth, green or white the colour of the water element, red that of the fire element, and blue of the air element. If asked what the colour of the ether element is the mystic would answer grey, because by grey one may think of anything one likes. It is most interesting for a student of colour to see that all colours are, so to speak, different shades of light; it shows that light itself has manifested in variety, in the form of many colours.

Another important question is that of line. Many lovers or students of art feel the great influence of a line, the effect that a line can have. A vertical line, a horizontal line, a curve, a circle, all make such a difference in the form. And the more one studies to what extent line makes a difference, the more one will find that the secret of all beauty is in the line. But it is difficult to say what form or what line is the right form or line, and man has to accept that what one cannot learn by study, intuition can teach.

The only explanation that one can give, from the mystical point of view, about the secret of line is that the effect of a certain line brings the inner and the outer planes of the human being into such a condition that, while he looks at the line, he is, so to speak, under the spell of that line. This can be understood through the secret of concentration: that every object man thinks about, even if only for a moment, has an effect upon his whole being.

There is a harmony of lines, and this is even more difficult and complex to understand than harmony of colour, for the harmony of lines reaches deeper than the harmony of colour. If a room is beautifully furnished with costly furniture, but these things are not kept in harmony according to the science of lines, we feel a kind of confusion in the room. It is the same with clothes. A dress may be very costly or beautiful in colour, but if it lacks line it lacks real beauty. Therefore in art line is the principal thing; it is the secret of art and of its charm, and only the artist who has conceived the beauty of line can express it in his art.

One aspect of art is shown when the artist tries to copy exactly what he sees. An artist is contemplative, and it is not a small thing to be able to copy the object exactly. Then the success of this artist is assured, because with all man's cravings for something new, what he really wants is something he has already seen. Is it not wonderful, is it not a great thing to be able to copy nature as it is, to produce in the soul of man that which exists in nature?

A further aspect of art is the improvement on nature which the artist makes by exaggeration; and the benefit of this art is more through attraction than impression. No doubt in this form of art the artist can fulfil his soul's purpose, but at the same time he may get far away from nature; and the further he goes the more he destroys the beauty of art, for nature and art must go hand in hand.

Art has still another aspect and that is symbolism. Symbolism has not come from the human intellect, for it is born of intuition. The finer the soul, the better it is equipped in some way or other to understand symbolical ideas. A fine soul always dreams symbolical dreams, and when the soul becomes finer still it can interpret the dream, understanding the meaning of that symbolism. The artist who produces in his art a symbolical idea has learned it from what he has seen in nature and has interpreted it in his art. This is real inspiration. The finer the artist is, the finer the symbols he produces.

In every work of art one can observe three factors: its surface, its length and width, and its depth; but I do not mean this in the literal sense of these words. The surface is what the picture itself is, the length and the width are the story that it tells, and the depth is the meaning that it reveals. Therefore the best way of studying and appreciating the works of an artist is to take these three elements into consideration. Art is a very vast subject.

CHAPTER II

THE DIVINITY OF ART

ART MAY be defined as having four aspects. One aspect of art may be called imitative art, the tendency and ability to produce as exactly as possible, on the canvas or in the clay something which one sees. This is the first stage, and one which leads the artist further on the path of art. In order to develop this faculty the mind must be fully concentrated. When the artist lacks concentration he cannot observe objects and their beauty keenly, and therefore he is not able to reproduce them exactly as he sees them. Concentration has such great power that a concentrated person can penetrate into an object, and can see not only the outside of it but also the inside. In other words a concentrated person not only sees the form but its spirit. That is the fullness of observation, and it comes by concentration. Whenever the artist cannot imitate nature, cannot copy an object exactly, it shows that he lacks concentration.

The next aspect of art is suggestive art. This can be divided into two kinds: first an art which directly suggests a certain idea, so that as soon as we see the picture we can see what it says, what it explains, what it represents; and the other kind which is expressed in symbols, an art which through a certain symbology expresses a great wisdom. This wisdom is covered; and the more one looks at the picture and the more one studies it, the more it reveals the idea, the wisdom, the thought that is hidden in it. Such art is a revelation. The art of ancient Egypt, of Greece, and especially the art of the Mongolians and of India, was chiefly symbolical art. In such periods, when other pictures were not produced and books were not printed, this was the only means of keeping wisdom alive and handing it on to the coming generations. This was done by the master artists who were inspired by spiritual wisdom and who tried to guide humanity. With hammer and chisel they carved in wood and engraved on the rocks, and left their work in the caves of the mountains and in the old temples and palaces, an art that expresses wisdom. When one visits one of these caves where wisdom is expressed in the realm of art, one will find that one symbol can reveal more than a volume of written manuscript. And in this way the sculptures of a temple or of a mountain cave were like a library with thousands of books. The one who can read, can find divine wisdom there, expressed distinctly and with great intelligence and wit.

The ideas of the Hindus about gods and goddesses and the different postures in which they stand or sit, the way Buddha holds his hands, all these express to him who knows a teaching which is connected with the culture of the spirit.

The third aspect of art is the creative aspect. In this aspect an artist creates a theme and improvises upon that theme as he goes on working. In this way the artist creates wisdom and power. No doubt, the higher the art the less it is appreciated and the less it is studied, and the majority will always seem to be ignorant of its meaning. Nevertheless, the artist who reaches that plane where he can create, can from that moment call himself an artist. Creating is different from imitating or suggesting. In the development of art imitating is the first step, suggesting is the second step, and creating is the third step.

In India fifty years ago there was an artist, the brother of the Maharaja of Travancore. After having read the sacred traditions of the Hindus, he wondered if it would not be a wise thing to reproduce these legends and stories in the realm of art. So he devoted all his life to this idea, and made perhaps twenty or thirty pictures of the ancient traditions. Since that time India has understood and appreciated its ancient spiritual traditions far better than ever before. By expressing the sacred traditions in the form of art he brought a new outlook and a new spiritual message to the people of India. This shows how much more effect art can have upon people if a spiritual idea is embodied in it.

The fourth aspect of art can only be developed through meditation, because it comes like a miracle. It is no longer only art but is a direct expression of the soul. This fourth aspect may be called giving life to the work of art. In the first three aspects the work of art is only art, but in the fourth aspect it becomes something living. And the artist who reaches this stage where he can give life to what he creates has reached the highest grade, which is the mastery of art. No artist can reach this stage only by the practice of his art; it is essential for him to know that in order to accomplish great things in the realm of art he needs spiritual development.

But in order to develop art in the real sense of the word, one need not be an artist, one need not have that particular vocation in life. Whatever be one's vocation, art is necessary just the same. It is wrong to think that art is not needed in one's social or domestic life, in business, in industry, in one's profession. It is because of the division that people have made between art and other walks of life that life has become devoid of beauty. And in this way art has been very much neglected, except by those who pretend to appreciate it and who have perhaps some leisure in which to give thought and time to it. But even they are very often ignorant of the real beauty and value of art; they take an interest in it only because they want to be able to say that they are fond of art. It is because of this that artists sometimes lack the opportunity of expressing their soul through their art, being hampered by this lack of appreciation. Others want to commercialize their art, but art is always above material values. When art has to be limited by material values and by seeking the approbation of those who do not understand it, it has to suffer; instead of evolving it declines.

But even in practical life art has great scope. Think for instance how much a woman can do in her everyday life in her home with her artistic gifts. She can make it beautiful and comfortable; she can train her children to have better taste; and whatever her means may be, even her manner can produce beauty, harmony, and happiness in her home. It is the same thing in one's office, in industry, in business, in whatever one does. If there is a regard for beauty and harmony one can make one's own business or profession, one's life and one's work, more beautiful, thereby producing greater happiness for oneself and for others.

When the spirit of art develops, this development does not produce anything outwardly, but it does so inwardly. And what is this? It is the art of personality. In a real artist a distinct personality is developed which expresses itself in everything he does. In other words, an artist need not paint a picture in order to prove himself an artist. When he has reached a certain stage of art his thought, his speech, his word, his voice, his movements, his action, everything he does becomes art. The value of the art of personality is so great that no one in this world, whatever be his occupation, can say that he does not need to develop or to learn it. If he is a business man, if he is a lawyer, if he is in industry, if he is a shopkeeper, or working in an office or factory, whatever be his position, this art of personality will help him. If he is a soldier he has a chance to become a general, if he is a worker in a factory he may one day be the head of it. Besides success he has the magnetism to win everyone he meets because of the art of personality. The art of personality shows in one's movements, in one's manner, in words, in speech, in thought, and in feeling. On the other hand, an awkward person does everything wrong. His movements are awkward, and every move he makes is unattractive. The one who has not yet acquired the art of speaking will offend even without intending to; and in everyday life do we not see people insulting others unintentionally because they do not know the art of saying without saying?

Other arts cannot be compared with the art of personality. Character is not born with a man; his character is built up after he comes here. Even if a person can call himself a human being, he has still to know that greater art which may be rightly called a true religion. For there is another grade to strive for, and that grade is the personality of God. As soon as one seeks for the personality of God, one sees that it is different from a human personality; for with the personality of man, man can only take a human point of view, whereas with the personality of God man has to take God's point of view. And it is those personalities with God's point of view who, whenever they have come on earth, have not only taught humanity, but have given an example to humanity by their lives. They came and went—some known, some unknown—but each one of them was accepted by some and rejected by others. None of them was accepted or rejected by the whole of humanity. Yet in spite of this, truth will prove by itself victorious, for victory belongs to nothing else. Victory which comes from falsehood is a false victory; only a true victory belongs to truth, and as man probes more and more into the depths of life and its secrets he will realize this more fully. Falsehood, whatever its apparent success, has its limitations and its end. For at every step the false person will feel falseness; and with every step a person takes towards falsehood he will feel his feet growing heavier and heavier when he encounters the truth, while those who walk towards the truth will feel their feet becoming lighter with every step they take. And it is by learning the art of life and by practising it that one is led on the path of truth to that goal which is the longing of every soul.

Finally there is the art of thought. The more one activates one's thought, one's imagination, the more capable one is of expressing them in the realm of art. Therefore the beautifying of one's thought is the greatest source of development in art. And when we have understood this, we will come to the conclusion that whether the outer works of art are poetry or music or painting or sculpture, it is the art of personality which is the greatest of all arts; but it is an art which cannot be perfected without developing the spirit of sympathy. This is the principal and most important thing in life. The deeper our sympathy, the greater our power and inspiration will become to bring our art to perfection.

CHAPTER III

ART AND RELIGION

VERY FEW in the world today link religion with art, or art with religion. But in point of fact art is much more important than the average person realizes it to be, in spite of the saying that art is what man makes and nature is what God makes. I would prefer to say that nature is what God makes as God, and art is what God makes as man. The artist who has arrived at some perfection in his art, whatever his art may be, will come to realize that it is not he who ever achieved anything; it is someone else who came forward every time. And when the artist produces a perfect thing, he finds it difficult to imagine that it has been produced by him; he can do nothing but bow his head in humility before that unseen power and wisdom which takes his body, his heart, his brain, and his eyes as its instrument. Whenever beauty is produced in art, be it music or poetry or painting or writing or anything else, one must never think that man produced it. It is through man that God completes His creation, thus there is nothing that is done in this world or in heaven which is not divine immanence, which is not the divine creation. It is the separating of that divine work which causes the perplexity that separates man from his Lord.

In the first place, everything that we see in this world, all the occupations that we engage in willingly or unwillingly, lead us to accomplish a certain purpose. But it is a fact that there are certain things in life by which we accomplish a greater purpose and which can only be accomplished by an inspiration from within. Art is a domain in which inspiration manifests with great facility. In order to become spiritual, to attain inspiration, it is not necessary that a man should be very religious or specially good; what is necessary is love of beauty. What is art? Art is the creation of beauty in whatever form it is created. As long as an artist thinks that whatever he creates in the form of art is his own creation, and as long as he is vain about his creation, he has not learned true art. For true art can only come on one condition, and that is that the artist forgets himself; that he forgets himself in the vision of beauty. And there is one condition through which his art can be still more valuable, and that is when the artist begins to recognize the divine in his art. As long as the artist has not realized this he has not touched the perfection of art.

In reality art is nature re-expressed, perfecting the beauty which is already there. Nature in no way lacks beauty; nature is perfect and therefore is most exalting. But it is beyond man's power to see nature as a whole. He only sees a part of it, and everything that is only seen in part is limited; it is this limitation which limits the beauty for us. As man sees only a limited beauty in nature his first impulse is to perfect it, and the means he adopts to improve upon it he calls art. The soul of man is the light of God, and so this impulse to improve upon nature which arises in the heart of man is also a divine impulse. Therefore art is divine, for all beauty is divine.

It is said in the Bible, 'God is love', and again, 'In God we live and move and have our being'. The word of the Prophet is, 'God is beautiful, and He loves beauty'. If we take these two teachings and unite them as one, we shall find that God Himself is love and at the same time beauty. This being so, in whatever direction man strives in life it leads towards a certain beauty. If he wishes to be rich or to have a high position, whatever may be his pursuit in life, in some form or other it is in order to have beauty. No doubt the idea of beauty is different for each individual; one considers beauty to consist of a beautiful environment, another that it means being dressed in beautiful clothes; yet another thinks that grace of movement, of manner, or of expression is beauty. One person sees beauty in character, another in virtue; one finds beauty in verse, another in the realm of music; one admires the beauty which is external, another seeks beauty within. And it is the method of creating beauty, under whatever aspect, which is called art.

Man is always seeking for beauty, and yet he is unaware of the treasure of beauty which is hidden in his own heart. He strives after it throughout his whole life. It is as if he were in pursuit of the horizon: the further he proceeds, the further the horizon has moved away. For there are two aims: the one is real and the other false. That which is false is momentary, transitory, and unreliable; wealth, power, fame, and position are all snatched from one hand by the other. Therefore in the language of the mystic this is called *Maya*; its nature is to change constantly. But our soul's longing is to hold on to something, to grasp something which we can depend upon. If man seeks a position, he feels, 'If only I could find something which would be permanent, something I could depend upon.' If he seeks a friend his first thought is to find a friend upon whom he can depend. Constancy is more valuable than anything else in friendship. Man wants something in life upon which he can rely; and this shows, whether he believes in a deity or not, that he is constantly seeking for God. He seeks for Him not knowing that he is seeking for God. Nevertheless, every soul is pursuing some reality, something to hold on to, trying to grasp something which will prove dependable, a beauty that cannot change and that one can always look upon as one's own, a beauty that one feels will last forever. And where can one find it? Within one's own heart. And it is the art of finding that beauty, developing, improving, spreading that beauty through life, and allowing it to manifest before the inner and outer view, which one calls the art of the mystic.

The artist, in the true sense of the word, is the king of the kingdom which is even greater than the kingdoms of the earth. There is a story known in the East of Farabi, the great singer, who was invited to the court of the Amir of Bokhara. The Amir welcomed him very warmly at the court, and, as the singer entered, went to the door to receive him. On coming into the throne-room the Amir asked him to take a seat. 'But where shall I sit?' said the singer. 'Sit,' the Amir said, 'in any place that may seem fitting to you.' On hearing this, Farabi took the seat of the king. No doubt this astonished the Amir very much, but after hearing the singer's art he felt that even his own seat was not fitting, for he understood that his kingdom had a certain limitation, whereas the kingdom of the artist is wherever beauty prevails. As beauty is everywhere, so the kingdom of the artist is everywhere.

But art is only a door, a door through which one can enter a still wider area. At different times the religious have considered art to be something outside them; this has very often been due to a kind of fanaticism on the part of religious authorities. It is not only in the East, but in the West as well, that one finds a tendency to separate art from religion. This does not mean that some great teacher of religion has taught it; it has come only from people who have not realized religion apart from its form. No one who has touched the depths of religion can ever deny the fact that religion itself is an art, an art which accomplishes the greatest thing in man's life. And there can be no greater error than to make this art devoid of beauty.

In ancient times in all the Hindu and Buddhist temples and pagodas there was music, there was poetry, there was sculpture, and there was painting. In those times there were no printing-presses, and no books could be published on philosophy and religion; but if one can find any scriptures expressing the ancient religious and philosophical ideas, they are in the ancient art. For instance, whatever sign can be found of the mysticism and the religion of ancient Egypt, of which so much has been said and so little is known, it is not in the manuscripts but in its art. Also the ideas of the Sanskrit age are still to be found in India engraved on the carved stones and rocks and temples. Travellers from the Western world often go to the East in order to see to what a degree of perfection Eastern art attained; but very few really know that art not only strove for perfection in those days, but that it was used as a means of communication by those who could not read.

The art of ancient Greece too is a sign and proof of great perfection in divine wisdom. Every movement that we see in Greek art is not only a graceful movement but has a meaning; and every statue expresses a certain meaning in its attitude, if only a person can read it. From this we learn that intuition is necessary both for the making of a work of art and for the understanding of it; and that is the very thing which the human race today seems to be losing more than at any other time in the world's history. One might ask why man has lost that intuitive faculty. It is because he has become so absorbed in material gain that he has become as it were intoxicated by the worldly life; and intuition, which is his birthright and his own property, is lost from his view. This does not mean that it is gone from him; it only means that it has become buried in his own heart.

We are vehicles or instruments that respond. If we respond to goodness, goodness becomes our property. If we respond to evil, then evil becomes our property. If we respond to love, then love becomes our possession. If we respond to hatred, hatred becomes our life. And if we respond to the things of the earth so much that our whole life becomes absorbed in worldly things, then it is quite natural that we should not respond to those riches which are within us and yet so far removed from us. Intuition is not something that a person can learn by reading books, nor is intuition a thing that one can buy and sell. Intuition is the very self and the deepest self of man, and it can be realized by that soberness which is so very desirable in life. Absence of intuition means absence of soberness.

CHAPTER IV

YESTERDAY, TODAY, AND TOMORROW

IT IS MOST interesting to notice that East and West have a different or perhaps contrary opinion on the subject of the world's evolution. While in the West man thinks that we are becoming more evolved, that we have progressed and are going forward compared with our forefathers, in the East man believes that compared with our forefathers we are going backward and downward, that we are worse.

What is the truth about this? From one point of view there have never been such good communications in the world as nowadays: the telegraph and telephone, ships like palaces floating on the water, aeroplanes, the gramophone, and then the radio uniting mankind in one moment at any distance; besides the development that is taking place in every branch of science, of art, there are also the modern systems, organizations, and classifications. When one looks at all this one cannot doubt for one moment that according to modern opinion the world is evolving but when we come to delicate thought and sentiment, good manners, knightly chivalry, kingly attitude, nobleness of spirit, generosity of heart, the tendency to sacrifice, depth of feeling, and keenness of insight, we are certain that what the man of the East says is true.

We learn from this that both opinions are right. We are evolving, and yet at the same time going backward. In certain things we are evolving, and in certain things we are going backward; and this brings us to the philosophical conception that it is not only the world which is round, but that everything is round; that everything moves in circles. For instance the early dawn is not very different from the late evening, age is not very different from infancy, when we realize how innocence develops as one grows old and one arrives at a stage where one shows the same expression of the angelic spheres which one had as an infant. It is just like the octave: seven notes and then the key-note comes again. It is not going upward or downward, it is going in a circle. But we are accustomed to say of everything that it is either going upward or downward. We may agree with those who say that we are going upward, or we may agree with those who hold that we are going downward, but in reality progress does not mean continually going upward; progress means going upward and downward at the same time; progress should be described by a circle and not by a straight line. If we look at it from this point of view, everything in the world has a circular aspect, for the real picture of motion, of movement, is a circle.

There are three aspects of knowledge: self-knowledge, the knowledge of another person, and the knowledge of the collectivity. Also, there are three ways of looking at the world: its past, its present, and its future. By yesterday is meant the past; by today is meant the present; and by tomorrow is meant the future. The knowledge of the past gives wisdom; the knowledge of the present gives power; the knowledge of the future gives peace. The one who is anxious to acquire knowledge must consider all these three aspects to be equally important.

For those who are treading the spiritual path it is as necessary to think of the world, especially at the present time, as it is to think of someone else and of themselves. No one should think that by position or rank, by profession or occupation, by condition or situation, he is too limited to think of the world; but each of us should realize that we are a self-sufficient particle of the whole. Each particle is responsible for the evolution of the world in proportion to the place it occupies in the cosmos; and everything a man naturally knows first about himself, and then about another, is of the greatest importance when he also begins to know something about the world at large. What he should know is what the world was, what the world is now, and what it will be in the future.

In the self-knowledge of past and present and future one has to learn what was the origin of the soul, how the soul has formed itself, how it has come to manifest, the knowledge of the process of manifestation, and the different stages through which it has passed towards manifestation. Regarding the present one should learn one's own condition, the condition of one's spirit, of one's mind and body, one's situation in life, and one's relationship to others; one should also realize how far the soul reaches in the spiritual spheres. And regarding the future one should find the answers to the questions, 'Am I preparing for something that is to come, and what is there to come? If life is a journey, what is the object of this journey? What is the destination and how shall I reach it? What preparations must I make for this journey and what must I carry to make the journey easy? What are the difficulties that I may meet on my way?' It is the understanding of these questions which is the knowledge of the future. And it is self-knowledge which helps man to know the past, the present, and the future of another. For those who know themselves another person is like an open book; they can read him clearly; his past is clear to them, and also his present and his future.

There are many ways in which people try to know about past, present, and future: by astrology, by palmistry, by physiognomy, by reading the features, and in many other ways. Although all such methods can often be helpful and give us some knowledge— for knowledge is within our reach and we only have to ask for it and it is given—yet by self-realization we can understand this knowledge so clearly at a certain stage, that no other method is necessary. It becomes natural; as it is natural for the eyes to see, so it becomes natural for the heart to see into the past, present, and future.

Looking into the past is just like looking deep down from great heights. It means probing the depths of life. Looking into the present is just like observing a wide horizon, as wide as we can see. Looking into the future is like looking upward to the zenith. And the feeling we experience is different with each of these three ways of looking. One gives knowledge; the other gives power; and the third gives peace, as I said before. Knowledge is man's birthright and it is the sustenance of the soul. It is to gather knowledge that the soul has come on earth; the acquisition of knowledge is the only purpose the soul has in coming here. In knowledge lies the satisfaction of the soul, the fulfilment of the purpose of life.

CHAPTER V

THE IDEAL OF ART

WHEN WE study the art of the Middle Ages and the psychology behind it, it seems that the principal aim of the artist at that time was to produce an object of worship. Restricted within the laws of conventionality, having a deeply rooted belief in the sacredness of the artist's task, he considered his art as the expression of his greatest devotion. And any sensitive person will certainly feel that the art of the Middle Ages has an atmosphere, a feeling, a magnetism which grows day after day. No doubt one can only appreciate this art if one does not compare it with the art of today; as Majnun said, 'To see Leila you must borrow my eyes.' So we must borrow the eyes of the people of the Middle Ages, the feeling of the people who lived at that time, and then look at their art; for in its primitive development there is a mystery hidden which could not be reproduced today.

When we think about the Middle Ages and the Renaissance, we notice that the wave coming from ancient Greece to Italy brought new life; yet the art which was once made for worship was then made for admiration. Art rose to great heights, bringing the spirit of classical antiquity into a new realm of expression. Nevertheless, one can say that in the Middle Ages art was directed towards God, that in the art of the Renaissance God was included, but that afterwards it was produced without God. And without God essentially there is no art. The gulf that we find between our time and the time when art was in its greatest glory, is because the art of today is without God. The artist of the Renaissance had not given up God, but afterwards God was forgotten.

Painting, sculpture, any form of art, if it is not directed towards a higher ideal must go downward; it cannot rise because there is no ladder. It is the ideal which helps everything to go upward, and without the ideal everything goes downward. One can see the reason why people become more materialistic: beauty naturally belongs to heaven; on the earth it is only reflected; and when the connection with heaven is broken, when the back is turned towards heaven, then the eyes become focused on the earth and slowly and gradually beauty begins to disappear. Thus in a way the divergence between the Renaissance and our time has been caused by materialism, by commercialism, and by the lack of heavenly inspiration.

No doubt the need that has been felt in the hearts of the lovers of beauty has been working on the inner planes, and now today it is beginning to show itself. But how? Not in the form of beauty; it is the absence of beauty that is now beginning to be felt. And the result of this is that the artist thinks that there should be a new start in the world of art, that a new kind of beauty should be found, a new expression; but when he tries to find it he mostly misses the mark, for when inspiration is lacking and the work of art is forced by effort, what is produced is mechanical. One artist thinks, 'Everything must be in angles; that creates a new beauty'; and another says, 'No, everything must be just colours; everything must be expressive by itself'; another artist says, 'Everything must be just lines without any detail; everyone should find out for himself what it represents'; and again another says, 'Everything must remain in an unfinished state; that is very artistic'. In this way it is just like many horses trying to take different directions in order to arrive at a certain place.

There seems to be no ideal today, but the day when the ideal again directs the hand of the artist, art will progress more rapidly, and the promise of the art of the future will then be fulfilled. That something which begins with a promise of touching the heights, of manifesting in perfection has another voice; it has another soul and another expression. Today the artist is striving for it, his soul is longing for it, but he has not yet found it. And the very reason why he has not found it is that he is thinking too hard. Art does not require hard thinking, nor does poetry or music. True art always comes with ease, with relaxation; it comes naturally. The artist should not be fighting with beauty or struggling with inspiration.

What is most to be deplored at the present time is the unconscious and yet predominant commercial influence hovering like a cloud over the art of today. There is a general feeling that every month a new fashion must arise; there must be a new fashion in everything; and this inclination, saturated with commercialism, destroys the roots of natural and beautiful art. Why strive for something new? Life is always new and always old. It is always the same and yet it is always new.

To think that we must forget, overlook, and destroy all the thought of the past is a still greater error. When artists start with this error, always wanting to make something new, then they make commonplace things, things which are far removed from beauty. And the admirers of art, those who buy, do not mind as long as it is new. Most of them only acquire a work of art because it is the fashion, not because it is beautiful; and thereby a great load of responsibility is laid upon the artist as well as upon those who present his work to the world. It is this pressure which spoils the work of artistic souls, who should have time to think about beauty and who should have leisure to feel deeply. Instead of this anxiety is thrown upon them, a responsibility is forced upon them to bring out something new. The day when the world of art forgets the word 'new', a new life will come into it.

It seems a pity that one aspect of art is much neglected nowadays: the making of frescoes. It is to be hoped that one day it will be developed again and take a more prominent place in the world of art. But fresco painting should be finished like any other way of painting, as it was done by the great masters in Italy who did

M

not leave anything unfinished. In any form of art there should be a desire on the part of the artist to finish his work, not to keep it unfinished, which is against perfection. The lack of desire to finish something is only laziness, lethargy, negligence. All of us human beings have our limitations. It is very easy to say, 'It may be unfinished, but just look at it, it is beautiful!' But it is not right. Everything we do we should wish to finish to the best of our ability, even though it will always remain unfinished when we look at it from the point of view of beauty itself. We do not need to keep it unfinished on purpose; it remains unfinished without our trying, when compared with perfection.

Contemporary decorative art[1] seems to represent a new step towards the unknown. No doubt the aim of decorative art should be to produce an impression without going into detail. But all the same it should first be produced in the depths of the artist's own heart, and then he should put his thought-power into the lines that he draws. If an artist only wants to make an effect externally, by trying to make something attractive through making it different, it will never look beautiful and it will never suggest what he wants it to suggest.

Today when an artist tries to express an idea in decorative art, he tries to avoid all details and depict his subject by only a few lines. But when those lines have not sprung from the depths of his heart, when they are not inspired, they do not become a universal language, they do not make another person feel at once that this is the idea which the artist intended to produce. It must be given extra thought, so that these lines are not only lines, but that they express something, are suggestive of something, are living; and then they instantly produce the meaning of the artist in the mind of the one who looks at them. If an object in decorative art is not made with this inspiration, it is not complete, and then it does not suggest anything but is bewildering and will confuse many people. And at this time, if even art is confusing, where else can one go? There is nowhere else. Art should be revealing and inspiring instead of confusing.

[1] Hazrat Inayat Khan uses the term 'decorative art' not only in the usual sense, but also to denote sketches and paintings in which the subject is suggested rather than elaborated in full detail.

There was a time when decorative art was highly developed, for instance in China where it reached its zenith. When the Chinese artist wished to decorate an object with a picture of the sky, he drew it with one line; and one can feel it. Where does it come from? From a mental effort? It comes from inspiration. It is one thing to think about an idea and another thing to feel the idea, and once the artist begins to feel the idea he is able to express it. Even if it is not finished, it is finished in the feeling of the artist, and that completes the lines. Those who want to will see the truth of it; they will be able to read it; they will know the object of the picture.

There is a new aspect of art nowadays which is called clairvoyant, mediumistic, or spiritualistic art. One may speak of the bewildering effect of art, but this is the most bewildering of all! One day a person put some colours on paper, and showed it to me, saying, 'People cannot understand this deep idea, but you will understand it. It is very deep, it has come from some clairvoyant source.' I looked at it; there were many colours, that was all one could say, and they were not even blending harmoniously with one another; they were only striking. The person who had painted it looked at me and waited for my opinion. He said, 'What do you think of it?' So I said, 'It is a picture of the end of the world.' And he was very pleased with this answer. Some people who claim clairvoyance try to paint what they call the other side, but to do this they would have to bring the paint and canvas from the other side too. The clairvoyant cannot paint the other side with the brush of this world; if he tried it would be a mistake.

Very often people also produce confusing patterns in decorative art. Maybe that in that pattern there is a flower, and perhaps that flower looks like a man's face; and if one looks at that flower from another angle, it is like the face of a monkey or of a tiger. If this is not confusing, what is it? And such patterns are often commercialized and used for wallpaper and other decorative purposes. It is this confusion of the artist's mind which commerce has taken over and made use of, and if confusion is used for commercial purposes, then where are we going if not towards confusion, greater and greater confusion helped by art, by so-called art?

The combination of inharmonious colours has very often an inharmonious effect on the nerves, on the thought, on the mind; and this gives scope to those imaginative artists who are, however, without beauty, without art, without knowledge of life, without any psychological conception of it. It makes their art popular; by claiming that it is quite different from anything else, they can sell their art better. Art should be simple; it should be expressive; it should also be inspiring and revealing.

CHAPTER VI

PAINTING

THE ART of painting is as ancient as the human race. It has existed in all ages, though not in the same form as today. There was a time when the Tibetans and the Chinese produced the most wonderful paintings. In these paintings the principal motive was to give a form to abstract thought; and therefore very often, especially in Chinese painting, there are forms which we do not recognize. They were meant to be the personification of power, of compassion, of joy, of sorrow, and similar concepts. They pictured joy or sorrow as an animal; the imagery of the Chinese artist even went so far as to create the form of a new creature to represent a certain idea. Thus the Chinese dragon represents power, and is at the same time a conception of the Almighty. And the Chinese dragon is a symbol of unity, for it has the tail of a fish, the wings of a bird, the fangs of a lion, and the face of a mythical animal, together with the eyes of a man.

This shows that all the different aspects of living beings together make one being; and one being means the oneness of the whole of manifestation. It is a lesson in unity taught by the symbolism of the Chinese dragon.

In India the upper end of the sacred Indian instrument, the vina, was often carved in the form of a dragon's head. The reason for this custom was to remind the listeners that when a musician played his music and they heard it, they should not think that it was the artist who played and that the instrument was only a vina, but their impression should be that it was the music of the whole being, of the divine Being, so that music might be considered not as a kind of pastime but as a source of elevation.

The most wonderful aspect of Chinese art has always been its drawings. The more one studies Chinese art the more one admires the fineness of the line. The greatest artists of China could give an impression of the sky in only a few lines. It is a wonderful art, a very suggestive art. And how very effective it is, the making of something beautiful in just a few lines, drawn with inspiration and intelligence, and suggesting a certain form, the artist only indicating the detail!

Japan followed China. The Japanese are an artistic people, and they have tried to produce even better things. What is good about their art is that they love daintiness, fineness; everything that comes from there is very delicate and refined. But even that will only continue for a certain time; the present condition of the Japanese shows the great interest they have in the things of the world, and this will increase; even what little art is left there now will disappear. It is one thing to be an artist, and it is another to be materialistic; these two do not go together.

The Tibetans have the same kind of art as the Chinese, but not as developed. The reason is that in China there was an empire, and there was luxury, appreciation of art, and a high ideal; in Tibet there was only religious thought. And in all periods and in all countries, if religious thought alone has been the central theme of life, then it has hampered the progress of art. Nevertheless, Tibetan art has always had the same depth that the Tibetans have in their character. One may take any Tibetan picture and one will always find that there is a magic hidden behind it. And the use the Tibetans made of colour is a magic in itself. It is not only the fancy of the artist; it is the attempt of the artist to express the mystery of the object through colour. In ancient paintings from Tibet, however primitive, the colour or the form always expresses a certain mystery of life.

Ancient Egyptian art developed in its own way, and in accordance with its own character it reached a great height. No doubt as the people of that time were more psychic, more mystical, they did not give the same attention to detail and to the things of the earth as is done today, although the colouring of the old Egyptian objects is exquisite. Colour meant a great deal to ancient peoples. They chose colour as a medium of expression in a way which is no longer seen. But in order to appreciate the art of the ancient people we must look at it from their point of view.

The Indians did not develop the art of painting in the same way as the Chinese or the ancient Egyptians. They were more drawn to other aspects of art, to sculpture, music, and poetry. Nevertheless there are to be found ancient Indian paintings where the colours are expressive of the five elements; everything expressed by these pictures, every idea or colour, has something to do with the five elements. Yellow represents earth, green represents water, red represents fire, blue represents air, and grey represents ether.

It was in Persia that art first developed into something finer and more beautiful than in India; but when Persian art was later brought to India it became richer in colour. The pictures of the Moghul emperors and of their families, sometimes painted on ivory, show how conscientious were the artists in reproducing every little detail. Even in the smallest picture one sees that every detail has been painted in. The combination of Persian and Indian art achieved very wonderful results. At the time of the Moghuls a picture was a luxury, and that is what the Moghul paintings were.

Nowadays[1] there exists a school of art in Calcutta under the direction of Abanindranath Tagore; this school tries to produce work in the same style as that of the ancient Moghul school. The modern versions that come from this school, however, cannot be compared with the old pictures; yet when we compare them with other modern conceptions of painting we find many things which are quite different. There is at least an extreme fineness about the pictures, a great delicacy of colour, and much attention has been given to the line; one discerns an attempt to reach perfection through delicacy. But by all that is said above I do not wish to indicate that ancient art was necessarily superior to modern art; I have only tried to point out what was good in it.

An interesting development in the Western world was the

[1] 1925.

introduction of the idea of light and shade into painting. This was not applied by the ancient artists, and it brought a new life to the world of art and made art more natural. But in modern Western art it often happens that an artist gets hold of an idea and thinks that it is the only idea there is and that there is nothing else besides it. He does not realize that any idea is a part of other ideas, and that many ideas together will make a whole. This has resulted in artistic movements such as cubism, which is derived from a certain impression one may get from the light. Light strikes out in straight lines and forms angles; and so these artists wanted to paint all the different planes of their pictures in angles. They painted as if the whole world was made like that, in angles.

Other artists say that in painting only colour is important, that it is colour which must make the form. This also is unnatural. However beautiful colour may be it is not sufficient; the picture cannot be complete when it is painted in that way. It is again stubbornness, obstinacy on the part of the artist. He wants to paint something which will strike us, and no doubt colour will strike us; but art is not only for striking, art is for giving some beautiful impression, for uplifting our soul; it is for inspiring, not for striking. In painting form is more important than colour; the colour is an addition to the form. No doubt colour touches the emotional side of man, but that is a different thing and is very material. It is not the mission of art to bring man down to earth.

All this shows that the world of art today is in great confusion. The souls of the artists want to bring something new to the world, but at the same time the artists are looking for this where it is not to be found. It is just like looking for the moon on the ground. They are eager, they are striving, they are in earnest; yet they are looking for what they want in the wrong direction. Even if they worked for a hundred years like this, one can be sure that there would be no progress.

Are they wrong in their ideas? No, they are not wrong, but they are limited. They have got hold of one idea; it may be a very good one, but they have pinned themselves to it. They cannot go forward, because they are limited to their own idea; whether people like it or not is irrelevant to them. Besides, though art can be most charming it can also be most deluding. If an artist is strong-minded and convinced of the quality of his own art, he can make people believe that he has invented a new form of art. But where does this new art lead us? What is the mission of art? Is it to delude us, to produce confusion? If there is no beauty, no harmony, no deep feeling, then what is its purpose? If it only strikes our emotions and our passions, or if it only strikes our eyes, then it has nothing to do with art.

No doubt there will come a time when the modern artist will be frightened of his own pictures, and he will awaken to the fact that he must find something else, that this is not the road to follow. The greatest example that we can follow is before us night and day, and that is the work of God. What can be better than God's creation itself? And the artist who bears this in mind that he should imitate the creation of God, is the one who will produce beautiful things.

When God's creation seems to be going to the North and the artist goes to the South, he thinks that he is creating new things. But they are not new, they are wrong. Suppose there came a new wave of musicians who said, 'We are not going to accept the seven notes as they are, but we are going to make other notes.' Perhaps they will have a following. Some will say, 'How interesting, it is something new!' And yet it will not be beautiful, it will not be exalting, it will not help humanity.

The peculiar state of the world today is due to spiritual poverty. It is this which causes all the restlessness and confusion. The extremes in modern art are the result of lack of balance. The soul wishes to express something, but if the soul cannot express what it wants to then there is no contentment, then there will always be suffering. The more a person works, the more he suffers; he suffers because his soul wants to express something and cannot. That is why in the lives of artists there is always so much suffering, because their soul has been born on earth with some ideal which has made them artists, but when they cannot produce that ideal before their eyes, then the soul goes through tortures. Until they come to that stage where they can produce their art to the satisfaction of their own spirit, they will always fall short of the ideal.

The artist has a great mission in the world. He cannot be compared with other human beings, for he is the instrument of God.

His mission in life is to create something that will inspire people and will elevate humanity; his work should be an education for the world.

It seems that the general trend of the artist's mind is to become more and more fanciful. No doubt this is natural, yet it would be well if it were remembered that nature is perfect in itself, and that the greater the art the more natural it is; the best art is the simplest. For instance one might point out that Egyptian art makes use of symbols which are not natural at all. But the ancient Egyptian civilization was flourishing at a time when the world was still in a very primitive condition, and therefore we cannot compare the art of that time with modern art which is supposed to be much more evolved. When we look at the pictures of many Indian gods and goddesses, for instance those of Sarasvati and Lakshmi, we see that they have four arms, which certainly is not natural. Yet there are no angles, and no attempt is made to produce something unnatural; every attempt is made to show that even with four arms they are natural beings. In this they are quite different to modern art, where even a man with two arms seems to be most unnatural.

Symbolism is the mature or ripened aspect of art, and if symbolism is used at the time when art is only beginning to develop, it is a drawback; then this art will not flourish. When art is in its infancy it should not touch symbolism, for symbolism should appear as the result of a natural development. It is an inspiration; it becomes natural when the artist becomes natural; then everything he does has a symbolical meaning. But when the artist begins by thinking, 'I must apply some symbolism', then he destroys his art. Symbolism should come by itself. It is not something that one can study or learn; it is nature's language, it is spiritual inspiration, it is in itself revelation. And when a person has spent his life developing his thought and feeling it springs forth naturally, since it is a divine spring of beauty. Then alone the artist is entitled to produce symbolism in his art.

Symbology expresses ideas which are complex and on which one has to ponder, but it has nothing to do with deformity, for deformity will never bring us higher thoughts.

No doubt when there is a continual striving to produce

something new, this will sooner or later have a result and will bring art up to a higher level; and perhaps that will be a step forward in evolution. But it will not come very soon. Evolution sometimes takes a wrong direction and sometimes a right direction, though in the end it will surely reach its destination. At the same time, the artist could find the way to bring about that result sooner, if he would only keep his thoughts more in the spiritual realm.

CHAPTER VII

SCULPTURE (1)

IN ALL periods of history art has played a prominent part in the life of humanity. With every rise and fall, and with all the different changes that art has gone through, it has always been the soul of life. It cannot be otherwise, for art is an improvement on nature. It is said that nature is made by God and art by man, but at the same time nature is made by God and art is made by God through man; in other words, art finishes nature. Therefore the artist, whether one considers him evolved or unevolved, is indeed the hand of God; for that which is not to be found in nature the artist adds, and that is why art has often proved to be the stepping-stone to God's shrine.

The Sufis have seen God in the realm of love, harmony, and beauty. The tendency towards art shows itself in all three; for beauty is produced through harmony, and if the arrangement of lines or the composition of colours is not harmonious, a thing cannot be beautiful. Harmony creates beauty, and love of beauty results in art; thus art is the practice of that philosophy which Sufism teaches: the philosophy of love, harmony, and beauty.

Today we notice on every side an increasing appreciation and love of the art of sculpture. A great effort is also being made by modern sculptors to produce the art which the soul of the world is seeking for; yet it seems that they are continually seeking for something that is still missing. Today many sculptors look at

Greek art with envy, and with the anticipation that they may one day produce again what was produced long ago.

The drawback today is the method of development. Before trying to imitate ancient art, it is first necessary to open the inner eye, to look at life as it really is. A statue is something dead; if one tries to make something exactly like it, it is like imitating something that is dead. The first thing one should understand is what has produced the statue, and one will see that it was inspiration; it was the opening of the inner eye that produced the art of yesterday, and now the sculptors find it hard to produce anything like it. In spite of all the development in sculpture, one finds that fineness, magnetism, and attraction are lacking; and that is because today art is approached from a practical point of view.

Also art cannot be accomplished in the first place by effort; art should come from inspiration. The life of the artist should be easy, without anxiety and worry, without pressure to produce something; he should be passive, so that the work of art may come naturally. Then the Creator Himself, who is the Lord of beauty, can use the artist as His pen. No doubt suffering can purify a person and make him more capable of inspiration, but when an artist wants to produce a beautiful work of art, he does not open himself to inspiration by hardening himself and by straining his will.

In ancient times people were very often inspired through their love of subtlety and beauty. When we study Greek art we find that the Greek people were fine and subtle in perception. From their statues we can observe that they did not lay down their philosophy in rigid, prosaic words. They made a shrine for wisdom in the form of legends and myths; they put the words of truth in a beautiful frame. This shows us the subtlety of their nature, and out of this subtlety a wonderful art was born.

Some of the most ancient statues are to be found in India and China; and by studying these we find that the sculptors had not only finished them in every detail, but had also put magnetism into them. Hundreds and thousands of times people have experienced that some of these statues possess great magnetism, and this shows that the artist of those days was not only an artist; his art also had magic, and an influence that would last for thousands of years. Whenever we go near such statues they have a certain effect; merely by being in their presence, by looking at them, by sitting before them, we can feel their influence which is like that of a living being, or even stronger.

It is therefore not surprising that the Hindus have kept for ages in their temples the images of Brahma, Vishnu, Shiva, Rama, Krishna, and many others. Even with all their great philosophy and comprehension of life, this art has always helped and inspired them, for it has given them this wonderful influence. When a statue has been worshipped in a shrine for a very long time, this too will magnetize it; yet the statue must have something to attract in the first place in order to make intelligent people inclined to bow before it. It is as if the statue called out, 'Come here with all your intelligence, man, and bow before me! I am sitting here full of life and influence, though I do not speak.'

Many stories are told about a sculptor of long ago whose name was Azar. The peculiarity of his art was that as soon as those who were antagonistic to idol-worship saw a statue of a god or a goddess made by Azar, they followed that particular religion. Art conquers humanity without words.

The art of ancient times was almost entirely symbolic. In those days when printing had not even been discovered, the only way in which an idea could be bequeathed to later generations was through the medium of art; so by different symbols the artists expressed the inspiration and the wisdom that were to be left for humanity. That is why we so often find that ancient works of art contain a message. The day will come when people will not be curious only about the artistic aspect of the ancient sculpture, but will begin to read this art as a scripture. No doubt there is already much curiosity everywhere about such art, and a great desire to go and study it in the East, in Egypt, India, and China. So far there is only appreciation of the skill and great fineness and beauty with which it was produced; but the day when the lovers of beauty look at it from a spiritual point of view, they will find in that ancient art an expression of divine wisdom which will again become a source of revelation.

To some extent symbology can be learnt, but symbology does not come to one only by learning; it comes by intuition. Symbolism is a language of intuition; it comes by itself; and suddenly one begins to understand the meaning of the different forms and colours. When it is said that the Twelve Apostles began to know different languages, it only means they knew the language of each person.

Suppose there were a book on symbology, and the book explained the meaning of different symbols; this would only be the opinion of the man who wrote the book. Perhaps all he said was wrong. But when symbolism comes by intuition, then the true meaning of the symbol is revealed. Therefore the knowledge of symbolism is not a form of learning. First the intuitive faculty must be opened and then the whole meaning of the symbols will be understood; and often it will be quite a different meaning from what the object seems to represent. It is a different language; it is learning the language of life.

Essentially symbols have the same meaning for everyone, yet according to the direction in which people are looking their meaning differs. Under the same sun we all see everything more or less alike, and in the same way in the light from within we all can see the meaning of the symbols; the only difference is that between individuals, in other words limitations. This is the reason why the wise very often spoke in symbols; even their jokes were symbolical.

In ancient art one often finds faces that are unlike those of human beings. This only means that the artist adopted an exaggerated way of picturing the features of different human beings in order to bring out their characteristics. Besides when a man looks at a statue which is not very different from the human form, it is just like looking at one's own kind; and when there is no difference one does not get such a clear vision. Clear vision comes from difference. Some artists, especially those of China, therefore adopted this particular method of making sculptures not exactly like human beings, but a little different; and by making them somewhat different they produced a clearness of vision which enabled man to see through it and recognize what he would not have recognized otherwise.

In the same way they made animals of different kinds. Sometimes in ancient art we see animals which are unlike the animals we know; but if they had been familiar animals they would not convey a certain idea to us; making them different helps us to concentrate our mind on some idea. A sculpture like this speaks to us louder than one which we can easily recognize. When the mind sees an object with keen sight and interest, it is ready to receive the lesson which the object is meant to give. That is why many ancient statues appear unusual.

We also see that in ancient works of art great attention was given to detail; wonderful skill was used in producing every detail. Then, when we look at the materials of which the sculptures were made, it is still more wonderful. Many statues made thousands of years ago look as fresh as ever today.

There is no doubt that the art of sculpture stands out and attracts our attention more than any other kind of art. And as soon as the unrest of the world lessens and this age of labour and strife begins to decline, there will be an improvement in the realm of art. People will come to value it more, they will appreciate the artist more, and art will attain greater prominence. As the world evolves there will surely come a time when art will recapture its ancient glory and will again become the means of expressing the divine wisdom. On that day words will not be necessary; art itself will be the source of revelation.

Furthermore, whether the artist knows it or not, what he makes always has an influence. Once when I was visiting Berlin I saw some statuary round the Kaiser's palace, and when I looked at it I thought that it was no wonder that this empire had collapsed. It could not have been otherwise; it was as if the statues had been put there on purpose in order to ruin it! The symbolism which, either consciously or unconsciously, the artist had embodied in these statues was nothing but a source of ruin. Even now or at some future time, if anyone lives there, there will be a downfall; it cannot be otherwise.

Can it be that a thing is beautiful and yet has a bad influence? It is very difficult to say what is beautiful, and sometimes that which one person considers beautiful another thinks very ugly. Also, something which appears most beautiful to many people may have an effect which is just the reverse, like a fruit which looks delicious, but when one eats it, proves to be quite bitter. Therefore one can say that something that is not beautiful in its effect is not really beautiful.

CHAPTER VIII

SCULPTURE (2)

IN ALL art there are three stages, and especially in sculpture. The first stage is conception; the next stage is composition; and the third stage is production. If the artist is not capable of conceiving an idea, he cannot go any further. He may try hundreds of times, but he will not arrive at the desired result. The outer world may help to bring about such a conception, but it must actually spring from within. It depends upon the stage of the artist's evolution; according to his evolution he is able to catch, to sense, the rising stream of inspiration which comes from within.

The sculptor's work is of very great importance, for it is an imitation of the art of the Creator, and not always in miniature form. The sculptor's first idea is to make a life-size statue, or perhaps even larger than life-size; and if it is smaller his task is to put so much life into it that it may take the place of a living creature. Thus sculpture is imitating God.

Composition comes from another faculty. Conception is the work of intuition, but even if a person has enough intuition to form an idea, he still needs the faculty of composition to express it. A gifted artist is he who has the gift, the capacity, to compose in his mind that which he wants to bring out. There are many intuitive artists who owing to their particular stage of evolution can perceive an intuition, but if they are not gifted they cannot compose it. That is another talent. No doubt a lover of nature, a keen observer, an admirer of line and curve, a real artist, all have such a gift—the aptitude for composing that which intuition brings in the form of an idea.

The third stage is the production. If a person is not qualified to produce something with his hands, then he may have intuition and he may have the gift of composition, and yet he cannot produce a work of art. That is something else, that is skill; and skill is learned by practice. Human nature is such that it considers everything easy. If one has intuition, one readily thinks that one can also compose; and if one is able to compose a work of art in one's mind, one believes that one can produce it; but, again, producing requires another kind of talent.

Which is the most difficult stage? This cannot be determined for one artist has talent but is without intuition; another artist can compose in his mind and yet is without skill in producing; and there is yet another who has intuition but is lacking in composition and production. In order to combine these three faculties one must be not only an artist, but one must become art itself. Then to the one who is so absorbed in his work that he forgets himself, that capacity, that intuition, that skill, will come naturally; then he begins to do wonders, and his art becomes a perfect expression of what he had in mind.

In the ancient art of Egypt one finds an extraordinary atmosphere. One may take a simple statue which seems to have been made with little skill when compared with the art of ancient Greece, but when it is studied from a psychological point of view, one finds something living in it. It is not only a work of art but life has been put into it; and this shows that the tendency of the ancient artists was to give life to their thought. Their sculpture may not show a high degree of skill, yet it is a phenomenon. If a piece of rock which was carved thousands of years ago can produce an atmosphere, this proves that the artist who made it gave it life. And the more man investigates the ancient history of Egypt, the more he will find that the Egyptians possessed the art of putting life into objects.

Coming to the art of India, the artists there made use of sculpture to produce scriptures; every work of art in India is a scripture, and we can read one or another philosophical truth in it. The carvings and engravings in the temples, the gods and goddesses, their several hands each holding some symbolical object, all have a deep meaning, and by the study of this meaning one may arrive at realization. Thus the ancient temples of India were not only places where people worshipped; but they were at the same time scriptures, places where people were inspired if their insight was keen enough to observe what was behind the symbols. The tourists who go there now and admire the artistic aspect of these sculptures, do not see what is behind them nor with what idea they were made. The artists did not give their attention only to the artistic side, for the principal motive behind these sculptures was to express certain aspects of the philosophy of life.

One finds this form of art all over India, for instance near Bombay in the caves of Elephanta, and in a place called Ajanta near Aurangabad. There are also examples near Darjeeling and in Nepal and its surroundings; and when one goes farther into Tibet, one finds that the ancient philosophy has been preserved for thousands of years in the form of sculpture, ready to be revealed to souls which are evolved enough to read what was written there.

In the East, ancient China was considered to have the highest artistic skill. What is most estimable in the art of China is its imagery; the Chinese artist produced the picture of patience, of greed, of wrath, the image of war, the image of peace, all kinds of abstract ideas like these, in the form of an animal or of man. It is a peculiar talent which is not to be found in every artist, as man naturally is inclined to picture what he is familiar with; but an artist who can imagine something entirely different from what one is accustomed to see has quite a different talent. When we look at it from this point of view it is very admirable, and the Chinese were indeed able to make most interesting works of art in this way.

All that we are accustomed to see is easy to admire, because our eyes are used to it; but any form that is different seems odd to us, something strange. The Chinese have given beauty to forms which have never been seen but which attract the eye and the mind all the same; and the thoughtful will stop to think what is behind them. By their imagery the Chinese artists attempted to bring the abstract into objective form. And to a greater or lesser degree the world has admired the ancient art of China, and yet has not wholly understood its meaning. Nowadays experts on Chinese art are trying to explain it to Western art lovers, but it is not the art expert who can explain the art of China. It needs psychological explanation, it needs the mystical touch; for it has come from a mind which is deep and thoughtful, the mind of a people which has suffered for thousands of years and has been in quest of the truth.

N

But as to beauty, there is no art that can be compared with that of Greece. Ancient Greek art stands alone in its beauty, in its fineness. Its peculiarity is the movement in it. It seems as if movement had been given to the statue and that the statue has been moving for thousands of years. The gracefulness, the delicacy, and at the same time the mysticism of ancient Greek art is wonderful. Every action that we can observe in this statuary reveals some meaning. Greek imagery, too, fills us with wonder and admiration.

When we come to the art of sculpture today, it seems as if the artist is searching; he is trying to reach something which he knows is absent. The soul of the sculptor is seeking for something which seems lost. First of all, by lack of appreciation around him, the artist is discouraged, and next he is put in the midst of the business world; and that relief which should be given to the heart of the artist, so that he may think of art and nothing else, is not to be found today. There was not so much thought of competition in ancient times, there was not a fixed price for art. Art was invaluable. The admirers of ancient art never considered a work of art as having a fixed price. They always thought that they could never give enough for real art. In that way art progressed; it was admired.

Besides the direction of art today is not of the same nature as in ancient times. The direction of ancient art was towards spiritual realization. Love, harmony, and beauty the artist saw in their highest aspects. And when the artist loses that direction then he comes down to earth; instead of going upward he is going downward. There is no doubt that humanity nowadays is less religious. Every step that we think we are taking in a new direction seems further removed from religion; in everything we see that humanity is forgetting religion, and the educated and intellectual people even wish to avoid any conversation on the subject. Many feel that to pronounce the name of God puts a great burden upon them; they think it is so heavy; and when this subject comes up in a conversation, they say 'higher forces', 'higher powers', or sometimes with great difficulty they say 'gods'. Simply to say 'God' is too simple; they believe they are much too evolved to say 'God'.

A wrong conception of democracy has also resulted in modern

writers writing against the ideal of God, an ideal which was pictured and beautified by the great prophets of Ben Israel and all the saints and sages. That ideal was the stepping-stone for them; but these writers say that by speaking, for instance, of the wrath of God, God was pictured in a cruel form. They think that the intelligent people of today would have expressed it better, would have given it a more beautiful form; but instead of giving it a more beautiful form they have destroyed the ideal and thus impoverished mankind. With the ideal lost, there is nothing to hold on to except objects which the senses can perceive and touch.

This does not mean that Western art has not developed since the Renaissance. It has evolved at every step, but still it seems that there is something lacking; and what needs to be added to modern art is not yet there. Modern art needs so much to make it perfect, and no one can feel this as deeply as an artist feels it today. The scientist is sooner contented with what little he discovers, but the better the work of art is the more the artist feels that there is something still missing; his heart is longing all through his life to produce something more than that. Consciously or unconsciously every artist is craving for that something which is missing. And if this goes on, no doubt the artist will find it; and on the day when the mystery is found, art will again become a language.

The meditative quality and the practice of concentration should be developed in art, and also the higher ideal; but this material world forms a barrier to all these. It stands in the way of the artist's progress. Nevertheless, there is no doubt that a real artist is always spiritually inclined; he is only hindered by the world, and therefore it is possible that tomorrow the art of sculpture will evolve; it will evolve in fineness and in beauty, and sculptors will also develop their imagery. Then art will culminate in that great achievement when the artist will really be able to produce a living statue.

The motive behind the whole of creation is to put life into everything; that is its sole object. In other words, every rock is longing for the day when it will burst out as a volcano, and when all that is valuable in it will come out. Sulphur, diamonds, gold, and silver, everything that is in its heart must come out one day; that is its purpose.

Every tree is longing for the day it will bear fruit. Love expresses itself through every channel, and it manifests outwardly in order that God may see Himself face to face. And so it is with a work of art. People think that it is the artist who has made it; in reality it is God who has perfected it. As it is God's pleasure to create the world, so it is also God's pleasure to create through pen and brush and chisel, to give life to what is lifeless. If there is life it is God. And what is God? God is love; and thus the desire of that love is to manifest in the form of beauty in the realm of art.

CHAPTER IX

ARCHITECTURE (1)

S C U L P T U R E and painting complete architecture. The idea of building a home did not develop only with the creation of the human race; it had already begun with the first manifestation. And if we look into life and its laws with keen insight, we shall see that the whole of creation is built on this one principle: that of making a home for every word, for every thought, for every sound, for every idea, and for every colour. No colour, sound, or thought could be recognized, no feeling could be distinguished, if they did not have a home to live in. For instance it is the breath which manifests as the voice, and it is the voice which manifests as a word; but in order to manifest as the voice the breath must have the mouth as its home; and for the voice to manifest as a word, as a sound, all that the mouth contains is necessary. That again is a home; it is a home conveniently made for the voice to turn into a word.

Then the voice, the word, needs a home in order to become audible; and that home is the ear. If something of what the ear should contain is missing, then the sound is not fully audible. The breath must have lungs and tubes through which it can manifest; they are its home. The blood must have channels through which it can circulate for the same reason, and in the same way the mind is the home of thought, the heart is the home of feeling, and the soul is the home of the divine light, the divine Spirit.

From the moment that the sound begins its journey and passes through the different spheres, turning into an individual, the entire phenomenon of this process consists in making a home. First the soul makes a home of the body which is taken from the angelic spheres, and by taking that body it becomes an angel. A being, a life which had no name and no distinctive features, obtained them when it gathered round itself a cover and took that cover as its home.

In the same way in the sphere of the jinn the soul gathers round itself a home that gives it an accommodation; and that home is its being. It is the same with the human body. The soul has gathered round itself another home, and it is of this home in which the soul lives that man says, 'It is I'. The Hindus have called this home an Akasha, which means accommodation. Thus accommodation is not only a need but it is indispensable; nothing can be born, composed, constructed, or moulded without its accommodation. The Sufis have called this accommodation the temple: there is a temple of breath, a temple of sound, a temple of hearing, a temple of seeing; and there is a temple of God's spirit which is the body. And each part of the body is again a temple which accommodates a thought, a feeling, a faculty, or a sense.

When we look at it in this light, we see that when man made a home for himself to live in, it was the second step. The first step was that he made himself, the next step was that he made a home to live in. It is his second step because the four walls and the roof, all that is in front of him and around him, form his personality, his character. Today, when there is so much hotel life everywhere and home life is much less known, when the home is so little appreciated, people cannot understand how sacred the idea of house-building really is. Besides the uniformity of these times takes away a great deal of the beauty of the home. We change the world into a prison when we begin to lose our conception of a home: then we think in terms of pigeon-holes where a thousand or more pigeons can be put in and locked up in the evening.

Even when man first began to build the accommodation for himself to live in, the sense of architecture was already advanced, for even the birds very often have greater skill in making nests than man has in what he does. A beautifully built nest is a miracle in itself. The skilful weaving, and the patience with which it is done, the perseverance and good sense that the bird shows, all these teach us that the spirit has developed the art of building a home even before man was created, and thus from his most primitive state he possessed the inborn quality of being able to build proper accommodation for himself.

The art of architecture began with people digging holes in the ground, piling up stones, and making use of mountain caves as houses to dwell in. And the first idea which inspired them to do this was not how it could be made more comfortable for them, more convenient, more beautiful; instead of this their first idea was how it could be made in such a way that they could think more of God. It is with this idea that the art of architecture began. Cutting stones and carving wood, the people made symbols or works of art, pictures or figures that would remind them of spiritual perfection. This was the first thought of primitive man.

Afterwards came the thought of how their home could be made more comfortable, how it could be made so that it would protect them against the weather—storms, excessive heat, cold, and rain. And so the next idea which influenced the building of the house was consideration of the weather, and that influenced all kinds of construction.

But unconsciously the people felt that the house should not be too different from the picture of the world. Naturally, therefore, because the horizon is round, they dug holes which were also round. In ancient Persian poetry they speak of *Gardish-i Dunya*, which means the roundness of the world. And *Gardish* does not mean only roundness, but a round action, a circular movement.

The houses were not always round, for sometimes there was an improvement, for instance when an oval opening was made. Even now one will find that among primitive people there are round dwellings; always their first idea is to build their house as they see the world, round, and then later they make it oval. This suggests that first they thought of the world around them, and only later did they think of themselves; for when we look at the form of a human being we see that it is not round but oval.

Then there came the tendency of building steps up to the house. Where did this tendency come from? It was an inherited faculty of the soul to feel that it had descended many steps, so that it had to climb up many steps again to reach the highest temple. The house was the picture of the temple, and the steps were suggestive of going towards the temple, each step being a symbol of a different plane of existence. The most wonderful part of this is that from the most primitive times no house was made without a religious conception of some sort or other. Perhaps the religion was of the lowest type, a very primitive conception of God, yet the house was always at the same time a temple. Later when the people had built more houses they constructed a temple for the community, thinking it would be better to come together in one building for worship. But their first conception was to use their own house as a temple.

The next important thing was the kitchen. There was an ideal behind using one's house as a temple, but the kitchen was a necessity, because in the kitchen the offering was prepared. There again the people had the idea that what they needed was at the same time an offering to God. So in some houses there was worship, and in others there was the kitchen in which to cook food and to offer it to God; and then to eat the food they had prepared for God as it were a blessing, a sacrament. That was the origin of the idea of sacrament, that no one should cook his meal thinking only of how to appease his hunger; and that man should realize, what he had already intuitively felt from the beginning, that there was someone else to offer his food to, who was better and higher and greater than himself and whom he should try to please.

And what was the origin of the idea of sacrifice? There were times when there were famines, when people could not obtain any food except animal food. And the most cruel thing that man can do, to kill an animal, struck even the most primitive man as not being right. But in order to save himself from starving, the only thing he could do was to go hunting, so what he brought home he placed before his gods as a sacrifice.

Naturally the necessity arose for a storeroom in the house, and also for a separate place in which to sleep; later it was thought that those who came to visit should not be taken into the kitchen

or into the room where one slept, because these were sacred; yet
they had to be taken into the house and not left out in the rain or
heat. Therefore a room was made and set apart for guests; and
with these few essentials in mind they built their houses.

When primitive people began to think that instead of living in
holes in the ground or in caves they should live on the ground,
they attempted to make houses of dry leaves, of straw, of reeds,
and then of bamboo; a still further development was that they
began to cut wood and make boards to build their houses with.
And so architecture developed more and more.

The first thing that helped architecture to develop was the
worship of God, the second was necessity, and the third love of
beauty. Then people discovered the art of painting and the art of
sculpture. The latter was dedicated to religion, to their belief, to
God; the art of painting was principally dedicated to making
pictures of the myths and legends of their race. Nearly all the
ancient legends are connected with metaphysics and religion; they
are symbolical. Even if they were primitive legends, coming from
the earliest races who had not yet developed their symbology,
they were symbolical just the same. Every religion contains symbology, and it belongs to metaphysics. That is why the ancient
people painted their books of philosophy on their walls in the
form of legends, and by their primitive sculpture they gave form
to the objects of their belief and of their worship.

Colour can be expressed in two ways. One expression of colour
is striking and the other is harmonious; one expression is soothing
and the other is exciting. And it seems that the primitive people
mostly used exciting colours. The more primitive the race, the
more exciting the colours they used. This was because they
wanted to feel that they existed, which is a hidden tendency in
every soul. If a person sits quietly, thinking about something,
imagining something, then generally after some time he begins
to move one of his legs up and down, or he begins to scratch
himself, or to drum on the table. He must be moving in order to
give evidence to his consciousness that he is still alive; that is why
he performs those actions. Inactivity gives him a thought of death,
and action gives him a thought of life.

The purpose of the use of striking colours by primitive races was this, that as soon as a man came home or somebody else came into the house, he should feel that there was a home. In Japan the doors are still painted red, in order that before the host comes to meet a visitor with his warm heart, the red door may welcome him with its warmth. In all ages the striking effect of colours has, naturally, been felt and appreciated most, while their more peaceful, healing, and harmonious effects were not generally understood as the people were mostly not evolved enough to enjoy them. This is why striking colours were mostly used in the beginning of architecture.

As to the furniture and objects that were in use in the houses of the ancient people, they were made of anything that could be obtained from their surroundings: skins of animals, straw, clay for pots and vessels, and other materials. They used pumpkins and animal guts for their musical instruments, bamboo and reed for flutes. In this way a happy home was made which was a kingdom in itself. There they had their kingdom, their God, their temple, and they were as happy, perhaps more happy, than man can be today.

One may ask why, if primitive people were happier than we are, do not the primitive races today show the qualities of the Golden Age ,but rather of savages. It is because they are affected by the condition of the human race as a whole. Children, animals, and the ignorant, all three, are more affected by the general condition of the world than others; therefore, if the general condition of the world is that it is full of conflict, they will reflect it more. In other words, when new wars are being plotted, the savage people will already be quarrelling and fighting among themselves. It is the condition of mind in the world that affects them, and then they act. Here there is only the planning, while there they are killing and dying.

Will humanity ever return to simple living? Life is an intoxication; and the more intoxicating it is, the more it proceeds from simplicity to complexity. It is the nature of life's intoxication to lead man from simplicity to complexity, and man chooses complexity for himself. When he finds himself surrounded by complexity he thinks that he is caught in it, and then it is very difficult for him to get out of it.

The sages of India give a very beautiful example of this. They say life is like a spider's web; the spider weaves a web, making it more and more complex, weaving and weaving until it is completed. But when the web is finished, then the spider itself is caught in the web and cannot free itself. Its motive was to live there and to catch all the insects that might stray into it. But in the end the spider does not see its desire fulfilled; the end is that the spider itself becomes captive in its own web. And so it is with the ideal of man on earth. He perseveres and tries to make it as complex as possible for himself, and he then enjoys that complexity, he sees it as an improvement, as something wonderful, and he becomes more and more interested in it. But what is the end? That one day he is checked by something, and then he begins to feel that if he had been without all this complexity it would have been a thousand times better.

CHAPTER X

ARCHITECTURE (2)

IF WE look at the Egyptian pyramids with open hearts and illuminated souls, they speak to us of the past. They tell us that even if the architecture of that time was not so advanced theoretically, yet it had reached a highly spiritual stage. They stand there as a token of the intelligence of the ancient people, and not only of their inspiration but of the depth of their mind. And if today or in the future, people inquire about the site that was chosen for the pyramids, they will find that it is exactly in the centre of the solid part of the earth's surface. At that time communications were not as they are now, and the study of geography was hardly known to the world, yet the Egyptians were able to find the exact centre and to construct something there which is unsurpassed in history. What was the meaning of placing the pyramids in the exact centre of the earth? The real heart is the solar plexus, and that is to be found in the centre of the body which is the shrine of God, and that is why it was necessary for the sacred temple to be in the centre of the earth.

The ancient Egyptians had a symbolical point of view in their architecture, and their influence became the principal source of inspiration for the civilizations that followed. Very little is known about ancient Egyptian drawing or painting; nevertheless, in the examples that remain we always discover some mystery, some atmosphere, some magnetism, something very wonderful. And the excavations which are being made today are proving that the Egyptians of that particular period had reached a stage where they were more advanced in art and architecture than any other peoples, and that they were also able to inspire later civilizations.

Egyptian architecture is expressive of mystery. It was a mystical age, and everything the Egyptians did was done without mechanical power; it was done with spiritual power; and that is the reason why what they have made will last after all that others have made has been destroyed, and when all other buildings have vanished from the earth. And it would not be surprising if on the last day, when everything else has been destroyed, the pyramids still remained standing.

It is very interesting to notice that the architecture of the Mongolian races is distinct and peculiar to them, and that it has no resemblance whatever to any other architecture. And what stands out as being most expressive of the people's character is Chinese architecture, including that of Tibet, Assam, Burma, Siam, and Japan. There is a peculiar line, there is a peculiar curve, and there is a peculiar taste in colour. This shows the exclusiveness of the Mongolian character, a character which is very distinct and remote. They have followed their tradition to such an extent that every insignificant form that the Mongolians have made has that particular character. They are so attached to the form that belongs to them, that they have been able to retain the type, the character of their architecture for thousands of years. They have never abandoned that form, and they do not change it nor add to it from outside, but they develop it in its own character. In this way Mongolian architecture stands out as something different and distinct, peculiar to itself.

The architecture of Persia was influenced by Arabian architecture;

and the peculiarity of Persian and Arabian architecture is the dome, which is called in Arabic the *Gunbad* and the *Mehrab*. Gunbad means dome, and Mehrab means an arch used in windows and doors which is not exactly round, but is formed of three or five parts; in other words, in five half-circles with the top made by two lines going upward and joining in the centre. The interpretation of this form was given by the mystics of Arabia, who called it *Qasab-e Kousein*, which means the meeting of the eyebrows. When a person looks upward, naturally his eyebrows come closer to each other. The idea is, that as the spirit soars upward the tendency of the soul is to rise from duality to unity, and by working with these two particular forms they have arrived at such perfection that if the same form were continued for a hundred thousand years one could never tire of it.

During the time of the Moghul emperors this architecture of Arabia and Persia was perfected in India. The Moghuls, who were worshippers of beauty and very fond of splendour and grandeur, spent enormous wealth in building something which would remain as a token of beauty. In India today the most unique and beautiful signs of the past to be found are the Moghul buildings, for instance Moti Mahal, the mosque in Delhi and, best of all, the Taj Mahal in Agra. It was because of the emperor's great love for Nur-i Jehan that he wished this love to be remembered for ever afterwards, and also he wanted the people to know that he really loved beauty. He spared no effort, no money, no time, to make this building perfect; and when it was finished it became the tomb of Nur-i Jehan. When one looks at it, it not only inspires one with its greatness and richness, but it also tells one of love, of beauty, of patience, of endurance, of an ideal, of joy, and of peace; these are all there. It speaks without a tongue, and it will go on speaking as long as it stands beneath the sun. Every little detail, the smallest piece of marble, was worked most carefully. There is not one inch in the Taj Mahal, of floor or wall or ceiling, which had not been made perfect.

This shows a love of perfection, a love of finishing something, a love of creating something beautiful. Would it have been possible to make such a building if the workmen had been on strike ten times a year? Not even in a century. And if the workmen had insisted on week-end entertainments? No, their pleasure was in what they were making. Each workman realized that what he was making would live for centuries, that it was the greatest blessing, the greatest privilege to be allowed to work at it. That was the spirit of every man who worked there. It was built with joy. One can still find this in its atmosphere, for as soon as one comes near the Taj Mahal one begins to feel joy; it is something living.

The builders have gone, but the work remains, and every artist who has a real sense of architecture will appreciate this. What is earthly gain compared with the thought that the work that one has done will live on and give joy for ages to come? This in itself is a great joy for the artist, because a real artist is not born for this earth; he is born in the sphere of beauty and he lives in that sphere. The things of the earth do not count for him.

In ancient Greek architecture, the Doric, which shows Jelal influence in its character, is expressive of power. And where there is Jelal there must be Jemal too; thus the Ionic architecture is expressive of Greek wisdom and beauty and fineness. And where one finds Jelal and Jemal, one will also find Kemal, and this influence is seen in the Corinthian architecture. No doubt when Jelal and Jemal clash, then there is something lacking on both sides; nevertheless these three aspects of Greek architecture are expressive of Jelal, Jemal, and Kemal.

When we compare the architecture of the Middle Ages with the Roman and the Greek, there again we find these influences. The Jelal influence of Roman architecture shows the ancient Roman characteristics: law and rule; the Jemal influence in Greek architecture shows the Greek love of beauty and wisdom. Gothic is the Kemal expression; however, Gothic architecture has taken its own peculiar form in every country. It seems as if the soil inspired the builders, both the architects and the workmen. The Gothic churches in France are different from those in Germany, and even if there is some resemblance between French and Italian cathedrals, yet there is an individual feeling in every cathedral wherever it may be. Gothic architecture has reigned over the Western countries for a long time, and although by now its influence has disappeared, it has made itself felt in a hidden way during many centuries.

It is very difficult to describe modern architecture.[1] We hesitate to call it beautiful; but to say that it is not beautiful—no, we cannot say that! So instead of calling it beautiful we might call it wonderful. If there is any wonder it is in the immensity of the buildings. They are indeed enormous; the ancient people would never even have dreamed of such buildings. They would be horrified if they saw them. They are also wonderful because in spite of the many floors they consist of, they yet stand so firmly; and then the way in which everything possible is pre-fabricated in order to build very quickly—all this is most wonderful. Yet it is a drawback that only vertical and horizontal lines are to be seen, and when a traveller passes through countries where he finds the same kind of architecture in every city, it is just like looking at the same house over and over again; there is no difference. Instead of wandering through the city he might just as well look at one house and be contented with that. Everyone must have the same kind of house built on the same plan, but we are not all made the same way. Every person is different and that is what makes life interesting. When every person is different, why should not every house and building be different? As the architecture of every country is expressive of the character of that country, so the architecture of every house should be expressive of the particular character of the owner of the house and of the man who built it. But when the law of uniformity is forced upon people then there remains no choice in the matter; the choice has been taken away from the architect as well as from the owner of the house.

No doubt one sees a continual effort on the part of modern architects to produce something new; and it seems that this effort is working as much in their minds as in the minds of painters and other artists, to produce, to create something new. No matter what direction architecture takes, there will come a time before long when a better approach will be found. But what is necessary for this is the development of spirituality. The architect should not think that it is the study of different architectures that will make him capable of producing something new; it is the heart, it is the

[1] Inayat means more especially the sky-scraper architecture of his time.

spirit, which must reveal to him what he should create. The work of the architect is of the greatest importance; it comes through inspiration and its origin is spirit, not matter. A house is built with matter, but made with spirit. And as the spirit of the world evolves so architecture will evolve also.

In the future one can foresee two improvements. One will be the giving of more scope to the personality of the individual to express itself; and the other will be the evolution of an architecture which does not discard all that belongs to the past, but blends some of its best characteristics with the architectural conceptions of the present.

CHAPTER XI

POETRY (1)

IN POETRY the rhythm of the poet's soul is expressed. There are moments in the life of every human being when the soul feels itself rhythmic, and at such moments children, who are beyond the conventionalities of life, begin to dance or to speak in words which rhyme, or to repeat phrases which resemble each other and harmonize together. It is a moment of the soul's awakening. One person's soul may awaken more often than another's, but in the life of everyone there are such times of awakening, and the soul which is gifted with the means of expressing thoughts and ideas, often shows its gift in poetry.

Among all the valuable things of this world the word is the most precious. For in the word one can find a light which gems and jewels do not possess; a word may contain so much life that it can heal the wounds of the heart. Therefore poetry in which the soul is expressed is as living as a human being. The greatest reward that God bestows on man is eloquence and poetry, and this is not an exaggeration; for it is the gift of the poet which culminates in time in the gift of prophecy.

There is a Hindu idea which explains this very well, and it is

that the vehicle of the goddess of learning is eloquence. Many live
and few think, and among the few who think there are fewer
still who can express themselves. Then their soul's impulse is
repressed, for in the expression of the soul the divine purpose is
fulfilled, and poetry is the fulfilment of the divine impulse to
express something.

No doubt there is true poetry and there is false poetry, just as
there is true music and false music. A person who knows many
words and phrases may fit them together and arrange something
mechanically, but this is not poetry. Whether it be poetry, art, or
music, it must suggest life; and it can only suggest life if it comes
from the deepest impulse of the soul; if it does not do that, then it
is dead. There are verses of the great masters of various periods
which have resisted the sweeping wind of destruction; they
remain ageless. The endurance of their words was in the life that
was put into them. The trees that live long have the deepest roots,
and so have the living verses. We only read them in the same way
in which we look at the trees, but if we could see where the roots
of those verses are we would find them in the soul, in the spirit.

What is it that awakens the soul to this rhythm which brings
about poetry? It is something that touches in the poet that pre-
disposition which is called love. For with love there comes harmony, beauty, rhythm, and life. It seems that all that is good and
beautiful and worth attaining is centred in that one spark that is
hidden in the heart of man. When the heart speaks of its joy, of its
sorrow, all of it is interesting and appealing. The heart does not
tell a lie; it always tells the truth. By love it becomes sincere, and
it is through the sincere heart that true love manifests. One may
live in a community where there is always amusement, pastimes,
merriment, and beauty; one may live that life for twenty years;
but the moment one realizes the movement in the depths of one's
heart, one feels that those whole twenty years were nothing. One
moment of life with a living heart is worth more than a hundred
years of life with a heart that is dead.

We see many people in this world who have every comfort
and good fortune and everything they need, and yet they lead an
empty life. Their life may be more unhappy than that of someone
who is starving. He whose soul is starving is more to be pitied

than he whose body is starving; for the one whose body is starving is still alive, but the one whose soul is starving is dead. Those who have shown the greatest inspiration and have given precious words of wisdom to the world were the farmers who were ploughing the soil of their heart. This is the reason why there are so few real poets in this world. For the path of the poet is contrary to the path of the worldly man. The real poet, although he exists on this earth, dreams of different worlds from whence he gets his ideas. The true poet is at the same time a seer, otherwise he could not bring forth the subtle ideas which touch the heart of his listeners. The true poet is a lover and admirer of beauty. If his soul were not impressed by beauty he could not bring it out in his poetry.

What stimulates the gift in the one who is born with the gift of poetry? Is it pleasure or is it pain? Not pleasure; pleasure freezes the gift. The sensitive poet's soul has to go through pain in his life. One may ask whether it would then be a wise thing to seek pain if one wants to be a good poet. But this would be just like thinking that crying was a virtue if one hurt oneself and cried a little. Who, with a living heart, can live in this world as it is and not suffer and not experience pain? Who, with any tendency to feel, to sympathize, to love, does not go through pain? Who, with any sincerity in his nature, could experience daily the insincerity, falsehood, and crudity of human nature, and yet avoid suffering? At every step he takes the poet will meet with suffering. A poet begins with the admiration of beauty, and his talent is the cause that he naturally tends to shed tears over the disappointments that he meets with in life. When he has passed that phase, then comes another phase and he begins to smile and even laugh at the world.

The further one advances in life, the more does life offer things that can give one a good reason for enjoying and amusing oneself. And the first thing that can make one smile is seeing how everybody is running after his own interests: how a man finds his way along devious routes, how he knocks another person down in order to go forward himself, how he pushes another from behind, and how he silences the next one. Is there anything that we cannot find in human nature? Biting, kicking, and fighting, it is all there. There is nothing of the animal nature that is not in the human

o

being; man even excels the animal. All this, however, only makes one smile; the laughter comes afterwards, when one can see where it all ends. If one is capable of seeing all the various endings, in the end there will be laughter.

It is in this period of a poet's advancement that in some way pity, sentiment, and the sympathy that he already had turn into smiles and laughter. It is like something which is turned inside out. The pity and the shedding of tears which were at first outside, are now inside; and outside is the smile and the laughter. Thus both exist at the same time: laughter or a smile on the lips, and pity in the heart. When the poet is laughing his heart is crying at the same time; this is his nature.

The poet rises above tears when he has shed enough. This does not mean that he becomes critical, that he sneers at life, but that he sees the funny side of things and that the whole of life, which he once saw as a tragedy, now appears to him in the form of a comedy. This stage is a consolation for him from above, after his moments of great pain and suffering; but then there comes yet another stage where he rises higher still, where he sees the divine element working in all forms, in all names, where he begins to recognize his Beloved in all forms and names.

This experience in the life of a poet is like the joy in the life of a young lover. It inaugurates another period in his life. Whatever be his condition, rich or poor, in comfort or in need, he is never without his Beloved. His divine Beloved is always in his presence. When he arrives at this stage he pities the lover who has only a limited beloved to admire, to love; for now he has arrived at a stage where, whether alone or in a crowd, whether in the North or the South, the West or the East, on earth or in heaven, he is always in the presence of his Beloved.

And when he goes one step further still, then it becomes difficult for him to express his emotion, his impulse, in poetry. For then he himself becomes poetry. What he feels, what he thinks, what he says, what he does, all is poetry. At this stage he touches that ideal of unity which unites all things in one; but in order to reach this stage the soul must become so mature that it is able to enjoy it. For an infant soul would not be able to enjoy this particular consciousness of all-oneness. From this time on one will find in the poetry of that poet glimpses of prophetic expression. Then it is not only the beauty of the words and their meaning, but his words become illuminating and his verses become life-giving. There are souls in this world who are pious, who are wise, who are spiritual; but among them the one who is capable of expressing his realization of life, of truth, is not only a poet but a prophet.

CHAPTER XII

POETRY (2)

THE POET was born first and poetry came afterwards; poetry was born in the spirit of the poet. It is said in the East that as one can already see in the cradle what features the child will have later, so one can recognize a poet before he learns to speak. And poetry came before language, for it is the poetic spirit in man which made language. Thus the poet is not the son of language but its father; instead of only taking words he makes them. If it had not been for the poet, the language of all races would only have been shouting and howling. In all the different aspects of life we can recognize the signs of inspiration most fully in the poet; and there is no doubt great truth in the saying that the poet is a prophet, though it would be still better to say that the prophet is a poet.

Poetry is the best art there is, for besides everything else it is also drawing or painting with words. The mission of poetry is the same as the mission of the other forms of art. Poetry is a living picture, a picture which says more than a picture on canvas; and its mission is to inspire. Poetry comes to a poet through the suffering caused by disappointment; but any pain or suffering is a preparation, and just as in order to be able to play on a violin the violin must first be tuned, so the heart must be tuned in order to express wisdom. The heart is tuned by suffering, and when the heart has suffered enough pain, then poetry comes. The natural birth of poetry takes place on the day when the doors of the heart are opened. Poetry comes from the heart quality; it is an expression of the love nature.

There is an example in the Sanskrit language of what has been said above, that poetry comes before learning, for in Sanskrit many everyday words rhyme. Mother and father rhyme: *matr* and *patr*. Also brother and friend rhyme: *britra* and *mitra*. And if one goes through the Kosh, which is the Sanskrit dictionary, one will find that all the words which are related to one another in some way rhyme, and this shows that for the ancient people poetry was the everyday language; in other words, their everyday language was poetry.

There is a Sanskrit saying which is perhaps an exaggeration, but it is significant: that a man without any interest in music and poetry is like an animal without a tail. If we wish to compare music with poetry, we can only say that poetry is the surface and music is the depth of one and the same thing. As with mind and heart the surface is mind and the depth is the heart, so it is with poetry and music. The ancient poets were not only poets but also singers. They composed poetry and they sang, and the perfection of the soul could be seen in these two faculties: the faculty of poetry and at the same time its expression in the form of music. Those who separate music from poetry are the same as those who separate religion from life; they are interested in separating everything.

When we study the earliest Sanskrit poetry, we see that it was composed of words which had a fixed measure, each word containing three consonant root-letters to which different vowels were attached. This divided them into two kinds: words of one syllable and words of two syllables. For instance, to the consonant root *mtr* could be attached one vowel *a*, giving *matr*, mother; or two vowels *i* and *a*, giving *mitra*, friend. The arrangement of the words thus composed formed a metre, and there were a great number of these metres in use.

The rhythms in which the ancient people composed their poems were taken from the rhythm of nature: the rhythm of the air, the rhythm of running water, the rhythm of a flying bird, the rhythm of waving branches—all these rhythms were taken from nature, and on them the poets based their poetry. They tried to keep near to nature, so that nature could teach them. And to each of these ancient rhythms or metres they gave a name which was related to something in nature. For instance there is a rhythm called *Hansa*, after the sound of a bird of that name. Poets used the rhythm of the Hansa's call in the composition of their poetry.

Thus the Sanskrit poets were very particular about the psychology of rhythm, words, letters, and syllables. They found that poetry had a mantric effect, which means that poetic inspiration creates a certain effect in the same way as mantrams, sacred words, and that thereby a person might unwittingly bring about bad luck or good luck for himself or for others, or be the cause of harm or success for someone.

There are superstitions that when a certain bird makes a sound it is a warning of coming death; this superstition exists in many different countries. It means that the sound this bird makes creates a destructive rhythm, and whenever that sound is heard it causes a destructive vibration. It is the same with poetry: the arrangement of words, syllables, and letters—all has an effect. When the wind blows from the North, from the South, from the East, or from the West, when it blows straight, slanting, zigzag, upward, or downward, it causes different conditions in the atmosphere. It may bring germs of a plague, it may culminate in a storm, it may create heat or cold, it may change the season, or it may cause destruction, good health, cheerfulness, or depression among people. And when by his breath, which can be likened to the wind that blows in the world, the voice of a singer pronounces a certain letter, then that breath has to take a certain direction. Either it goes upward or downward, to the right or to the left, straight or zigzag; and in accordance with this direction it has an influence upon a man's life.

One might think that if breath has such an influence on man's life, it is only for himself, whereas the influence of the wind is for the whole country, perhaps for the whole world; but man is more powerful than the world, though he may not realize it. The ancient people used to say that one man can save the world and the thought of one man can cause a ship to sink. If one wicked thought can cause a ship to sink, what a great power man has! The reason is that the wind is not so directly connected with the divine spirit as is the breath of man, and therefore man's breath is more powerful than the wind. And when we consider words and their meaning, modern psychology supports the idea that the meaning of every word acts upon our life and has an influence on the lives of other people. Poetry can thus be considered to be a psychological creation, something with psychological power, either for good or for ill.

What was most remarkable about the poets of the Sanskrit age was that all their life they practised diction, the right pronunciation of every syllable and sound. Everything had to be in rhythm; besides it had to be of the right tone and it had to create the right vibrations. And the most learned men, not only among poets but among doctors and others, spent half an hour or longer every day in practising and pronouncing different syllables and words, so that they could speak with greater fluency. Just as a singer today practises pronouncing every word clearly, so did the poets of that time, because they believed in the influence of sound: how it is produced, and what effect it has.

The Vedas which are supposed to have come from the divine source are all in verse, as are the Puranas and other sacred scriptures of ancient times. This shows that when the divine mind wished to express itself, it did not do so crudely; it always expressed itself in a fully poetic, rhythmic, and lyrical form. So often we meet people who proudly and boldly say, 'I speak the truth. I do not care whether anybody likes it or not. I have the courage to tell the truth no matter if it hurts or kills.' But they do not know what truth means; they do not know that truth comes in the form of poetry, of music, of delicacy and fineness.

After the Sanskrit age came the Prakrit age. Poetry became more human, not as philosophical and scientific as in the Sanskrit age. At this time the poet began to conceive in his mind different pictures of human nature and character; this was called *Rasa Shastra*, the science of human nature. In writing lyrics they distinguished between three aspects of love, and they classified the female and male natures in four different aspects.

It has always been the poet's natural inclination to set the feminine aspect of life and of nature on a high pedestal; it is this which inspires the poet to give a beautiful form to all that he creates. Thus poets of great repute in all ages have always been attracted by the moon; they have not written so many lyrics about the sun, as they had more appreciation for the feminine aspect of creation. For the same reason the crescent was the sign of the Prophet, for if a prophet were not responsive to God as the crescent moon is to the sun, illumination would not come to him. It is through his response to the voice of God that a prophet receives or conceives in his spirit the message which he then gives to humanity.

Kings at all times have been very much interested in knowledge and learning, and their association with poets softened their character and balanced their warlike tendencies, their roughness and crudeness. The poets helped the kings to look at life in a different way. It was the poetic inspiration of the emperor Shah Jehan which made the Taj Mahal. If it had not been for poetry he would not have become such a great lover.

The one who reads poetry, the one who enjoys poetry, and the one who writes poetry must know that poetry is something which does not belong to this earth, that it belongs to heaven; and in whatever form one shows one's appreciation and love for poetry, one really shows one's appreciation and love for the spirit of beauty.

CHAPTER XIII

POETRY (3)

VERY LITTLE of the ancient Egyptian poetry has come down to us, and we can only trace some of it through what we know about the character of the Egyptians of those times, who expressed the mystical and musical aspects of the soul in a symbolical way. Hebrew poetry is little known too, except what one finds in the Old Testament. It was the Arabic lyrics which became best known to the Asiatic world as being the most inspired and beautiful. Also, the Arabs were a metaphysically and philosophically inclined people, and their poetry combined philosophy with lyricism and romance.

Poetry found its highest expression in Persia. The Persians had a natural gift for poetry and poetic inspiration, and their language yielded poetic form for the expression of their souls. When Firdausi wrote the history of Persia, he wrote it entirely in verse, showing thereby how the inspiration and language of the Persians blended with poetry. Sufis, especially from the time of Farid-ud-Din-Attar, have given God's message and have interpreted religion to the people of Persia in the form of poetry. Jelal-ud-Din Rumi's wonderful work, the Masnavi, and the poetry of his teacher Shams-e Tabrèz, all show that the spirit of poetry was incarnate in Persia at the time when Hafiz was born and when Sa'di wrote his *Rose-Garden* and his *Garden of Fragrance*, in which he taught ethics from beginning to end. In this period great poets were born, one after another, but after that they ceased.

What gave rise to this subtle, deep, and symbolical poetry was the fact that the Persian rulers suppressed all free thought and utterance; and therefore the great philosophers who felt a deep inspiration and also an urge to interpret the secret of life by the means of words, had to look for some way in which they could express themselves. In the end they found it, and that way was by expressing their philosophical ideas in the form of lyrics. This gave birth to a new form of art. It was like painting: all poetry became a picture of life; with different lights and shades and colours the poets composed pictures of the various aspects of human life. That is why Persian poetry has always been known as an individual, a unique, and a most wonderful and beautiful art. It is still considered to be so, though that inspiration seems to have vanished a long time ago.

The poetic wave from Persia came to India, and it was with this wave that the poetry of India changed its character. The Hindus, who have always been exclusive and remote, and followers of tradition, did not at first adopt the Persian form, so that in India two different aspects of poetry were developed. One aspect was the poetry written in one of the Prakrits, the vernaculars which had superseded Sanskrit both as a spoken language and in some forms of literature. It is said that the Prakrit languages were formed by Yogi powers and spiritual inspiration. The poets expressed wonderful ideas in Prakrit poetry, and they generally followed the same metres as in Sanskrit; they used many Sanskrit words, although the languages as a whole were Prakrits. Only in rhythm a new form was introduced, in which the vowels attached to different consonant letters were not heeded any more,[1] and words and ideas were arranged so as to follow only the beat of the rhythm. In this way they were quite free to express themselves as long as they could beat the time in their minds, without being tied to the rigid system of syllables prevalent in Sanskrit poetry, as explained in the previous chapter.

There is an amusing story about two great Hindustani poets whose habit it was to speak in poetry. Poets who were able to do this were called *Shigrakavi*. One of them came to the village where the other poet was living; and one was very thin while the other was very stout. The fat one asked the thin one, in verse, if he was well. And the other answered, 'The temple which is meant for God to live in does not need flesh; one must be thankful that there are bones!' And he added, 'But you look quite well.' Whereupon the stout poet answered, 'When I had not yet found my beloved I also was thin, but the moment my beloved had come to me I became fat.'

The other aspect was the poetry written in Urdu-Hindustani which developed later. With the birth of this language poets found a great facility in expressing their souls, for it was composed of many languages, and this gave them a vast scope of expression. There were perhaps ten words for the sun and about twenty for the moon, and there was a great variety of expressions for any idea. In one way this made poetry easier, but in another way more difficult: easy for the gifted ones and difficult for those who wanted to make poetry mechanically, because the choice of words is not an easy thing. When there is a variety of objects in a shop it is difficult to make a choice, and to make a choice of words demands greater inspiration.

The poetry of Persia was enriched by the ideas of the Sufis, and Hindustani poetry was also developed by the same Sufi influence.

[1] Hazrat Inayat Khan refers to a peculiarity of Dev Nagari and similar scripts used in Sanskrit and Prakrit literature.

Many of the great Hindustani poets were Sufis, and there was no end to their success; the whole country was in ecstasy over their poems. It grew to such an extent that in conversation every literate man quoted verses from some well-known poet. This custom exists even today; an educated man when he is conversing even for a short time with another of his kind will always quote a few verses. In this way he uses the words of the poets to support his arguments.

When we look at the other side of the world, the Greeks of ancient times were as great in their poetry as they were in art. Every race that reaches a higher consciousness shows signs of its development in the form of art, music, and poetry. Greek poetry, therefore, will always remain an inspiration for poets and lovers of wisdom. Latin poetry too contained a great deal of mysticism. And in spite of the great gap of years, Dante showed the flame of the same inspiration which was so apparent in antiquity. It is most wonderful to see that in the same period on the one hand there should be such a wave of poetic inspiration in Persia, and on the other Dante should renew the art of poetry in Italy.

As we go further we find that from poetry came dramatic art, which became so highly developed in the time of Shakespeare. In his work we recognize the flame in spite of some passages of darkness. We can feel in the words of Shakespeare the ancient voice of the prophets. Whether people dwell in the East or in the West, in reality they come neither from the East nor from the West; nor do they go in the end either to the East or to the West. The source and goal are the same, and so is inspiration. And whoever reaches the truth and realizes the truth, whether in the East or in the West, realizes the same truth; the guidance comes from the same Spirit of Guidance. It seems as if there is weight in every word of Shakespeare, as if behind every word there is something else; and the more one thinks about it, the more one sees that his words are a kind of veil, hiding what is behind them. Added to this there is great dignity in Shakespeare's work.

When we come to modern poetry, we see that there have been symbologists and expressionists and other schools, but it seems that it will take a long time before the poets will reach the real symbols, before they will become real symbologists. Symbolism is born of an unconscious feeling which springs from intuition. When this happens, then the symbolism which the poet or artist has expressed in words or in some other form, inspires even the one who has expressed it.

A poet was once reading a very deep poem, a symbolical poem, written by a friend of his. And when he saw his friend he said, 'What a wonderful poem! I was so impressed by its symbology. Will you explain to me what you meant by this line?' And the poet looked at him and said, 'Really, I cannot tell myself what it means.' When a poet writes mystical poetry and he himself is unconscious of his mysticism, then his mind must be a machine. Indeed, an obsessed poet can do this; but then it is some other poet who composes and he is only the pen. The poet writes what his soul dictates, and he writes according to the evolution of his soul.

No doubt in modern times much thought is given to rhythm, but on the other hand there are many poets who want to free themselves from rhythm. Both inclinations are right if they are used rightly. If rhythm binds one's thought and ideas and holds them back, it is just as well to be free from this bondage; but at the same time one should not forget that rhythm comes from the dancing of the soul. When the soul begins to dance, every word, every expression of a person becomes rhythmic. Rhythm, therefore, must not be forgotten, for rhythm inspires other souls also to dance.

Modern writers have a tendency to seek the expression of power rather than of beauty. When birds turn into animals, which happens according to certain theories, they become heavy and dense; and in the same way people, after having sought beauty, may turn into pursuers of power. Seeking beauty means going upward, but pursuing power means going downward; and when the birds come down the sparrows turn into barnyard fowls. It is owing to the materialism and commercialism of our time that poets are becoming more dense. Also, nowadays there are so many writers and so few poets. This itself shows that instead of going upward we are going downward.

One day I was introduced to a very well-known poet by a friend, immediately after I had given a lecture. And this poet asked me, 'Is it really true that inspiration is required for poetry?' He, a well-known poet, did not believe in inspiration. And I met another poet who had made a great name for himself, but neither his expression nor his movements, words, or thoughts showed any sign of his being a poet. Why was this so? Because to become well known and enjoy momentary success, a man nowadays has to come down to the lowest mentality; that is what makes him a great man in the eyes of the people today. But it is a mistake. Why must one impress common people? It is better to impress the best people, the people with the purest mentality and highest spirit, and let the others appreciate what is shallow. In this way one can raise the ordinary people to a higher standard instead of stooping to reach them on their own level.

In New York a newspaper reporter came to see me and asked questions for half an hour, questions on philosophy and mysticism, and I was so interested in the questions he asked that I answered them extensively. Finally the journalist said, 'How shall I put all these things that you have told me to the man in the street?' I said, 'If you have come here in order to put these ideas to the man in the street, please do not use any of them; just put what you like.' And so he did.

Poetry is the dance of the soul; and when from a poet's heart an inspiration wells up and he writes it down, even his prose will be poetry. But it is difficult for a writer of prose to write poetry, for it is not his line. Life has become so mechanical for us. We are thrown into this struggle of life from morning till evening; everywhere we turn we are caught up in a certain mechanism; and the depth of life, the high imagination, the lofty ideal, all seem to be missing. It is because of our everyday life. Under such conditions, what happens is that those who are really talented and worthy of praise are not noticed; only those who succeed in making an appeal to the most ordinary mentality are well known. No doubt this will not last and a change will come; but it can only come when the readers of poetry change. It seems that general education conceals the beauty of the art of poetry, because education is principally given for commercial purposes: to fit a man to protect his own interests in his worldly struggles. How can such a man appreciate poetry? And it is not only so in the West; in the East it is still worse. Poets have died of hunger for many, many years. Very few Rajas today have any appreciation of poetry, and the general public is not developed enough to appreciate it; therefore a good poet must die of hunger and only those who can make an appeal to the general public are successful.

But by their success the mentality of the whole race is being lowered. The day when education takes another form and is given with another ideal, the poetry of the world will change also. In order to write poetry or appreciate poetry, the poetic spirit must be awakened. It is not that the human race has lost inspiration, but that it is not awakened. The spirit today is awakened to business, but when it comes to higher ideals and principles, beautiful imagery, wonderful symbols, depth of thought and feeling, then it seems that the race is not making any progress. And this should be remembered: that the day when poetry improves and becomes more appreciated and more instructive and illuminating, that day we shall see and feel the promise for the human race to go forward once more.

CHAPTER XIV

MUSIC (1)

IN ALL AGES the thoughtful have called music the celestial art. Artists have pictured the angels playing on harps; and this teaches us that the soul comes on earth with the love of music. In Arabia there is a story that when God commanded the soul to enter the body, the soul refused saying that this body seemed to it a prison. Then God asked the angels to sing and dance; and as the soul heard this music it was moved to ecstasy, and in that ecstasy it entered the physical body. It is an odd story, and yet it gives the key to the secret of music: that it is not after being born on earth that man learns to love music, but that the soul was already enthralled by music before it came to earth. And if one asks why then every soul does not love music, the answer is that there are many souls which are buried. They are alive, yet they are buried in the denseness of the earth; and therefore they cannot appreciate music. But in that case they are not able to appreciate anything else, for music is the first and the last thing to appeal to every soul.

The heaven of the Hindus, Indra Loka, is filled with singers. The male singers are called Gandharvas, and the female singers Upsaras. In Hindu symbology music seemed the best symbol to express paradise with.

Why does music appeal so much to man? The whole of manifestation has its origin in vibration, in sound; and this sound, which is called Nada in the Vedanta, was the first manifestation of the universe. Consequently the human body was made of tone and rhythm. The most important thing in the physical body is breath, and the breath is audible; it is most audible in the form of voice. This shows that the principal signs of life in the physical body are tone and rhythm, which together make music. Rhythm appeals to man because there is a rhythm going on in his body. The beating of the pulse and the movement of the heart both indicate this rhythm.

The rhythm of the mind has an effect upon this rhythm which is going on continually in the body, and in accordance with its influence it affects the physical body. The notes appeal to a person because of the breath; breath is sound and its vibrations reach every part of the body, keeping it alive. Therefore, in having an effect on the vibrations and on the atoms of the body, sound gives us a sensation.

This is only an explanation of the appeal of music to the physical body, but music reaches further than the physical body; it only depends on what kind of music it is. There is a tradition that the first language in the world consisted of music; after that a language of words came into being. Even now among primitive races there is a language of sounds; also, the more musical languages of the world are more expressive, whereas the languages which have less music in them are less so. It is not only words that convey a meaning; very often the tone of the voice conveys it much better, and sometimes the same word can have two or more meanings depending on the tone in which it is spoken.

It is said that Shiva, or Mahadeva, was the first inventor of a musical instrument. When he was wandering about in the forest, engrossed in his spiritual attainment, he wanted to have some source of amusement, a change in his meditative life; and so he took a piece of bamboo and two gourds, which he attached to the bamboo; and the strings he made out of animal guts. When he had fixed these on the instrument he had invented the vina; that is why the Hindus call the vina a sacred instrument, and for many years they did not allow any strings except gut-strings to be used. Afterwards this instrument was improved and made more refined, and now steel strings are mostly used; but the reason why gut-string is appealing to the human soul, is that it comes from a living body, and even after being separated from the body it still cries out, 'I am alive!' Thus the violin gives out a more living sound than the piano. The piano may drown the violin, but the life that comes from the gut-string manifests as a voice.

There is a Chinese legend which says that the first music was played on little pieces of reed. The great musician of ancient times who introduced music in China, made holes in a piece of reed at a certain distance from each other, the distance between two fingers; and so the flute of reed came into being. From this came the scale of five notes: one note was the original note produced by the reed, and the four other notes were made by placing the fingers on the holes. Afterwards many other scales were developed.

Hindu philosophy distinguishes four different cycles of humanity, of the human race: Krita Yug, the Golden Age; Treta Yug, the Silver Age; Dvapar Yug, the Copper Age; and Kali Yug, the Iron Age. This cycle in which we are living now is the Iron Age. In the Golden Age there was the music of the soul, a music that appealed to the soul itself and that raised it to cosmic consciousness, the music of the angels, the music which was healing and soothing. And the music of the Silver Age was the music of the heart, the music which appealed to the depths of the heart, creating sympathy and love of nature, inspiring man and helping the heart quality to develop. The music of the Copper Age appealed to the mind, to the intellect, so that one could understand the intricacies of musical science, the difference between the many scales, the quality of the rhythm. Finally the music that belongs to the Iron Age has an influence on the physical body; it helps the soldiers to march and moves people to dance.

A story told in India illustrates this idea. At the court of the last emperor, Mohammad Shah, a singer came who had invented a new way of composing. And when this man sang his new compositions, he won the admiration and praise of everyone at the court. The singers and musicians were simply amazed to think that there could be a new development in music. But one of the old musicians who was present said, 'If your Majesty will pardon me I would like to say a word. There is no doubt that this is most beautiful music, and it has won the admiration of all those present, and also my own. But I must tell you that from this day the music of the country, instead of going upward will go downward, because the music which was handed down to us has weight, it has substance, but now it seems that this has been lost and that the music has become lighter. Therefore from now on it will go downward.' And so it happened; step by step after that the music was brought down.

A well-known writer said, 'There are four intoxications: the intoxication of physical strength, the intoxication of wealth, the intoxication of power; but when it comes to comparing these three with the fourth, the intoxication of music, they are all as nothing'.

One day the Emperor Akbar said to his chief singer, Tansen, 'You are such a great singer and there is such wonderful magic in your voice, I wonder how great your teacher must have been.' 'Please,' Tansen said, 'never compare me to my teacher, there is no comparison.' Akbar said, 'Is your teacher then so great? Is he still alive?' Tansen said, 'Yes, he is living dead.' 'Where can one find him?' asked the emperor. 'I should like to hear him.' Tansen said, 'I will try, but I am afraid that his spirit might revolt if he saw that he had to sing before the emperor.' Then Akbar said, 'I shall come disguised as your servant.' Tansen said, 'In that case, it might be possible.'

Akbar went with Tansen, and after travelling a long way they found this teacher in the mountains, in solitude. Although Akbar was dressed as a servant the sage recognized him; still, the emperor's humble attitude appealed to him. And then he sang, and both Akbar and Tansen became spellbound; the sphere of the earth was lost from their consciousness.

When they came to their senses they saw that the sage was not there any more. 'Where is he?' asked Akbar. Tansen said, 'He has left this place for ever, fearing that we might come again and trouble him.' Akbar could not say one word in praise of the music he had heard.

After their return to the palace, one day the emperor said, 'Tansen, I feel such a longing to hear him again!' Tansen said, 'We can never find him again now that he has left that place.' 'But,' said Akbar, 'I feel so restless, I long so much to hear that voice again. Do you not know that raga which he sang?' Tansen said that he did know the raga and began to sing it. But when he had finished the emperor said, 'It is not the same. Why is it?' And Tansen felt hurt and said, 'It is because I sing before you, but my teacher sings before God!'

This incident awakened in Tansen's heart such a feeling of independence that he saluted the emperor and bade him goodbye. He saw that the source of his imperfection was the relationship he had with the court; and he could no longer bear it. And so he left, and the rest of his life he wandered through the country and led a meditative life.

The stories told about singers who could charm the birds and the animals, and about the miracles that were performed through the power of their music, are not only stories. Music can do even more than that; tone and rhythm are the source of the whole of manifestation.

CHAPTER XV

MUSIC (2)

THE ANCIENT Greek music seems to have been largely the same as the music of the East. The Greeks had certain scales like the ragas in India, which also resembled the Persian scales. In this way there was a similarity in the music of the human race; but there came a division between the music of the East and of the West when the Western music, especially the German, progressed in another direction. In the traditions and the history of the world, as far as one can trace, one finds that melody was considered the principal thing in the East as well as in the West; and the composers, according to their stage of evolution, enriched this melody as much as they could. At first the melodies were chiefly folksongs, but sometimes also more elaborate compositions, and as such they were the expression of the soul. They were not compositions in the sense of modern, more technical, compositions; they were in reality imaginations. An artist made a melody, and that melody became known after he had sung or played it; and then it was taken up by others. In this way one melody was sung by perhaps ten different musicians in various ways, each retaining his liberty in singing that melody. No doubt it was difficult even to recognize the same melody after four or five persons had sung or played it, yet each of these had his freedom of expression, right or wrong.

Music in the East was based on ragas, which means a certain arrangement of notes, a theme which was recognized and distinguished as a certain raga. These ragas were composed by four different classes of people: by those who studied and practised folk-songs, and out of these folk-songs arranged certain themes or ragas; by mathematicians who mathematically worked out many hundreds of ragas; by poets and dramatists who composed ragas and their wives, raginis, as well as sons, daughters, and daughters- and sons-in-law, creating in this way families of ragas in their imagination; and finally by musicians who out of the three above-mentioned kinds of ragas composed new ones with their musical gift. On these ragas the music of India was based.

The credit for every song a musician sang and for every theme he played went to him, because while the theme might consist of only four or eight bars, he improvised extensively on it and made it more interesting. Therefore a performer in India had at the same time to be a composer, although in these improvisations due consideration was given to the original theme and rhythm of the raga, so that the audience might be able to recognize it. Even to-day, if a musician sings a raga which is not exactly as it ought to be, there may be someone among the audience who while not knowing precisely what is wrong will yet feel immediately that it does not sound right; just as in Italy when an opera singer makes one little mistake, someone from the audience will immediately show his disapproval. This is because the music of the opera has become engraved upon the spirit of the lovers of opera, and as soon as it seems slightly different from what they are accustomed to hear they know there is something wrong.

But what is most remarkable is that the mystics played such an important part in the development of Indian music. They used it for their meditation, as it was invented and taught by Mahadeva. Music is the most wonderful way to spiritual realization; there is no quicker and no surer way of attaining spiritual perfection than through music. The great Indian mystics such as Narada and Tumbara were singers; Krishna played the flute; and thus music in its tradition and practice has always been connected with mysticism. Musicians have always held to the principle that modern scientists have rediscovered: that the ear is incapable of fully enjoying two sounds played or sung together, and that is why they enriched the melody to such an extent for the purpose of their meditation.

When Persian music, with its artistry and beauty, was brought to India, it was wedded to Indian music; and there resulted a most wonderful art. The desire of the people of all classes and ages has always been and still is, that music, no matter whether it is technical or non-technical, theoretical or non-theoretical, should touch the soul deeply. If it does not do so, the technical, theoretical, and scientific side of it does not appeal to them. Therefore it has often been very difficult even for the great masters of music who had developed the technique and science of music, and who were masters of rhythm and tone, to please the audience; because the audience, from the king to the man in the street, everyone, wants only one thing, and that is a great appeal to the soul from the voice, from the word, from melody. Everything expressed in music should appeal to the soul; and this is true even to the extent that when a beggar in the street does not sing a song that appeals to the passers-by, he will not get as many pennies as another who is more appealing.

No doubt the music of India has changed much during the last century. That which the Indians call classical music, or music with weight and substance, is not patronized any more, because of the ignorance of most of the princes and potentates of the country, and therefore the best music is no longer understood. Then people have taken to smoking and talking while listening to music, and music was not made for that. It seems that the spirit of the great musicians is dead; for a great vina player, who considered his instrument sacred and who worshipped it before taking it in his hand, practising and playing it for perhaps ten hours a day, regarded music as his religion. But if he had to play before people who are moving about, smoking, talking with other people as at a social gathering, then all his music would go to the winds. It was the sacredness with which the people of ancient times invested music that kept it on a higher level.

When Tansen, the great singer, left the court, hurt by a remark of the Emperor Akbar, as was related in the previous chapter, he went to Rewa, a state in central India; and when the Maharaja of Rewa heard that Tansen was coming he was perplexed, wondering in what way he should honour him. A chair was sent for Tansen, to bring him to the palace, and when he arrived Tansen expected the Maharaja at least to receive him at the door. So as soon as he got out of the chair he said, 'Where is the Maharaja?' and the man whom he asked replied, 'Here is the Maharaja!' pointing to the one who had been carrying the chair all through the city. Tansen was most touched, and he said, 'You could not have given me a greater reward.' From that day Tansen saluted him with his right hand, saying, 'This hand will never salute anyone else all my life.' And so it was. Tansen would not even salute the emperor with his right hand. Such was the appreciation, the acknowledgment of talent in ancient India.

Now a new music has come to India which is called theatrical music. It is neither Eastern nor Western; it is a very peculiar music. The themes of march and galop and polka, and airs which no one wants to hear any more in the Western world, are imitated, and an Indian twist is given to them. Thus they are spoilt for the ears of the Western listener and also for good Eastern ears. Since the masses have not been educated in the best music and for them there is only one source of entertainment, the theatre, they are becoming as fond of this music as they are of jazz in America.

Pope Gregory I, after whom the Gregorian scales are named, co-ordinated those beautiful melodies which had come from ancient Greece via Byzantium to form the religious music of the Church. This is all that remains as a relic of the music of those times, though one finds traces of this Gregorian music in the compositions of the seventeenth and early eighteenth centuries— for instance in Handel's *Messiah*; later composers, however, created a type of music which was quite different. No doubt in this way they laid the foundation for Western music and helped it to evolve, but evolve in what way? Mechanically. They were able to make use of large bands, either brass bands or string bands, and also of an orchestra in which hundreds of instruments could be played at the same time. This naturally made a great impression, and it gave the world of music much opportunity and scope for the development and evolution of music. Nevertheless, there was one thing which was lost and which is being lost more and more every day: the appeal to the soul, which is the main purpose of music.

Debussy was looking all his life for something new to introduce into modern music; and Scriabin once told me personally, 'Something is missing in our music, it has become so mechanical. The whole process of composition nowadays is mechanical; how can we introduce a spirit into it?' And I have often thought that if Scriabin, with his fine character and beautiful personality, had lived longer, he could have introduced a new strain of music into the modern world.

Will someone else try to do what Scriabin wanted? When there is a need, if there is a real desire for its fulfilment, it must come. It only seems that we do not need it enough; that is the difficulty. We become so easily contented with what we have. If the world feels a greater need for a better kind of music, then it will come; but if people mostly enjoy jazz, and if that is sufficient for them, then naturally it will only come slowly, because so few want anything better.

The music of the future will be different from the music of the past in this way: the ancient music developed only in one direction, and that was that every instrument was played alone and every song was sung alone; there was no other instrument or voice. And the modern development is that there is a variety of voices and there are many instruments playing together; the development of music in this direction has its origin in what is recognized as classical music. It certainly has its value, but on the other hand something has also been lost. In order to make music perfect, its ancient aspect should be developed more.

There is music which makes one feel like jumping and dancing; there is music which makes one feel like laughing and smiling; and then there is music which makes one feel like shedding tears. If one were to ask a thoughtful person which he preferred, no doubt he would say, 'The last, the music which brings tears'. Why does the soul want sad music? Because that is the only time when the soul is touched. The other music, the music which reaches no further than the surface of one's being, remains only on the surface. It is the music that reaches to the depths of one's being which touches the soul. The deeper the music reaches, the more contented is the soul. No doubt a person who is very cheerful and has had dinner and a glass of wine could be quite happy with some dance music. But then he need not have serious music, for him jazz will be quite sufficient.

The modern revival of folk-music is an effort in the right direction. But it should be carried out without spoiling the folk-music; for the tendency of most composers is to take this music and then put too much of their own touch into it. If, however, they can preserve the folk-music without spoiling it, it will be something worth while. Composers sometimes take folk-music and attach modern harmony to it, and this spoils it too, for generally folk-music is the expression of the soul of that particular time when there was no harmonization such as there is now. And the modern method of harmonization, when it is applied to folk-music, takes away its original atmosphere.

We can observe two principal tendencies in modern music. One is the tendency to make the music of our time more natural, and in that way to improve it. And this can surely be developed more and more, as there will be a greater appreciation of solo music, for instance of the 'cello or the violin. Musicians will again go back to the ancient idea of one instrument playing or one voice singing at a time. And when they again come to the full appreciation of this idea, they will reach the spiritual stage of musical perfection. People today like music which has more than one voice because they do not listen enough to solo music. But the more they hear it and the closer they come to it, the more they will forget the other kind. There are big symphony concerts given in the concert-halls of London, New York, Paris, and all the large cities, but if one notices carefully what the audience likes best, it will be a solo on the 'cello, on the flute, or on the violin.

People are accustomed to hear music of many sounds, and after the solo concert is over they will enjoy the other kind of music; but in the depths of their being they will surely still prefer the solo music, for the human soul is the same now as in ancient times, and the same in the East as in the West. The ringing of one bell has a greater appeal than the ringing of many bells. One sound always goes deeper than many sounds. The reason why two sounds are in conflict with each other is that however much they are tuned to one another, yet they are two, and that in itself is a conflict.

But then there is another tendency which is working hand in hand with this one, and which is dragging music downward. And that tendency is that the composers are not contented with the chords that the great masters such as Mozart or Beethoven or Wagner have used in their music, but they are inventing new chords, chords which tend to confuse thousands of listeners. And what will be the outcome of this? It will have an unconscious effect upon the nervous system of humanity; it will make people more and more nervous. And as we often see that those who attend good concerts only go there out of vanity, they will accept any kind of music. But, as Wagner has said, noise is not necessarily music. It is not the newness of the music which will give satisfaction in the end; it will not do any good to the souls who have gone to the concert-hall only to satisfy their vanity. Music should be healing, music should uplift the soul, music should inspire; then there is no better way of getting closer to God, of rising higher towards the spirit, of attaining spiritual perfection, than music, if only it is rightly understood.

CHAPTER XVI

DRAMA

WHEN ONE thinks deeply about the origin of drama one finds that drama belongs to the origin of life itself; that not only has man invented dramatic art, but that God has produced a play in the form of this manifestation. Very often inquiring souls raise the question why, if God is kind and loving and merciful, must there be these tragedies in life, suffering, disappointments, and failures. And the best answer that could be given to this question is that He has arranged this play. Would we say that it is unkind to give someone the part of the victim in a play, or that it is wrong of the producer to give an actor the part of a murderer? But when we look at it as a play, we see that all these different parts are given in order to produce one effect, in order to get to the essence. For every character in the play, from beginning to end, the king and the slave, the murderer and his victim, the lover and the one who hates, the cruel one and the one who is kind-hearted, the one who is just and the other who is unjust—they are all helping to produce one ultimate effect, and it is for this effect that the whole play has been arranged.

It is the same with God and the creation. The whole of manifestation is arranged, with all its desirable and undesirable aspects, with its right and wrong, and with all the kindness and cruelty that we see on the surface of this earth; all this produces in the end one single effect for which the whole play was made. One might say that if this is only a play then it is nothing, but if this is nothing then there is nothing else that we can call anything. If anything exists at all, it is this manifestation; one may call it everything or nothing, as one wishes.

When we trace the origin of dramatic plays back to the Sanskrit age, we find that religious ceremonies and rituals first took place in order to give human beings the impression which they needed for their development: to console them, to bless them, to reveal the truth gradually to them; for everything that was necessary for their development was given to them in the form of ceremonies or rituals. Then the same tendency took another form, and the result was the putting on the stage of the palace, the court, the king, and the courtiers; and later the officers and soldiers of the army were added. It was all a production, but a production for a purpose, for in life drama is necessary; life is a drama and it needs drama.

When we consider our own individual life, is it not a drama? In the dream a play is performed; for hours on end a certain life is experienced, but when the eyes are opened the curtain has fallen and the play is over. That which was real at that moment becomes a dream as soon as the eyes are open and the sun has risen.

The ancient drama was performed by reciting, singing, playing music, and acting. One man told a tale and acted it at the same time, helped by those around him; and in this way it developed into a form of story-telling. Man's artistic sense embellished it more every day, to make it as pleasing as possible to the eyes and ears. The great Hindu scriptures of Valmiki became most popular, because they presented philosophy and religion in the form of tragedy; and that tragedy was then performed by those who were capable of giving full expression to it. The dramas of Kalidasa, the great Indian playwright of the Sanskrit age, have always appealed to the Hindus as dramas of most wonderful character and ideal. As later in the dramas of Shakespeare, we find in them great substance and the full expression of character.

In opera much of the ideas and of the plot is sacrificed in order to make continual singing possible. The result is somewhat unnatural. On the stage when a man is happy he sings; and when a man is sad he also sings; whether a man is anxious or at peace, from beginning to end he is singing. No doubt it is most interesting to hear singing all the time, but it is also one-sided, it does not give one a full idea of the play; it only gives one an occasion to hear singing.

It seems that the more material humanity has become, the more superficial is the drama of today. And in comedy every attempt is made to amuse the man in the street. Imagine a play during which the audience has to laugh from the beginning to the end! What can a play like that teach mankind? There is a roar of laughter all through the play, and hundreds and thousands of people come to see it and to become hysterical in the end. That was not the idea of the theatre. The idea of the theatre was to awaken man from his intoxication of life, and to make him realize life's deeper aspects, showing him an aspect which was hidden from his eyes, so that his eyes might be opened and he might see it; that was the object of drama and the theatre.

There is a feeling, called *Vairagya* in Sanskrit, which is produced by throwing a full light upon life, and this Vairagya was the central theme of the ancient playwrights. Among the Greeks there was a custom that in the midst of a feast a mummy was brought into the assembly; the idea was that when people were enjoying life and drinking and playing, intoxicated with life, one brought before them something to distract their mind from the pleasure and joy of the surface of life, and to draw their attention to its beginning and end, and to its reality. That was the real purpose of drama: that men who are busy in their factories and offices and industries, or with their studies, might have an opportunity to look at life from another point of view; that they might be able to see more clearly those sides of life which are veiled from their eyes because of their everyday occupations.

Nowadays there is not only the theatre, but in addition there are moving pictures; and they are only for distraction and to pass the time. And in that distraction the degenerate side of life is shown, so that very often children and young people get wrong impressions. Hundreds and thousands of people go to see these plays, but what do they gain? In fact it is a great loss. Life was already so material, and the cinema makes it even more so.

At the same time we see that the theatres and opera-houses and music-halls are built more splendidly than ever before in the whole history of humanity. The stage is so cleverly illuminated and the scenery is made to appear so real, that one can say that never in the world has there been such an advance in this field as today. It is wonderful to observe how anxious are the artists to do their best on the stage, and also the talent of acting is far developed. If only in the artistic world, and especially in the world of actors, a spiritual ideal could be introduced, if their interest could be drawn to the real side of life, they could render a very great service to mankind at this day when the stage is a central object of interest to humanity.

One cannot say what the future will be. But as today one sees such numbers of people quite satisfied with what they get at the theatre, and as very little effort, or none at all, seems to be made to deepen the dramatic ideal, it must obviously take some time to introduce a spiritual ideal. But with the development of art, literature, music, and poetry, drama will also develop in its own time; and the development of drama will become a most important factor in the evolution of humanity.

The effort that a playwright makes today is to show the present condition of life to the world. But the present condition of life is already known; it need not be shown again. People see it from morning till evening; the street, the café, the station, the train, all these things they see and none of these are new to them. Giving the picture of life as everyone sees it all day long is not helpful. One should bring before the people the sides of life which are hidden from the generality and which can help them in their evolution; then no doubt drama would take an important place in education.

When one speaks to people on this subject, they say, 'People do not like to have anything philosophical in a play, because if they want to learn philosophy they will read books. They do not want anything religious; if they want religion they will go to church.' Then what do they want? Pastime. But those who never open a book of philosophy and yet for whom philosophy would be very helpful in their lives, can be benefited by a little touch of philosophy in the play. At the same time, whether it is the church or the stage, whenever wisdom is given it helps humanity. It does not matter in which way it is given.

Plays today are made as if in a mould, and if they are not made according to this mould, then it is not considered to be good playwriting. But an ideal is something which cannot be confined to a mould, which cannot be limited to a certain design or a certain form. The higher the ideal is the larger the scope it requires, and it cannot be accommodated in a small design or form. Not only drama, but also music and poetry often suffer because of a fixed mould that is forced upon the composer or the poet. The production of art has become material. Whether it is poetry, music, or drama, it can only be true art, really inspired art, when it is made just as it comes, and when it is also completed in that way.

THE PROBLEM OF THE DAY

CONTENTS

CHAPTER I

THE PROBLEM OF THE DAY (1)

THE HUSTLE and bustle of life leaves a man very little time to think of his general condition. The only news he receives is from the newspapers, and so he depends upon the papers for his ideas; and the intoxication of life leaves him very little time to think about the real meaning of life. When he looks around him and considers the condition of the nations today, he finds that in spite of all the progress there is an increase in ill-feeling between them. Friendship exists only for self-interest. A nation only thinks about its own interest whether it has to deal with friend or enemy; and if he considers the world as a body, he can say that poison has been put into its heart, owing to the hatred which people feel towards one another.

No period like this can be traced in the history of the world; this age has accomplished a much greater destruction than ever before. It reminds one of a spider, which weaves its web for its own comfort but cannot get out of the web it has made for itself. And if one goes to the root of this subject one sees that all this disorder has been caused by the spirit of materialism. Money seems to be the only gain and the only aim. It is undeniable that when one is continually thinking of such a subject all one's thoughts and energy will go in that direction, and perhaps in the end man awakens and finds that all his life he has given his thoughts to something which does not last, which does not even exist, and which is only an illusion.

No doubt this pessimism is the bridge from one optimism to another, and it may be said to be disinterestedness, or *Vairagya*, as it is called in Vedanta terms. It is not the man who leaves the world who is great, but the one who lives in the world, understanding the difficulties and troubles that belong to humanity. It is he who sees not his little self, but the whole. Jesus Christ taught us to think of our fellow-men, to love our fellow-men. And what do we see today? Difficulties arising between masters and workmen;

peace conferences where nothing can be decided concerning peace. And all this because the point of view is not there which makes people say, 'I will do something for you and you will do something for me.' 'No,' says everyone, 'I will look after myself and you will look after yourself.' To serve one another, to love one another, to work for one another, should be the aim of life, but man has lost hold of it altogether.

Look at the central theme of the education of today. Only a short time is given to the child to prepare him for the kingliness of life and the freedom of the spirit. And when the child's intellect grows, every year more and more it sees life before it like an ocean which it has to cross, like something dark awaiting it. And later when the child has become a man, he gives all his time to his work, to his office, and there is no time even for love or friendship; yet at the end he cannot take all these things with him. After sacrificing all his life to these things, what has he really gained? Through his external life in the world the complications of life have only increased.

In spite of all the progress of modern civilization that has been made in all departments of life, such as commerce, industry, politics, and economics, the question still remains whether we have really progressed. If one observes the superficiality of the life which man lives today in the so-called civilized parts of the world, one will certainly find that he is far removed from nature both within and without, and he has become an exile from the ideal state of life. The more laws that are made, the more crimes are committed; the more mechanisms that are prepared, the more work increases, and yet little is being done; the more lawsuits that are brought in court, the more cases occur; the more physicians, the more diseases. Cupidity has come to the fore so that whether one has an aristocratic or a democratic system, justice seems to be absent.

Also, in spite of the regard for the rights of women which have been established in this age, woman's responsibility in life has much increased. She has to fight her battle in the open field, which naturally exhausts her energy and courage, causing her to lose her inherently fine nature as she has constantly to rub against the rough edges of life. The prejudice, hatred, and distrust that exist between nations whether friends or foes, every nation being absorbed in its own interest regardless of the people in general, have reflected on the mentality of individuals and have made life difficult for both rich and poor. Everywhere one turns one sees material strife; every ideal, every principle has to be sacrificed for it. And yet no man can be deprived of his human inheritance. There is a treasure in himself which has to be found. Religion should have helped man, but the religious authorities have very often failed to uphold the inner qualities of their religion. The question is not what religion one follows, but how to live one's religion. When religion has lost its hold on inner life and faith, there is nothing left. Many people, especially among the intellectuals, have lost their religion, and among the younger ones there are a good many who even dread the name of God.

What is needed today is an education which will teach humanity to feel the essence of their religion in everyday life. Man is not put on this earth to be an angel. He need not be praying in church all day long, nor go into the wilderness. He needs only to understand life better. He must learn to set apart a certain time in the day to think about his own life and doings. He must ask himself, 'Have I done an honest deed today? Have I proved myself worthy in that place, in that capacity?' In this way he can make his everyday life a prayer. Among politicians, doctors, lawyers, merchants it might be possible to have love as the battery behind every deed, every action, together with a sense of harmony behind all these activities.

We need today the religion of tolerance. In daily life we cannot all meet on the same ground, being so different, having such different capacities, states of evolution, and tasks. So if we had no tolerance, no desire to forgive, we could never bring harmony into our soul; for to live in the world is not easy and every moment of the day demands a victory. If there is anything to learn it is this tolerance, and by teaching this simple religion of tolerance to one another we are helping the world. It is no use to hold on to the idea that the world is going from bad to worse, that the germs of disease will spread and bring greater calamities. Every man's being is good; in the depths of his heart there is something definitely good.

There are teachings about healing, but the best way is the way of character healing, healing one's own character; in this way instead of accomplishing miracles, one's whole life can become a miracle. The lack of religion today has created strange beliefs about communicating with ghosts or fairies, and things one does not and cannot understand; but all this has very little to do with religion. The Bible is full of simple things and one would be happy if one could accomplish one of them. There has been a great demand for knowledge and for occult powers, but with all his intellectuality what has man achieved beyond the destruction of his brother?

The need of the world today is not learning, but how to become considerate towards one another. To try and find out in what way happiness can be brought about, and in this way to realize that peace which is the longing of every soul; and to impart it to others, thereby attaining our life's goal, the sublimity of life.

CHAPTER II

THE PROBLEM OF THE DAY (2)

THERE has been a great upheaval in the world, beginning at the time of the Reformation and culminating in our own times. It seems that there is continual unrest in every direction of life; there seems to be a great turmoil; and in spite of all the progress which has been made during the last years civilization does not seem to have succeeded. The difficulty has been the adjustment of the new idea of democracy to the foundation of aristocracy on which it was based. The outcome of this difficulty is felt now more than ever before; there seems to be confusion and chaos rather than the understanding of how to live life to its best advantage. The reason is that the character of aristocracy and democracy is not generally understood from the point of view of the mystic, and as long as this lack of understanding remains, a thousand democracies or aristocracies would always fail in the end.

When we study nature we find that there is a model of life, a design, for us to follow: the interdependence of the stars and planets and how they are sustained in heaven by each other's magnetism, how the light of the sun functions in the moon and how the light of the sun is reflected by all the different planets, and at the same time how the planets differ in their light and character and how every planet in the universe fulfils the scheme of nature. Call it aristocracy or call it democracy, there is a model of life that nature has produced before our eyes.

To some people the word aristocracy, when not understood, often sounds very unpleasant, but the real aristocracy is not necessarily the picture of its abuse, its degeneration. And what is democracy? Democracy is the fulfilment of aristocracy; in other words democracy means complete aristocracy. But when democracy is sought without aristocracy having been understood, then democracy cannot be fully understood either, for then it is not complete. Man is born in this world ignorant of the kingdom which is within himself, and true aristocracy is the attainment of that kingdom. To recognize that kingdom in another person is aristocracy, and to see the possibility of that kingdom in oneself and to try to fulfil that ideal of life is true democracy. Aristocracy means that one person is king, democracy means that all are kings; but when a person does not know one king, he does not know all kings. What I mean by this is that we should realize that the object of life does not lie in revolting against someone who is more advanced than ourselves, and by this revolt pulling him down to our own level—that is not democracy. Real democracy means recognizing the possibility of advancing just as others have done, trusting in that possibility, and trying to advance to the same level as that of the others.

The problem of the day should be studied by all sections and classes of humanity. It seems that through being absorbed in a more comfortable life, many have neglected their part in all the different aspects of life both at home and outside. There are certain classes who have been unaware of the tasks that life demands at home and in the world; and now the time has come when they meet with difficulties because they find themselves more dependent on the very things which they have neglected in their lives.

They have always shown unwillingness to do certain things which seemed beneath their idea of dignity, and now humanity is being turned upside down; what has happened is that one class is being submerged by the other class and its place is being taken by the other. In this way instead of more comfort chaos is being manifested.

The way out of it would be to imitate some of the ideas of the ancients, for if this is not done, although life will perhaps become settled in a certain way, it will become a hotel life and there will be no more of that joy and happiness and pleasure which is found in home life. The difficulties of modern living will before long bring about a situation where in every district there will be a kind of hotel arrangement, and in that way all individual progress, culture, and joy will be hampered. Man's individual choice will be sacrificed to the mechanism of living.

The method I mentioned which might be followed is a method which was used in ancient times by the Hindus, and even now some part of it exists. Among the different communities of Brahmins, a Brahmin may be in a high position and be very rich, yet he knows how to cook himself. The women in the household, even in the home of the Prime Minister, attend to the kitchen themselves. There is nothing in the home which they do not like to do. In ancient times they were trained to sew, to knit, to weave, and to cook, keeping the house neat, decorating it, cleaning it, painting it, all these things were accomplished by everyone. No one possessed a house at that time who did not know everything about taking care of the house, quite independently of the housekeeper. Perfection of life means perfecting oneself, not only spiritually but in all the different aspects of life. The man who is not capable of attending to all life's needs is certainly ignorant of the true freedom of life.

The more we study the problem of the day, the more we shall realize that it is the strict division of work at the present time that has made people helpless. What is most necessary now is to introduce into education the spirit of providing for oneself all that one needs, and arranging for oneself all that is necessary in one's everyday life. The mechanical life of our times may show progress, yet it is not a complete progress. Imagine a person living from morning till evening in a factory and only making needles! Perhaps he does this for twenty years and what does he know of life? Only how to make a needle. Perhaps the benefit goes to the owner of the factory; but what benefit goes to this man who has been making needles all his life?

The ideal of life and its progress is to become self-sufficient, and the key to the secret of democracy is self-sufficiency. Spiritual perfection is the second step, and the one who has first made himself self-sufficient is entitled in the end to spiritual perfection.

The unrest which one finds throughout the world, the difficulties among the nations, the hatred existing among people, the cry of misery which comes more or less from all sides, the commercial catastrophes, the political problems, all these make one wonder what may be done to find a solution for the general cry of humanity. What happens today is that the different institutions try to extinguish the fires burning here and there, but that can never solve the problem of the world.

The first thing that should be remembered is that all activities of life are connected with each other, and if one does not heed this one finds that while one thing is put in order another thing goes wrong. It is just like a person who is ill and who needs sleep and good diet: if he gets sleep without that diet it will not do him good, nor will a good diet without sleep help him. While trying to straighten out commercial difficulties political problems creep in; while considering the social questions moral difficulties appear. The desire to serve humanity in the work of reconstruction is the duty and responsibility of every sensible soul whatever be his rank or position or qualifications in life; and the first question to be studied is what remedy can be found for all the maladies that manifest on the surface of life today.

There is one principal remedy and that is the changing of the attitude of humanity; it is this alone which can help in all aspects of life. This attitude can be changed by moral, spiritual, and religious advancement, and the work that the Sufi message has to accomplish lies in this particular direction; for it is a method which enables man to have another outlook on life.

The chief thing that the Sufi Movement tries to avoid is sectarianism, which has divided man in all ages of the world's history.

The Sufi message is not opposed to any religion, faith, or belief; it is rather a support to all religions, it is a defence for religions which are attacked by the followers of other religions. At the same time the Sufi Movement provides humanity with that religion which is in reality all religions. The Sufi Movement is not supposed to take the whole of humanity in its arms, yet in the service of the whole of humanity lies the fulfilment of the Sufi message. The Sufi Movement, therefore, does not stand as a barrier between a member and his own religious faith, but as an open door leading to the heart of that faith. A member of the Movement is a bearer of the divine message to the followers of whatever church or sect he may belong to.

The work of the Sufi Movement is not to collect all the rain-water in its own tanks, but to make a way for the stream of the message to flow and to supply water to all the fields of the world. The work of the Sufi message is sowing; reaping we shall leave to humanity to do, for the fields do not belong to our particular Movement; all the fields belong to God. We who are employed to work on this farm of the world must do what we have to do and leave the rest to God. Success we do not trouble about; let those who strive for it seek some other direction. Truth alone is our success, for the only lasting success is truth.

CHAPTER III

WORLD RECONSTRUCTION

ESPECIALLY after a war and the pain that the world has thereby experienced, people begin to think again about the subject of reconstruction. But no doubt every person looks at it according to his own mentality, and in this way the ideas about the reconstruction of the world differ very much.

If we consider the condition of the world as it is today, we see that its financial condition, which is most essential for order and peace, has become so involved that many people of intellect and understanding are helpless before this most difficult problem. No doubt there are those who will tell us that there is no remedy for the betterment of humanity other than the solution of the financial problems; but at the same time it seems that these problems are becoming daily more and more difficult and bringing nations and races and communities towards a greater and greater destruction. Before a solution is reached it will be no wonder if a great deal of damage is done to many nations. And although, absorbed by their own problems, men do not think enough about these things, nevertheless in the end the world in general will realize the weakness, the feebleness caused by this disorder and by the unbalanced condition of the financial world. Nations and people make profit out of the losses of other nations and people, and even if for the moment they may think that they are benefited, in the end they will realize that we human beings, whether as individuals or as a multitude, all depend upon one another. For instance, if because of one part of one's body another part suffers, in the end there will prove to be an unbalanced state, a lack of health in the physical body; and just as health means that all the organs of the body are in good condition, so the health of the world means that all nations, all people, are in a good condition.

Leaving this financial question and coming to the problem of education, in spite of all the progress that has been made in this field, any thoughtful person will be struck by the amount of work which a little child is given to do considering its age and its strength. It seems that in the enthusiasm for making education richer and richer, a load has been heaped upon the minds of the children. And what happens? It is like a dish which was meant to be cooked for half an hour but is being made ready in five minutes. It will perhaps be burnt, or perhaps it is underdone. The child knows too much for its age; it knows what it does not require, what it does not value, what is a load to it, what is forced upon its mind. And how few of us stop to think of this question, that childhood is a kingliness in itself. It is a gift from above that the child is growing and that during the time of its growth it is unaware of the woes and worries and anxieties of life. These are the only days for experiencing the kingliness of life, the days when the child should play, when it should be near to nature, when it should absorb what nature gradually teaches.

The whole of childhood is devoted to study, study of material knowledge; and as soon as the child has grown into a youth, the burden of life is put on its shoulders, a burden which is becoming heavier and heavier for rich and poor. The result of this is that there is strife between the political parties, that there is disagreement between labour and capital; and this life full of struggle to which the child opens its eyes never leaves it time to be one with nature, to dive deep within itself, or to think beyond this life in the crowd.

When we consider the problem of nations we become still more perplexed. The enmity, hatred, and prejudice which exist between one nation and another, and the antagonism and utter selfishness which are the central theme of the relationships and ties between nations, show that the world is going from bad to worse, and unrest seems to be all-pervading. There seems to be no trust between nations, no sympathy, except for their own interest. And what is the outcome of it? Its impression falls as a reflection, as a shadow upon individuals, turning them also towards egoism and selfishness.

Religion was meant to be the safest, the only refuge in the world; but at the present moment, with ever-growing materialism and overwhelming commercialism, religion seems to be fading away. A silent indifference towards religion seems to be increasing, especially in the countries foremost in civilization; and that being so, where can man find the solution of the problem of the day?

We can also consider this question from a philosophical point of view. What is construction and what is reconstruction? A construction is that which is already made. A newborn child is a construction. But after a disorder in the body or in the mind, there comes a need of reconstruction. In English there is an expression: to pull oneself together. The reconstruction of the world today means that the world has to pull itself together. Education, the political, social, and financial condition, religion, all these things which made civilization, seem to have been scattered; and in order that they may come together again, the secret of life must be studied. What is the secret of healing power? It is making oneself strong enough to pull oneself together; and that is the secret of the life of the mystic. The world has lost its health, and if one pictures the world as an individual, one can see what it means to lose one's health. It is just like illness in the life of an individual; and as for every illness there is a remedy, so for every disaster there is a reconstruction.

But people have different ideas. There is a pessimist who says, 'If the world has got to this state of destruction who can help it, how can it be helped?' This is like a person who says, 'Well, I have been so ill, I have suffered so much, I do not care. How can I be well now? It is too late.' In this way he holds on to his disease and he cherishes it, though he does not like it. And then there is the curious person, who is very anxious to look at the newspaper and see whether his investments have gone up or whether they have gone down, and to see whether there is the probability of war; and he will excite his friends about it. Then there is another person who says, 'Committees must be formed, there must be societies and leagues; congresses must be held, and many more meetings, many more discussions.' There seems to be no end to the discussions and disputes in order to find out the ways and means of how to improve conditions!

I do not mean to say that any effort, in whatever form, towards the reconstruction or towards the betterment of conditions is not worth while. But what is most needed is for us to understand that religion of religions and that philosophy of philosophies which is self-knowledge. We shall never understand the outer life if we do not understand ourselves. It is knowledge of the self that gives knowledge of the world. The politician, the statesman, however qualified, will dispute about things for years and years, but he will never come to a satisfactory conclusion unless he understands the psychology of life and of the situation. And so the education- ist will try new schemes but he will never come to a satisfactory conclusion unless he has a psychological knowledge of life, the knowledge which will teach him the psychology of human nature. But I do not mean by psychology what is generally understood by this word; I mean the understanding of the self, the under- standing of the nature and character of the mind and of the body.

What is health? Health is order. And what is order? Order is music. Where there is rhythm, regularity, co-operation, there is harmony, there is sympathy. Health of mind and health of the body depend therefore upon the preserving of that harmony, upon keeping intact that sympathy which exists in the mind and body. Life in the world, and especially as we live it amidst the crowd, will test and try our patience every moment of the day, and it will be most difficult to preserve that harmony and peace which is all happiness. For what is the definition of life? Life means struggle with friends and battle with foes. It is continual giving and taking.

And where are we to learn this? All education and learning and knowledge is acquired, but this one art is a divine art, and man has inherited it. Because he is absorbed in the outer learning he has forgotten it, but it is an art which is known to the soul; it is his own being; it is the deepest knowledge that he has in his heart. No progress in any line that man can make will give him the satisfaction which his soul is craving for, except this one which is the art of life, the art of being, the pursuit of his soul.

In order to further the reconstruction of the world the only thing possible and the only thing necessary, before trying to serve humanity, is to learn the art of being, the art of life, for oneself and in order to be an example for others.

CHAPTER IV

THE NEED OF RELIGION

EVERY man is born on earth with a certain object to accomplish, and the light of that object has been kindled in his soul. The day when he finds out his life's purpose he is stronger, more successful; his life becomes easier, he feels inspired, and a greater power pours out through him. And as a man develops spiritually, so there comes with the fullness of his soul a time when his service to the world and to humanity is a sign from the higher Spirit.

Those who have come at different times to the world to enlighten humanity and to awaken souls from their sleep of ignorance, have come from one and the same source. And although they are different souls there is but one spirit in them, and thus all that they have given to humanity is the same in essence. By studying the scriptures deeply and with sympathy, not only intellectually, one will find in Christianity, Islam, Zoroastrianism, Judaism, Hinduism, and Buddhism, in all these religions which have been followed by millions for ages, that in spite of having a different outer form, they all have one and the same inner sense. The inner teachings of Buddha are the same as the teachings of Krishna, although their followers may deny it. And so will the others; each one will say that the faith of the other is different from his own. This separation has always existed and still exists and it can only be removed by the understanding of the essence which is to be found in all religions.

But one might ask, 'What about the different histories of the great ones, the tradition of the life of Jesus Christ, the history of Mohammad, the life and story of Krishna, the legend of Buddha? They are all quite, quite different!' Yes, they are different in appearance because they came at different times and to different people. Mohammad came to Arabia, Jesus to Palestine, Zoroaster to Persia, Buddha to India. Because they have had to give God's message to different peoples they have had to adopt different terminology and different expressions. If there is any difference, it is only in the way they have presented divine wisdom, and not in the essence of divine wisdom itself.

Then people say, 'Yes, I can understand that all religions have the same essence. But at the same time I believe that one prophet is greater than another; please tell me who is the greatest.' But who can tell who is greater? Apart from the prophets, how can we even judge the greatness of musicians such as Beethoven or Wagner; are we equal to any of them? When we have a better understanding of their music our lips close. Since there is but one truth there is only one religion, and the different creeds which today appear as many different religions or churches are only special covers hiding that one truth which alone is *the* religion.

All through world-history there have been wars, for the very reason that there were differences in faiths, that certain people had faith in a particular creed or religion, or in a particular community. But the truth has always been one and the same. If the great masters such as Jesus or Buddha and all the other great ones who have given a spiritual message to humanity, had seen the Sufi Universal Worship, it would have fulfilled their ideal. And it was their prayer that one day the people of all the different religions might witness this service which includes all the different faiths. The Universal Worship, therefore, gives the promises of a world form of worship.

Religion is the greatest need at any period in the past or future. No doubt, the form of religion has changed according to the evolution of man, for the form depended upon the customs and ways of the country, and also on the psychology of the followers of any specific religion. These changes which were made in the different religions did not spring from the intellectual part of man's spirit. There is another part of man's spirit: the divine part; and the awakening of that part raises a fountain, a fountain which is religion. In the ancient history of India there are a great many examples of men who were in the position of kings and rulers and who wanted to introduce a new religion; but they never wholly succeeded, for religion does not come from that source. Its source is divine.

If truth and falsehood are distinct and different then what is the difference between them? Truth is God and the unreal is all this nature which we see before us. Therefore all that is from God is real. No doubt man's mentality has also played a part in religion, and every religion has come coloured by whatever mentality was expressed; but religion itself is from the divine source. The outside may be different but the depth is always the same. In this age it seems that one has science on one side and politics on the other, and that education is aiming at supplanting religion. But nothing can supplant religion.

There is a touching story of a scientist in France who all his life did not believe or admit to any belief in God, in the soul, or in the hereafter. But as he lived longer in the world, he felt the need of religion, although he did not feel he could accept it since all his life he had not accepted it. His wife on the other hand was devoted and religious. One day, stirred by profound sentiment, they were talking heart to heart on the question of religion. The wife was anxious that he should accept it and she asked him, 'Don't you ever feel the need of religion, of that devotion which is the only thing that is worth while?' And his answer was, 'I do not admit it, yet I believe in your belief, I enjoy your sentiment. That is my religion, my only religion in life.'

We do not know under what guise a person preserves his religion. It may be hidden somewhere in his heart; perhaps it does not show outwardly. No doubt, if no one were able to express his religious sentiment there would be no communication possible, and that is why it is very necessary in society that we should communicate our deepest religious sentiments.

CHAPTER V

THE PRESENT NEED OF THE WORLD

NO ONE with any sense who observes keenly the present condition of humanity, will deny the fact that the world today needs *the* religion. Why I say *the* religion and not *a* religion is because there are many religions in existence which might be called *a* religion; but what is needed is something else; it is *the* religion. Must this be a new religion? If it were to be a new religion it could not be called *the* religion; then it would be like many other religions. What I call *the* religion is that which one can see by rising above the sects and differences which divide men; and by understanding *the* religion one will understand all religions.

I do not mean that all the religions are not religion; they are the notes; but there is the music, and that music is *the* religion. Every religion strikes a note, a note which answers the demand of humanity in a certain epoch. Yet the source of every note is the same music which manifests when the notes are arranged harmoniously together. All the different religions are the different notes, and when they are thus arranged together they make music.

One might ask why at each epoch not all the music was given; why only a single note. The answer is that there are times in the life of an infant when a rattle is sufficient; for the violin another time in life is more appropriate. During the time of the Chaldeans, Arabs, Greeks, and Romans, different religious ideals were brought to humanity. To the few music was brought, to the many only a note; and this shows that this music has always existed, but that man in general was not ready to grasp it and so was given only one note.

The consequence was that the one who was given the C note fought with another who was given the G note, each saying, 'The note given to me is the right note!' But in reality all are right notes. Thus there is an outer substance of religion which is the form, and an inner essence which is wisdom; and when wisdom has blessed the soul, then the soul has heard the divine music. Those who tuned their hearts, who raised their souls high enough, heard this divine music; but those who played with their rattle, their single note, disputed with one another. They would have refused a violin; they were not ready for it and they would not have known how to use it.

Today the world is more starved of religion than ever before, and the reason is that some simple souls, attached to the faith of their ancestors, hold their faith in esteem, for they consider religion necessary in life; but many others, with intelligence and reason and understanding of life, rebel against religion, as the child when it grows up throws away its rattle, for it is no longer interested in it. So today the condition is that religion remains in the hands of those who have kept to its outer form through devotion and loyalty to their ancestors' faith; and those who are, so to speak, grown-up in mind and spirit and who want something better, but cannot find anything. Their souls hunger for music, yet when they ask for music they are given a rattle; and then they throw away the rattle and say that they do not care for music. Yet at the same time they have an inner yearning for the soul's music, and without it their life remains empty.

There are few who recognize this fact, and fewer still who are willing to admit it. The psychological condition of humanity has become such that a person with intelligence refuses the music, he does not want it; but because he still wants something, he calls it by another name. Travelling for ten years in the Western world, I have come into contact with people of great intelligence, thinkers, men of science; and in them I see the greatest yearning for that religious spirit. They are longing for it every moment of their lives, for they feel, with all their education and science, that there is an emptiness in themselves, and they want it filled. Yet if one speaks to them of religion they say, 'No, no, speak of something else; we do not want religion!' This means that they only know the rattle part of religion and not the violin part. They do not think that anything can exist that is different from a rattle, and yet there is perplexity in their heart and a spiritual craving which is not answered even by all their learned and scientific pursuits.

Therefore what is needed in the world today is a reconciliation between the religious man and the one who runs away from religion. But what can we do when even in the Christian religion we see so many sects, one opposing the other, while the Muslim, Buddhist, Jewish, and many other religions also consider that no religion is worth thinking about except their own? To me these different religions are like the different organs of the body, cut up and thrown apart. It seems as if one arm of the same person were cut off and were rising up to fight the other. Both are arms of the same person, and when that person is complete, when all these parts are brought together, then there is *the* religion.

Then what is the purpose of the Sufi Movement? To make a new religion? No, it is to bring together the different organs of one body which are meant to be united and not thrown apart. And what is our method, how do we work to bring about such a reconciliation? By realizing for ourselves that the essence of all religions is one, and that that essence is wisdom; by considering that wisdom to be our religion, whatever be our own form. The Sufi Movement has members belonging to many different faiths and who have not given up their own religion. On the contrary, they are firmer in their own faith through understanding the faiths of others. From the narrow point of view people may find fault with them because they do not hate, mistrust, and criticize the religion of others. They have respect for the scriptures which

R

millions of people have held to be sacred, though these scriptures do not belong to their own religion. They desire to study and appreciate other scriptures, and to find confirmation of the fact that all wisdom comes from one source, both the wisdom of the East and of the West. The Sufi Movement, therefore, is not a sect; it can be anything but a sect; and if it ever became one it would be quite contrary to the ideal with which it was begun. For its main ideal is to remove differences and distinctions which divide mankind, and this ideal is attained by the realization of the one source of all human beings, and also the goal, both of which we call God.

CHAPTER VI

EAST AND WEST

IN ORDER to distinguish East from West, it is natural first to give the points in which they differ. The people of the East, in all ages, have had only one object in view, and that was to get in touch with the deeper side of life. Some came sooner to that point, some later; some had to struggle along, and for some it was very easy. The result naturally was that for both the wise and the foolish there was less contact with the outer world. By this I do not mean to say that there are no people in the East who are pursuing material gain and material things, and that there are no people who love wealth and all that belongs to the earth. There are earth-worshippers in all lands, and hell-worshippers too. But when for instance one is among the most learned people of the East, one finds that although they have great knowledge of science and art, yet at the same time it all serves the purpose of gaining knowledge of the deeper side of life; in any work they are doing their whole motive is to understand this deeper aspect.

Even ancient Eastern politicians and warriors thought in the same way. We have as an illustration the history of the Prophet Mohammad, who was not only a mystic but a general of his army and a statesman, and who was the first in the history of the Orientals to set up a constitutional government, in Mecca. His people formed the first parliament in Medina, and every man and every woman in the city had the right to vote in that parliament; and this happened fifteen hundred years ago!

I have often come across a domestic servant, who had never had any education, who did not even know how to write his name, but who, as soon as one began to touch his sentiment and his heart, showed that he knew as much about the worthlessness of material life s a great philosopher. A man like this may perhaps talk to one on philosophy for an hour, from his deepest sentiment and with a full understanding of life.

All this does not mean that the East did not make any progress in material things, for if one takes for instance the science of medicine, the books of Avicenna have been the foundation of medical study for the whole world. Besides the music of the Vedas was not only music but a psychological expression of sound and rhythm; and therefore it was also a mystery, a science so perfectly formed that it was not only useful for worldly things, but for meditative purposes. In fact music became the most essential part of religious practice. Today people come and tell the world about the repetition of some word which will cure people from illness. Both the scientific and the unscientific worlds believe this to be a new thing, but if one goes to the East any man in the poorest circumstances will say, 'We have always known this, we do it every day; we know what the power of the word means!' They will not be able to give a definition; one must ask that of a learned man; but it is a science which has always existed in the East.

As to the Western world, in the first place the race which came from the ancient Aryan sources to countries with difficult climates, giving rise to greater responsibilities, became naturally more active. Being obliged to concern themselves more with material things these people found the means of communicating with matter. The result of this is in itself a phenomenon. All these inventions that we see today are no less than a miracle, but a miracle which has come from communication with the things of the earth, as the product of earthly things, and it is as visible and tangible as the earth. It is like a father with two sons: one son produces something all the time, one day a rattle, another day a bicycle, a third day an aeroplane; he always has something to show his father; but the other son may sit quietly, and while perhaps his thoughts and feelings are developing, he has nothing to show. Something may be developing in him which he himself cannot very well define, nor can others see it. Therefore it is natural that progress made in the objective world is visible and tangible, whereas in the spiritual realm it is difficult to see how far someone has progressed.

However, with all these differences human nature is always the same. Those who have developed in thought and in feeling are not only to be found in the East; there are many to be found in the West too. Also those who have a material inclination and produce things from matter, do not exist only in the West; they exist also in the East. In the West there is more scope for producing what one has invented or discovered, while in the East there is much less scope; and this is the cause of many difficulties.

Nevertheless, the actions of East and West are directed towards two different poles. The material progress of the East has been hindered by the climate, a climate which makes part of the day useless for active work. One would prefer to sit and dream rather than be active and work, and this also makes a difference in inclinations. Moreover very much of Western progress is due to the uniformity of the people, and much of the backwardness of the East is due to lack of uniformity. Every man in the East may have his own individual progress; but whenever there is individualistic progress, it may be very free, yet it will not be recognized by those who do not understand this particular way. It is like a scientist who comes with a new invention which is not understood by another scientist, who then will be sure to oppose him. In the East, therefore, whenever an intelligent person progresses in his own line, he has to face great opposition, and he finds no one who can quite understand him. But in the West it is the contrary. There are academies and associations and people who understand things and who can give encouragement. Yet on the other hand uniformity pulls people back from individual progress.

Now, owing to modern communications, East and West have been brought closer together, and this gives us great hope that

East and West, which depend for their progress upon mutual exchange and understanding, will soon unite. In industry, in politics, in all things they can unite and benefit from each other; but the greatest benefit that can come from the meeting of East and West is through the interchange of thought and ideal, through meeting in that light which is the light of intelligence and which is divine by nature.

The Sufi Movement has directed all its efforts towards this goal, that the East may be able to appreciate all that is good and worth while in the West, and that the West may understand and sympathize with all that is worth understanding in the East. Words cannot explain to what extent the world would benefit by the realization of this ideal. Just now the East is working in its own way and the West is working in its own way; this is like working with one eye open and the other eye closed. It is in the unity of East and West that the vision will become complete, and it is in this conception that the great disasters and troubles which have kept the world in such uneasiness will be rooted out. And by the unity of East and West in wisdom, one can look forward to a real peace.

CHAPTER VII

BROTHERHOOD (1)

ONE CAN see the beginning of the spirit of brotherhood when one looks at flocks of birds flying together in the sky, or at the herds of animals in the fields and the swarms of insects all living and moving together. No doubt this tendency of brotherhood is more pronounced in man, for man is not only capable of realizing the spirit of brotherhood, but also of fulfilling the purpose which is hidden in this natural tendency. There is one secret behind all this diversity which we call good or bad, right or wrong, sin or virtue; and it is that all that leads to happiness is right, good, and virtuous; and all that leads to unhappiness is wrong, bad, and evil;

and if there is any sin, it is the latter which may be called sin. Brotherhood is not something which man has learned or acquired; it is something which is born in him, and according to his development of this spirit he shows the unfoldment of his soul.

Coming to the religions which have been given to the world, we read for instance in the Bible the words of Jesus Christ, admonishing us from beginning to end to love our fellow-man, our neighbour. It was the moral of brotherhood that the Master taught and repeated constantly. If one studies what is the central theme of all the different religions which exist in the world, with their millions and millions of followers, we will find that it is brotherhood: to love one another, to serve one another, to be sincere to one another.

But while man is capable of loving his friend, he is still more capable of hating his neighbour. The first tendency, that of brotherhood, of love, brings satisfaction to him and happiness to the other. The other tendency of hating his brother brings dissatisfaction to him, and unhappiness to the other. Brotherhood creates happiness, and the spirit which is contrary to it produces sorrow.

When we read the scriptures of the great world religions, whether the Bible, the Kabala, the Qur'an, the Gita, or the Buddhist scriptures, we find that in some form or other, in the manner best suited to the people to whom the religion was given, it was the same moral, the same symphony, it was the same music which was performed before them. Were the great teachers specially engaged in giving mystical or occult teachings to the world? Were they engaged in discussing philosophical problems? Not at all, although they were mystics and knew philosophy and occultism, that was not the principal thing that they had to give. What they gave to the world was that simple philosophy which is never new to anyone and which even a child knows: to love one another, to be kind, to be sincere, to serve one another.

But if it is such a simple thing, so simple that even a child knows it, why was it necessary for the great ones, the godly souls, to come and teach it? Life is most simple and yet it is most difficult to live, and man will not accept any teaching from someone who does not live it, or if he accepts it, he will not hold on to it for long. Therefore they came on earth with the love from above, and they lived that simple moral, that simple philosophy of brotherhood. A Moghul emperor, Ghasnavi, who was a great poet, wrote, 'Born in a palace, and having reigned from the first day that I came on earth, I saw nothing but thousands and thousands of people bowing before me. But on that day in my life when I learned my first lesson of love, my proud head bowed as a servant before every slave that I saw standing before me. Then I felt that I was their slave.' What does this show? It shows that coldness of heart hardens one's feelings and closes one's eyes to that light which illumines the path of brotherhood.

There are many relationships, there are many connections in this world, by blood and also by law, but the greatest relationship is friendship; and it is the culmination of friendship which is called brotherhood. Brotherhood means perfect friendship.

But now comes the question: how may this principle of brotherhood be lived, how may it be practised? It is very difficult to teach this principle to anyone. The best way of teaching it is by living it oneself. The parents, either father or mother, who show their children that feeling of brotherhood, can best express themselves to their children in this way, and the children too are able to express themselves best to their parents through this feeling. A father may be most kind, a mother most loving, but as long as he or she maintains the attitude of considering himself or herself only as father or mother, as beings which are different from the child, it will perhaps grow to love them but it will never look upon them as friends. The child will look for friends elsewhere. And a teacher may be respected by his pupils, he may bear himself with great dignity before his pupils, but at the same time there cannot be established that communication of inspiration, of love, of sympathy, of understanding until he has practised the manner of brotherhood with his pupils.

In what way did the great ones, the prophets, the seers, the mystics, treat their pupils, their disciples? The story is known to all of Jesus Christ calling the fishermen to come and sit and talk with him. The Master never felt comfortable when they called him good. He said, 'Call me not good.' What he meant was, 'Do not consider me superior to you, I am one of you.' Think then of the Master washing the feet of his disciples; what does it teach us? It teaches us brotherhood. No miracle, no great power, no great inspiration, occult or mystical, can equal the phenomenon of that humility, of that fraternity, of that brotherhood with which the great ones have become one with all men.

The world appears to be going from bad to worse; it seems that the suffering that has been caused to humanity has not yet ended. No doubt life in the world is so intoxicating that man hardly stops to think about this; life such as it is just now has so many responsibilities; everyone, whether rich or poor, is so absorbed in his affairs that he hardly has a moment to think what is going on in the world. Nevertheless illness is illness, and the world is ill. A person may neglect his illness and engage his mind in something else, but if that illness is not attended to, it remains just the same. When we look for the cause of all these disasters we may be able to find a thousand causes, yet there is one principal cause and that is the lack of brotherhood.

One could have endured the absence of anything else; but the world can never be happy, nor can order or peace ever be maintained, in the absence of brotherhood. This brotherhood can be learned, and every person has facilities for learning it in his life. The master who is kind and loving to his servant, who considers his servant as his brother, is blessed. A family in which all the members, whatever be their relationship, realize the idea of brotherhood in sharing pain and pleasure with one another, how happy, how blessed that family will be! How blessed would be a nation, in which, whatever its government, whatever its constitution, there were this spirit of brotherhood between people of different position, of different rank or occupation! From whence does injustice come, from whence unfairness? It all comes from the lack of brotherhood. Think of the conditions today, the courts full of cases, the prisons full of prisoners! How many disagreements there are between people and inharmony between nations, all caused by the lack of brotherhood.

When we consider this question from a still deeper point of view, we shall find that in the spirit of brotherhood is hidden a way to illumination. A man who may live by great principles, or who prays all day or meditates in the caves of the mountainside, if he does not show the spirit of brotherhood, is no good to himself or to others, because brotherhood is the way to develop spirituality. It is not exclusiveness, it is not running away from the world which is the way of the really spiritual ones. Their way is to consider one's obligations, to keep one's word, one's honour, and to prove sincere in whatever minor capacity one may be working, faithful to friends and true to everyone. These are the merits which develop by themselves when the spirit of brotherhood has matured in man.

But when we come to the metaphysical point of view we see that an element attracts its own element. For instance two streams of water will be attracted to one another. But although there will come a time when they join together, efforts will have to be made by both. When fires start at two sides of a certain place, each fire will be attracted to the other and in the end they will meet and become one. In the same way an artist is attracted to an artist, a thinker to a thinker, a scientist to a scientist, and the man of action to the man of action. They are not only attracted because there is the same element in both of them, but because there is a comfort, a happiness in being attracted by the same element. Think of the joy when two people of the same thought meet together. It is greater than a joy, greater than a satisfaction, it is that happiness which is promised in heaven.

But behind all this world of various names and forms there is one life, there is one spirit. This spirit which is the soul of all beings is attracted towards unity, and it is the absence of this spirit which keeps the world unhappy. To a person who has just had some unpleasantness with his brother or sister, his food is tasteless, the night without sleep, the heart restless, the soul under a cloud. This shows that we do not necessarily live on food; our soul lives on love, the love that we receive and the love that we give. The absence of this is our unhappiness, and the presence of it is all we need. Nothing in the world is a greater healing power, a greater remedy, a greater happiness, than to be conscious of brotherhood and to be able to give that feeling to one's child, master, neighbour, and friend.

The humble efforts made by the Sufi Movement in the service of God and humanity, are towards brotherhood. In the form of devotion, of philosophy, of mysticism, of metaphysics, art, or science, in whatever form the Sufi Movement presents the ideal to the world of which the central theme is always brotherhood.

CHAPTER VIII

BROTHERHOOD (2)

BROTHERHOOD is not something which is learned or taught. Brotherhood is a tendency, a tendency which arises from a heart that is tuned to the proper pitch. And it is in this natural tendency that the real happiness lies from which rises harmony and which culminates in peace. The message of brotherhood is a message of sympathy, a message of harmony. But the person who is not in harmony with himself cannot be in harmony with another, with all the teaching of brotherhood and with all his learning, he will not be able to observe the law of brotherhood.

In the whole system of the world's creation one sees a blind impulse working like a kind of mechanism of the universe. This impulse is more apparent in living creatures, and its most pronounced form is agitation. If we study the lives of the lower creatures we find that they not only have a desire for food or a desire to move about with their mates; their first desire is to sleep. But besides this there is an inclination which manifests as agitation, and it is because of this agitation that the animals and birds fight among themselves. Their whole life is filled with that agitation. Furthermore, herbivorous animals are less agitated than carnivorous ones, while in the carnivorous animals there is more desire for fighting. The lion and the tiger are more inclined to fight than horses and cows, which shows that the herbivorous animals are a step more advanced than the carnivorous animals. The tendencies to eat or drink, to seek pleasure or enjoy comfort or become agitated, do not belong specially to the human being; he gets these characteristics from the animal. His special characteristic is sympathy, harmony; but this comes only when man rises above that agitation which, so to speak, buries the spirit of sympathy. No doubt man is educated, he is trained, he has some polish, he has been taught some manners, and therefore he does not always show his agitation. It is only at a time of weakness, when he cannot control his agitation, that it breaks out and manifests to his own view as well as to that of others, thereby proving that he is not yet ready to be called human.

One might ask if there is any time in a man's life when he rises above this. One person will get it under control sooner than another, but one will always master it when one really tries to. This spirit of agitation shows itself as intolerance, as rivalry, as jealousy, as a domineering spirit, as irritability, or as the tendency to patronize; all such qualities show agitation. When we study the lives of those who have served humanity, we see that this was the first thing that they had to conquer. When it is said that Krishna fought a battle with Kamsa, the monster-man, that monster was not outside of Krishna; that monster was inside him. It was this spirit of agitation. Krishna had to fight it, and it was only after conquering the spirit of agitation that he became the messenger of love.

In the Bible we read that Jesus Christ went for forty days into the desert, and that Satan was at his side. What is Satan? It is the same spirit which is the greatest enemy of the human race, the spirit of agitation. And Halima gives a symbolical, artistic, and picturesque description of an experience of the Prophet. She says that the breast of the Prophet was cut open and that some undesirable matter was removed. Symbolically this means that the spirit of agitation was taken away to make place for divine inspiration. This shows that man inherits the earthly characteristics, and among those earthly characteristics agitation is the principal one. A child sometimes shows it against its parents, a schoolboy against his friends, a youth against his companions, a grown-up person against his neighbours—and everyone has a reason to justify this wrong attitude. Agitation, therefore, is the sign of the false ego, and when this false ego is broken, when this very agitation has crushed itself, just as fire burns itself out, then begins the process of purification.

Man does not really notice how far this spirit follows a person on the path of spiritual progress. A person may arrive at the very gate of the heavens, and even to that length this spirit will travel with him. It may become weaker, but it is there; only, this spirit has no entrance into the shrine of God, and the soul which carries this spirit with it has no entrance into that perfect abode. He may advance as far as the gate of the inner temple, but he is not allowed in; he is held back by the power of that same spirit of agitation. For the shrine of God is called *Dar-e-Sala'm*, which is the same as Jerusalem. It means the door of peace, and agitation is not allowed to enter through the door of peace; it must stay outside. When the ancients said, 'You cannot follow two masters, God and Satan,' this meant that Satan is the spirit of agitation which is to be found within ourselves, while God is the spirit of peace in whom is our happiness; and we cannot follow both of these masters.

There are many movements and institutions for the promotion of brotherhood, and they are all doing what they can to further this ideal, for this is an ideal which is the essence of religion and the soul of spirituality. But how can one attain to it? By creating in oneself, and by trying to give to others, the idea of a natural sympathy; by strengthening ourselves, thereby giving power to others also to fight against this spirit of agitation which has always proved to be the worst enemy of mankind.

Where does this agitation come from? From disorder, either of the body or of the mind; if the body is not in its proper rhythm and proper tune, or if the mind is not in its proper rhythm and tune. And if the mind and body are not in tune with one another, if they are not in harmony, then also this agitation comes. Sometimes it is the reflection of the mind upon the body, and sometimes it is the reflection of the body upon the mind. How true it is that man is his own enemy; but where is that enemy? That enemy is this spirit; a spirit which is never contented, which does not appreciate, which does not respond, which does not sympathize, which does not agree, which does not endure, which does not tolerate, which does not harmonize. A spirit which stands against any influence of harmony, agreement, sympathy, or kindness.

Is this spirit a living being, is it Satan, a devil, or what is it? What is its explanation? What is its origin? The best explanation is that it is like a smooth silken thread which becomes tangled at one end and ties itself into a knot. But in the place where it is a knot and where it is very difficult to unravel, it is still the same silken thread; only, it is in a condition where it is difficult for it because it is not free, and it is difficult for others because they cannot unravel it. And so the same soul which has divine breath in it, which has come from heaven, which represents God on earth, when it is turned into a knot has difficulty with itself, difficulty with others, and others have difficulty with it. In this way it becomes inharmonious, and it creates inharmony; it finds itself in a kind of inharmonious condition. This only means that it has lost its natural, original condition, its smoothness and softness; and yet it remains silk, it has not turned into cotton, it is still silk. Call it Satan or devil or whatever you like, but if once one knows the source, the origin, one cannot call it anything else but a condition. Thus what is most important in the work of brotherhood, is to develop that spirit in ourselves by getting above all knots and difficulties, in order that we may not only be able to follow the rules of brotherhood, but that all which comes naturally from ourselves may express brotherhood.

In working towards the establishment of brotherhood, the main object of the Sufi Movement is to bring about a better understanding among the different classes, among the followers of different religions and the people of different races and different nations; but by this we do not mean mixing them up. If this were our idea, it would have been quite a different thing. We want to let the farms of wheat be farms of wheat; on the farms where rice grows, let rice grow; where there are woods, let there be woods, where there are gardens, let there be gardens—all are necessary. Our ideas have not reached to the extreme of wanting to cook everything in the same dish. We do not wish to stretch the fingers so as to make them all even, for their natural size is the proper size for them; our conception of equality does not conform with such an idea. Our only motive is that the East and the West, the North and the South, instead of turning their backs upon each other, may turn their faces towards each other.

We do not wish all the people in the world to be of the same religion or the same education, or to have the same customs and manners; nor do we think that all classes must become one class, which is impossible anyhow. We wish that all classes may blend with each other, and yet every individual have his own individual expression in life; that all nations may have their peculiarity, their individuality, but at the same time express good-will and friendly feeling towards one another; that different races may have their own manners and their own ideas, but at the same time understand one another; that the followers of different religions may continue to belong to their own religions, but at the same time become tolerant towards each other.

Therefore our idea of brotherhood is not in any way extreme. The motive is not to change humanity, but to help humanity on towards its goal. People may belong to one church and yet fight with one another; it is just as well that they should belong to different churches and yet understand each other, respect each other's religion, and tolerate one another. People may belong to one institution, and yet disagree with one another. Then what is the use of that institution? Therefore it is not at all the mission of the Sufi Movement to try and make the whole of humanity followers of one special movement, but to give to humanity what God has given us, so that we may serve in His cause.

THE INTERNATIONAL SUFI MOVEMENT

The International Sufi Movement was created by Inayat Khan in 1923. Its work embodies the flow of inspiration expressed in the Sufi Message: to activate and reflect the quest for the human ideal. Esoterically and exoterically it realizes expressions of the human life force where it meets the contemporary horizons of reach and intensity.

The Head of the Movement, the Representative General and Piro-Murshid, is counselled by an Executive Committee located at the International Headquarters in Geneva, Switzerland. Affiliated national and local centres coordinate the activity-divisions of the World Brotherhood, the Church of All, the Healing Order and the Sufi Order.

THE WORLD BROTHERHOOD

This is in essence a conceptual community, an open meeting place for those who share a desire for human brotherhood in terms of some unifying ideal. The different individual and group activities of the Brotherhood orient all inner deepening and outward unfolding towards a balanced achievement of this ideal. The Sufi Movement sees that the Brotherhood can only really exist if it is composed of whole people who are healthy in an eventual mental and physical sense and who meet, at an individual rather than a group level, in a true democratic spirit of considerate equality and shared commitment.

From time to time *Spring and Summer Schools* are held in different countries in different languages by the Head of the Sufi Movement and those designated by him. The International Summer School is regularly held in the Universel Murad Hassil in Katwijk aan Zee, Netherlands. Instruction and training is given in different aspects of work in the Sufi Order, the Healing Order and the Church of All.

The *School of Creative Leadership* derives its name from the recognition that human development originates in self-knowledge and self-leadership. The activities of the School are generally participatory; they involve lectures, discussions, active mental culture exercises, outside reading requirements and from time to time a public seminar organised by the participants of the School.

Workcamps are presented under the personal or assigned guidance of the Head of the Sufi Movement. These programs give psychological and spiritual training in a great variety of forms and locations. In general, workcamps establish in a non-material way the components of a universe, the raw material of which is available to the group and a few creative individuals within it, to receive, to transmute and to project.

THE CHURCH OF ALL

All the great teachers and founders of faiths the world over were without exception carriers of the same single message, which was expressed in ways adapted to the time, place and receivers of their teachings. All the messengers, the known and unknown, formed the embodiment of the one essential Master, the Spirit of Guidance. The Church of All was established by Inayat Khan in recognition of the need for ritual devotional expression in different suggestive forms that would reflect the abstract unity behind all religious teachings. They are in truth one single attempt to communicate with the Spirit of Guidance, to induce into an assembly of people, rhythmically tuned in receptive release, a manifestation of grace.

THE HEALING ORDER

This Order exists to guide and inspire all attempts within the Movement and by those interested to activate, contact, represent or invoke, in esoteric and exoteric, traditional and contemporary ways, and at all levels of physical, mental and spiritual being, the divine current that is the essential healing influence of unity in the universe: to lubricate the totality of being alive.

People may join the Healing Order independently of any other association with the Sufi Movement; they are admitted by healing Conductors if their basic aims are felt to be in harmony with those of the Order and the group.

THE SUFI ORDER

The Sufi Order is the inner school of the Sufi Movement. The Order represents the continuity in a line of succession of initiatic and evolutionary thought enchained in the Sufi tradition which connects it with its origins. Its aim is the cultivation of an inner wholeness, the heart quality, in which can flower the self-creative potential of human beings searching towards their deepest ideal.

The essential vehicle for this is a silent teaching, a tuning transmitted across the mutual bond of trust and responsibility which connects and unites an individual mureed or disciple with the murshid, teacher, or guide, and through them with the Sufic current.

Universel Murad Hassil

CENTRES

Local groups or centres are essentially expressions of the activity of the Sufi Movement within a connecting chain of leadership. These take the form of programs, communities or Khankahs, schools and buildings which integrate the ideal of allowing and encouraging social and cultural diversity.

A *Khankah* is a retreat where people who are bound in an emergent, non-explicit way by the thread of Sufism gather to live and work together. It is a place where one may come for a while to breathe afresh, to experiment responsibly and creatively with life solutions and then leave with a fuller sense of contact with the ideals of Sufism, and the goal of human becoming.

The *Universel Murad Hassil* is located on the dunes in Katwijk aan Zee, Netherlands, on a site said to have been chosen by Inayat Khan himself as a reflection of a deep current of inspiration. A Universel is a material consecration of projected ideals that draw forth the search for a higher unity in every human activity. The name Murad Hassil means 'wish fulfilled.'

The *Dargah* is the burial site of Inayat Khan in Delhi, India. It is a place of pilgrimage, as is the tradition for all great Saints and teachers, where on the 5th of February each year the 'Urs', the ceremony commemorating the anniversary of his death, takes place.

Enquiries concerning the activities of the Sufi Movement are welcome and should be addressed to:
The International Headquarters of the Sufi Movement
11 Rue John Rehfous
1208 Geneva
Switzerland

THE SUFI MESSAGE OF HAZRAT INAYAT KHAN

THE INNER LIFE
The traditional Sufic outlook on life's values and purpose is re-expressed by Inayat Khan in universal and contemporary concepts. Included are: *The Way of Illumination; The Inner Life; The Soul: Whence and Whither* and *The Purpose of Life.*

THE MYSTICISM OF SOUND
Sufism traditionally used music as a means of transmitting the essence of mystical insight. Inayat Khan expresses aspects of this musical tradition while recomposing a musical concept extending beyond the tradition of time or culture. Included are: *The Mysticism of Sound; Music; The Power of the Word* and *Cosmic Language.*

THE ART OF PERSONALITY
Inayat Khan suggests that the art of personality is the completion of nature and the culmination of heredity. Development of the personality is taken from before birth to the deepest aspects of consciousness in these talks which include: *Education; Rasa Shastra; Character Building; The Art of Personality* and *Moral Culture.*

HEALING AND THE MIND WORLD
The role of the mind in the totality of the being is a cornerstone of the Sufi Message. In these talks Hazrat Inayat Khan develops the idea of the mind and its power over the body which he sees as the essential healing effect. Included in these basic teachings: *Health; Mental Purification* and *The Mind World.*

SPIRITUAL LIBERTY
The Sufi Message of Spiritual Liberty; Aqibat: Life After Death; The Phenomenon of the Soul; Love, Human and Divine; Pearls from the Ocean Unseen; Metaphysics. Reports of earlier talks of Inayat Khan, mostly given during 1914–1918 in England.

THE ALCHEMY OF HAPPINESS
Inayat Khan herein suggests that spiritual aspirations are to no avail if life is not lived fully and deeply in all its different aspects. He points out that by living out all possibilities, true wisdom and insight are gained and a fulfillment or happiness is experienced.

IN AN EASTERN ROSE GARDEN
Talks given between 1918–1920 on a variety of subjects. Inayat Khan's ability to communicate the unity and relativity of his viewpoint on diverse subjects illustrates the essence of his mystical perception of life.

SUFI TEACHINGS
A collection of talks on various practical and esoteric aspects of traditional Sufi teachings developed by Inayat Khan in a modern and universal context.

THE UNITY OF RELIGIOUS IDEALS
Inayat Khan evolves his message of universal religious ideals by looking at the personalities of some of the great prophets of mankind.

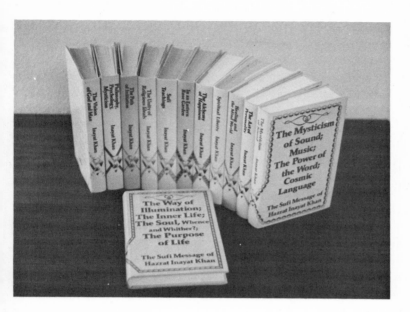

THE PATH OF INITIATION
Inayat Khan situates the traditional concepts of initiation, discipleship, spiritual teaching and other esoteric aspects of Sufism in today's world. Besides the main part consisting of: *Sufi Mysticism* and *The Path of Initiation and Discipleship*, these subjects are included: *Sufi Poetry; Art: Yesterday, Today and Tomorrow; The Problem of the Day*.

PHILOSOPHY, PSYCHOLOGY AND MYSTICISM
These later talks of Hazrat Inayat Khan, given in 1927, were an attempt to give to his disciples a clear overview of these topics in terms of his Sufic vision. The *Aphorisms* at the end are sayings noted down by his pupils which Inayat Khan expressed at different times and places to soothe or clarify the seeker.

THE VISION OF GOD AND MAN
The Vision of God and Man; Confessions; Four Plays. The first part of this volume deals with the relationship of man and God. The second part is autobiographical. The third part contains four short plays written by Inayat Khan for his pupils.

SACRED READINGS
Sacred Readings is derived from classes given by Inayat Khan to his pupils at different stages of their training. All of the material included is published here for the first time.

GHIZA-I-RUH
The 14th and 15th volumes will contain comprehensive biographical accounts of Hazrat Inayat Khan describing his cultural and spiritual heritage and will include more of his poetic work. Other teachings restricted to his pupils until now and regarded as deeper, more esoteric, will be published for the first time.

SELECTED PAPERBACKS FROM THE SUFI MESSAGE

THE BOWL OF SAKI
Thoughts for daily contemplation from the sayings and teachings of Sufi Inayat Khan.

Arranged attractively and practically to provide the perfect opportunity for a personal daily meditation, to recall something or someone special, or just to remember the value of each day.

THE DEVELOPMENT OF SPIRITUAL HEALING
Sufi Inayat Khan discusses the basic laws governing the subtle relationship between body and mind.

Emphasising the influence of the mind on the body the Sufi mystic describes various forms of spiritual healing, the psychological nature of diseases, and the development and applications of healing power.

EDUCATION: FROM BEFORE BIRTH TO MATURITY
Beginning with the unborn child (an approach only recently taken seriously in scientific and psychiatric circles) Inayat Khan explores the development of the mind, heart and body of the child through the formative years.

A wealth of knowledge and insight for parents and educators concerned with the needs of the child in a total sense.

MUSIC
Sufi Inayat Khan was a musician and mystic. His thought naturally attuned itself to melodic and rhythmic expression.

Music brings together in one book the essence of his experience of the intermingling of music and all life.

THE PALACE OF MIRRORS
'. . . This is a mirror land, living because the mirrors are living. It is not only projecting and reflecting that takes place in the mirrors, but a phenomenon of creation: that all that is projected and reflected is created at the same time, and materialised sooner or later . . .'

GAYAN, VADAN AND NIRTAN
Deluxe hard cover and paperback editions will be available in the near future.

MYSTICAL PSYCHOLOGY
'. . . Real psychology is the understanding of a law working behind the scenes. It is the understanding of cause and effect in everything. The one who cannot see the truth of mysticism is ignorant because he is backward in psychology.' Publication date to be announced.

In U.S.A. send orders to:
   Hunter House Inc., 748 E. Bonita Ave., Suite 105, Pomona, CA 91767.
In United Kingdom send orders to:
   Sufi Publishing Co. Ltd., 23 East Street, Farnham, Surrey GU9 7SD.
Please note that books may be supplied directly by the above companies or through their agents.
In all other countries orders should be sent to:
   International Headquarters Sufi Movement, 11 Rue John Rehfous,
   1208 Geneva, Switzerland.